THE LORD'S PRAYER
IN THE BIBLE

By H. G. MOSS

" A book which all can cordially recommend. It might seem impossible to find anything new to say about the Lord's Prayer, but Mr. Moss's suggestive, original and by no means lengthy work reminds us that there are new and interesting things being said continually about the Gospels. Mr. Moss has many things to say tending to throw light on common prayer and Bible study in general which are themselves marks of clearer teaching . . ."

"

"

"

"

"

"

"

"

WITH A FOREWORD BY THE BISHOP OF BLACKBURN

6s. 6d. net.

LONGMANS

THE PREACHER'S HANDBOOK

EDITED BY

GREVILLE P. LEWIS

B.A., B.D.

NUMBER ONE

THE EPWORTH PRESS

Published by

THE EPWORTH PRESS

(FRANK H. CUMBERS)

25–35 CITY ROAD, LONDON, E.C.1

*

New York	.	*Toronto*
Melbourne	.	*Capetown*

*

PRINTED IN ENGLAND BY
HAZELL WATSON & VINEY Ltd
AYLESBURY AND LONDON

LOCAL PREACHERS' DEPARTMENT

THE STUDIES BOARD

FOREWORD

by the PRESIDENT OF THE CONFERENCE 1948-9

THE Editor of this *Preacher's Handbook* makes the astounding claim in his Preface that the Local Preachers of the Methodist Church in Great Britain 'constitute the greatest lay ministry in the world'. Astounding as it may seem, I can vouch for its accuracy, if for no other reason than that the point was made during the discussions of the Amsterdam Assembly. That First Assembly of the World Council of Churches rightly emphasized the outstanding importance of the work of the laity in relation to the progressive activity of the Christian Church. But, apparently, until one of the Methodist delegates called attention to the fact, it had no conception of the extent to which the ministry of laymen is utilized in British Methodism. If I underline this fact it is in order that I may share with the Secretary of the Local Preachers' Department a strong emphasis upon the distinction and importance of this great service, and the urgent necessity for Local Preachers to share with the 'Itinerant Preachers', to use the old phrase, the responsibility of a teaching ministry as the basis of the evangelistic message and appeal. Recognizing this fact so keenly, I welcome this new *Handbook* enthusiastically and commend it to all the Local Preachers of our Church.

There are many interesting points connected with this publication which would be worth mentioning, but I will name only one. The Editor calls attention to the lack of continuity in the ministry of Local Preachers, which is often a definite weakness. I have myself seen the enormous advantage of team work of such a nature that, working together and without making more demands upon time than Local Preachers are able to give, it is possible for the congregations to receive the benefit of continuity of teaching. I hope very much that this book will be used as the basis for that kind of team work throughout Methodism.

It is a privilege to write this brief Foreword and to commend this volume to our Local Preachers with the hope that it may be widely used and result in a definite enrichment in the ministry of the pulpits of our Church.   E. BENSON PERKINS.

PREFACE

METHODISM had hardly come into being, when John Wesley realized that the small group of clergymen who were co-operating with him could not possibly maintain that increasing preaching-witness which was demanded by the rapid growth of Methodist Societies up and down the land. So, despite the fact that the law of the Church of England ruled that only episcopally-ordained clergymen were allowed to preach, when the call to preach the Gospel came to worthy laymen like John Cennick and Thomas Maxfield, Wesley, after an initial hesitation, affirmed the validity of such a call, and appointed a certain number of *lay* preachers.

The first Methodist Conference (1744) consisted of six clergy-men and four lay preachers. Two years later, the country was divided into seven 'Circuits'—London, Bristol, Cornwall, Evesham, Yorkshire, Newcastle, and Wales—and by 1753 the lay preachers, who now numbered forty-one, were divided into two groups:

(*a*) *Itinerant Preachers*, who gave all their time to the work of preaching, travelled from Circuit to Circuit, and later became the '*Ministers*' of Methodism.

(*b*) *Local Preachers*, who carried on their previous professions or trades, and preached mainly in their own *localities*. As the number of Circuits increased and their size decreased, the Local Preacher became, what he still is, a layman who is authorized by the Methodist Church to exercise a preaching ministry, chiefly and primarily in his own Circuit.

But that was two centuries ago. Today in the Methodist Church in Great Britain there are 26,230 Local Preachers (2,349 of whom are women) and 3,263 Local Preachers on Trial, and they constitute the greatest lay ministry in the world. They conduct more than 16,000 Sunday Services every week of the year, for the most part in the chapels of our country areas, and without their devoted labours Rural Methodism as we know it would cease to exist.

They belong to almost every profession and trade; they include solicitors and bricklayers, doctors and shop-keepers, Members of Parliament and miners, architects and nurses, journalists and business men, teachers and engine-drivers, housewives and factory workers, civil servants and farmers, office clerks and agricultural workers, soldiers, sailors and airmen —and so the list could continue—and that is why our Local Preachers have their own unique contribution to make to the preaching ministry of the Church. Day by day they grapple with the problems and temptations of the work-a-day world, many of which are only known to the average Minister by hearsay or imagination. Day by day they rub shoulders with men and women who, in the struggle and bustle of that world and so often in vain, are trying to discover their own true destiny; and it is to these fellow-citizens of Vanity Fair that, out of their own experience, our Local Preachers can cry,

> *O let me commend my Saviour to you,*
> *I set to my seal that Jesus is true:*
> *Ye all may find favour who come at His call;*
> *O come to my Saviour! His grace is for all.*

Yes, it is a great thing to be able to proclaim to struggling men and women a Living Saviour, whose redeeming power you have proved in that rough and tumble of daily life which you share with them—*but it is not enough.* The preacher must not only be able to declare that 'Jesus saves'; he must be able to explain *how* He saves, from what, to what, and all the rest of it. He must be able to bring the sinner to conversion, and then lead him onwards into that full Christianization of life which the older theologians knew as Entire Sanctification. But before he can even convert sinners, he must be able to give an 'apologia' for the primary affirmations of the Christian Faith, none of which can be taken for granted nowadays. He wants to reconcile the sinner to God, but first he must convince the sinner that he *is* a sinner, and that there is such a thing as sin. But perhaps the sinner doesn't feel the sting of sin and the horror of being a sinner, because he's not sure that there *is* a God against whom he has been sinning—and, if there is, whether we can know anything about Him. Yes, the preacher must go back as far as that, to the primary assumptions. But again, he will try to persuade the sinner that his decision—for or against Christ—will affect his destiny, not only in this life but through the everlasting years. But is there a future life? The preacher must be able to give a confident and convincing answer. But more than that. He must be able, and with authority, to expound the Christian Ethic—the Sermon on the Mount, and all that. He must also be able to show that Christianity is a Gospel for Society, as well as for the individual, and to champion that Gospel against every modern ideology—atheistic Communism, for instance—which would deny it or rival it.

But enough has been said to show that the preacher must be more than an 'evangelist'; he must also be a thinker and an apologist; he must be a Bible-scholar and an able exponent of all the great fundamentals of the Christian Faith. That is why we urge every Local Preacher on Trial, as he prepares himself for his great vocation, to give himself with unsparing devotion to our prescribed courses of study in the Old Testament, the New Testament, and Christian Doctrine, that he may begin his preaching ministry well grounded in the essentials of our faith—and knowing that, long after he has received his Long Service Certificate, he will still be making new discoveries of the wonder and power of the Gospel he preaches and the God whose glory he declares.

But there's the rub! How often, within a few years of his admittance on to 'full plan', the Local Preacher finds that his daily work is making increasing demands on his time and energy, and at the same time that he is being persuaded to accept this and that office in the Church, the Sunday-school, or the Youth organizations—not to mention this and that voluntary service in the local community. He has less and less time for reading and sermon-preparation, and finds himself living more and more on the capital of his early studies in the Bible and theology. Scholars are keeping abreast of modern thought and world-changes, and reinterpreting the Gospel and the Faith in terms which challenge the minds and meet the spiritual needs of modern men and women—but how can he (or she) find time to study the books of these scholars and keep in touch with their new interpretations of the Faith? He is told that even the simple message of the Evangelist needs to be expressed in new thought-forms, and that the old technique of Evangelism must be adapted to the mentality of each new generation—but he continues to preach the same sort of sermons which he preached when he first became a 'fully-accredited' Local Preacher, because he has no other message to preach.

No one suggests that this preaching is *ineffective*—but it is not so effective as it ought to be. Its vocabulary tends to become out

of date and somewhat unintelligible; and often it lacks the freshness and vigour that come only from new discoveries of the
wonder of the Gospel and the relevance of the Faith.

It is partly to meet the urgent needs of such busy and hard-
pressed preachers that this new venture has been planned; an
annual *Preacher's Handbook*. The individual Local Preacher will
find in it guidance for his thinking and reading, and many
suggestions for sermons on those fundamental Christian affirmations which are most relevant to modern needs. We hope also
that many Local Preachers' Fellowships will use the Manual as a
textbook for corporate study and discussion.

But lack of time is not the Local Preacher's only difficulty. He
has no *continuous* preaching and teaching ministry. At most he
preaches to the same congregation three or four times a year,
and he often feels that his message has no planned connexion
with the messages which precede and follow his own, and that
therefore it loses something of its effectiveness. The *Handbook*
should help to lessen this difficulty, and in two ways. Its fourteen
Study Articles on the Christian Year will help every Local
Preacher to prepare sermons which are relevant to the great
Christian festivals and seasons as they come round, and so could
ensure some measure of continuity in the messages which are
delivered by a great variety of preachers. Also, those preachers
who are prepared, after corporate study, to use the very helpful
scheme of Team or Continuity preaching will find this *Handbook*
an invaluable textbook.

This first issue, which will serve as a model for future numbers,
is divided into three parts.

Part One contains a series of Introductory Articles which give
guidance on matters which are of particular importance to every
preacher.

Part Two consists of a series of Study Articles on the Christian
Year—on Advent, Covenant Sunday, the Gospel of the Cross
(including Easter), the Holy Spirit (including the Trinity), and
Young People's Sunday. Each article will begin with a list of
Bible passages for preliminary reading and to help you in your
choice of Lessons, and will give frequent Bible references—there
will be no danger of all preachers choosing the same text!—and
many illustrations from the *Methodist Hymn Book*. Throughout
the *Handbook*, and especially in this Part, full attention will
be given to the Old Testament, in which we trace so many of the

ideas and hopes which came to their fulfilment in Jesus Christ and the history of the Church.

Part Three will always include (*a*) a series of Study Articles on one of the major doctrines of Christianity, with special emphasis on its practical importance for the solution of personal and social problems. This year, we deal with the Doctrine of Man, and derive from it the Christian answer to atheistic Communism and the Christian argument against the evils of Drink and Gambling. (*b*) A series of Studies on some subject which is of major interest to the student of the Bible. This year we have chosen 'The Life of Jesus'. In our next issue, we hope to present 'The Life of Paul'. Because this is our first issue, we are including, as an Appendix, the Standing Orders of Conference as they relate to Local Preachers' affairs, and we hope they will be carefully studied.

As the years pass, and your annual *Preacher's Handbooks* take a prominent place on your bookshelves, we hope that you will find that, in themselves, they constitute a miniature Preachers' Library, to which you will habitually turn whenever you need guidance in your sermon-preparation or in your reading.

The several lists of books which are given for further study are not intended to be in any way complete. Further suggestions on especial subjects can be had on application to the publishers of this *Handbook*.

My own personal thanks are due to all our gifted contributors, most of whom have written their articles amid the pressure of many other affairs and duties and with much burning of the modern equivalent of midnight oil, and none of whom has grudged the added labour; to the members of our very efficient Studies Board, who have been so generous in encouragement and so helpful in counsel; and to the Connexional Editor, the Book Steward, and the staff of the Methodist Publishing House, without whose sympathetic interest and unfailing co-operation this *Handbook* could not have been published.

GREVILLE P. LEWIS.

CONTENTS

PART ONE

Introductory Articles

---

1. The Preacher's Life of Prayer *

By DOROTHY H. FARRAR, B.A., Ph.D.

'*How shall they hear without a preacher?*' (Rom. 10 [14]).

'. . . *but as of sincerity, but as of God, in the sight of God speak we in Christ*' (2 Cor. 2 [17]).

'*Perhaps no sin of omission more frequently occasions this [the Wilderness State] than the neglect of private prayer; the want whereof cannot be supplied by any other ordinance whatever. Nothing can be more plain, than that the life of God in the soul does not continue, much less increase, unless we use all opportunities of communion with God, and pouring out our hearts before Him. If, therefore, we are negligent of this, if we suffer business, company, or any avocation whatever, to prevent these secret exercises of the soul (or, which comes to the same thing, to make us hurry them over in a slight and careless manner), that life will surely decay. And if we long or frequently intermit them, it will gradually die away*' (Wesley's *Sermons*, XL: 'The Wilderness State').

WE may say, 'If preachers do not pray they should not preach'; it would be more true to say, 'If preachers do not pray they cannot preach'. They may give admirable addresses on a variety of topics, searching analyses of the world situation, little talks with nice little titles, but they are not able to proclaim the good news about the Lord Jesus Christ. Local Preachers whose life of private prayer has become irregular, hasty or neglected may be Local Speakers; they are not Local *Preachers*.

Why not? Because our preaching must be a witness to God in Jesus Christ and we cannot speak of One whose call we have forgotten and of whose present working we are ignorant. Paul longed for his people that they should 'know', and without a

*Some of the material in this Article will be found in Dr. D. H. Farrar's '*The Life of Prayer*'; No. 10 of the '*Message and Mission of Methodism*' booklets (Epworth Press).

I

living communion with God we cannot 'know', because we cannot understand the Word of God in the Bible unless we allow God to work in our minds and hearts. *Insight into the Scriptures* is the very groundwork of our preaching, and this cannot be gained without prayerful reading. Studying for examinations is not enough; He Himself must open the Scriptures to us. Our subject-matter, our texts, and the thoughts which we must offer must be given to us, and they are given only to those whose minds are near to the Mind of God. A real sermon is begun, continued, and ended in Him. We cannot know the innermost needs of those to whom we preach, but He does, and so we need His constant help if we are to know how to offer the message of the Bible to our contemporaries.

Further, every Local Preacher is called upon *to lead in prayer*. This is impossible unless the preacher's own life of prayer is deep and steady. The reading of a Collect can be no more than words, while the extempore prayer which is the heritage of the Free Churches can become an address to the Almighty, an exhortation to the congregation, or a rambling discourse which actually prevents the weary congregation from praying. It is only by learning through prayer an ever deeper love for, and understanding of God and our fellows, that we shall be guarded from becoming 'sounding brass' and 'tinkling cymbals'. And in our own lives we dare not overlook Paul's solemn warning, 'lest by any means, after that I have preached to others, I myself should be rejected' (1 Cor. 9 27).

Any thought about the life of prayer brings us straight to *the question of time*, for He needs time with us as we with Him. The life of the monastic cell is not for the business man, the technician, the housewife, the student, or the Local Preacher. But it is quite wrong to believe that, without such conditions as services several times a day and hours of uninterrupted meditation, the deep communion with God cannot be theirs. Let us remember those who had to struggle to find time for quiet; above all, our Lord himself; or St. Paul in journeyings often with the care of all the Churches upon him; John Wesley toiling, travelling, writing, thinking, preaching; and ask whether or not it is possible to have deep communion with God under pressure and strain. It was said of one great Christian: 'Here was a man bustling, striving, organizing, speaking and preaching, with the dust and fire of the world on his clothes, but carrying his shrine with him everywhere.' We cannot have three or four hours a day for prayer and reading, but we can make half an hour, with moments of remembrance in buses or trains, and an upward look at the beginning or ending of a piece of work. Many people are working a five-day week and have more leisure; is any of it given to God?

To spend some time in quiet each day is, of course, a matter of *personal planning*. For those who live alone or spend hours of the day alone it depends on their own ingenuity. It can be done. But many people live in families or communities, often with little space or privacy, and here a real difficulty begins which is rarely faced. One of the first responsibilities of the members of a Christian family is to make it easy for one another to pray. But any one of us who cares enough will manage in some way to make a quiet place for God, the more so because He does not leave us to struggle alone, even in the planning of our prayers. He is there to guide, to comfort, and to bless: to bring new ideas to the mind, to smooth the path unexpectedly, and to give the courage to persist when the road seems to wind uphill all the way.

When we have faced this question of time and actually enter upon our prayer, let us remember first of all that God is more concerned with it all than we are, and that *He is intimately near* whether we feel it or not. Even though there seems to be a blankness before us, He is there, and we need not worry or fret. It is true to say of our little prayers as of the creation of the universe: ' In the beginning . . . God.' His servants in all ages have known that their dealings with God were all begun by Him. He spoke, they answered. We have lost sight of this amazing fact. We settle down to address God in praise or petition and never realize that our first 'O God', 'O Father', 'O Lord', is not a call but an answer. 'The Master is here and calleth for thee.' Our very impulse to pray is not our own: the fear, the restless dissatisfaction, the heart-break or the joy which turns our minds to Him is His summons. We have so easily accepted the idea that it is we who do all the seeking and the calling, that we tend like the prophets of Baal to call more loudly in order to bring Him nearer, forgetting that our own clamour rings so loudly in our ears that it drowns the Voice which says 'Come unto Me . . .'. A great Christian has said: 'For Thou didst first stir me up that I might seek Thee.' The beginning is always His, not ours, and we need to dwell on this fact at the opening of our quiet time. But what next?

We need *the Bible*, not only for preaching, but for our own souls, and there is no substitute. In it we find teaching about prayer given by Jesus himself, words in the Psalms which clothe our deep desires in words, but more than this; through it God speaks to our deepest needs and, above all, shows us through our Lord Jesus Christ what He is like. We do not realize this by quick superficial reading which does nothing but make the well-known words better known and less understood, but by slow prayerful consideration—the 'searching the Scriptures' of which John Wesley speaks.

There are certain points it is well to keep in mind about reading the Bible:

1. Have a plan. Almost any honest persevering plan will do, but there are schemes of Bible reading, such as the Bible Reading Fellowship leaflets, and others, which are helpful to many people. But it is good to draw up one's own scheme for a week or month.

2. Read slowly, and, especially in the Gospels, try to imagine the scene described.

3. Read sometimes in an unfamiliar translation of the Bible or perhaps in a different language, if possible.

4. When time permits, read a long stretch of the Bible at a sitting, e.g. St. Mark's Gospel or the Epistle to the Philippians.

5. Read expectantly. God has a word for us in the reading; it may be a word of comfort or pardon, or it may be a word of searching rebuke, but His love is waiting to reach us all as we read.

Many Methodists have never thought of using their *Hymn Books* to help their prayers, and yet Wesley in his Preface commends the book, not only for congregational singing, but to the Reader 'as a means of raising or quickening the spirit of devotion, of confirming his faith; of enlivening his hope; and of kindling and increasing his love to God and man'. Our hymns are very near the thought and the language of the Bible, and not only give us an outlet for feeling, but show us a spiritual experience deeper than our own which we can come to share. We can join with men and women of all ages and many nations when we speak to God in the words of the great hymns.

The Christian Gospel teaches us that loving intimate converse is possible between an ordinary sinful human being and the Father in Heaven, by whom through Jesus Christ it is sought and made possible. We both speak and listen as He speaks and listens to us. How should we speak and of what may we speak? St. Paul has told us: 'In nothing be anxious, but in everything by prayer and thanksgiving let your requests be made known unto God.' Many need this counsel, because speaking to God is for them a dull, conventional business. In their right desire to be reverent, their language may be stilted or semi-biblical and is far removed from their usual way of speaking. Certain subjects are permitted to enter their prayer, others are rigidly excluded as being unfit for God to know. Anyone who has spoken with people in trouble knows how often the question, 'Have you told God about this?', meets with a surprised 'No'. We must be open with God. We so easily deceive ourselves, and our insincerity kills our prayer before we realize what is happening. Often we act a part before the world, but to pretend to God is intolerable. The true communion is as rich and varied as life itself for 'in everything' includes hopes and fears, worries and excitements, shame and pain, new and lovely thoughts of God or base resentment against Him. Let Him hear all, for we need not banish from our prayer anything that matters to us. But we must hear what He says about it all and let Him tell us where we are wrong, mistaken or ignorant.

A great German theologian has said: 'Everything must come to this: right hearing, and hearing again, and better hearing.' We must attend to such a word, for most of us know that we are *too talkative* in prayer, and that what God has to say to us is far more important than what we have to say to Him. Some have said that 'listening to God is a strain' and that against their reason they have expected an audible voice. So they give up the uncomfortable effort, concluding that they are not the right type for such prayer. There is no need for such perplexity. We use the word 'listening' because it is natural and has become part of the language of devotion, but we know that it does not describe the many ways of communication between God and ourselves. Our friends convey much to us without direct speech and God has more ways of reaching us than we dream. Words read, or spoken by friends, a song, a mountain, a sunset or the sea may be God's messengers. In our own thoughts, God may use a memory of the past, a sudden new idea, a plan or hope for the future, and can make us realize that He is speaking through it. We can sometimes see how these thoughts come, sometimes it is a mystery: sometimes a thought which we believe holds a message from God comes with force and urgency, sometimes in slow and tranquil manner. In our times of quiet, He uses these inner ways of reaching us, and as we follow Him we learn to distinguish with growing assurance His presence in our thinking and our praying and to 'hear Him inly speak'.

Men and women who have loved God have never been able to think of their communion with Him as ending with their death. On the contrary, they have longed for a deeper communion, when they would see God more clearly and love Him more perfectly than is possible in this life. Their longing has a curious certainty about it as though they had some inner assurance from God Himself that their hopes would not be disappointed: 'For to me to live is Christ, and to die is gain . . . having a desire to depart, and to be with Christ; which is far better' (Phil. 1 21–23).

> Yet onward I haste
> To the heavenly feast:
> That, that is the fullness; but this is the taste;
> And this I shall prove
> Till with joy I remove
> To the heaven of heavens in Jesus's love.

No words about ordinary daily prayer would be complete which did not end with the communion of saints and the vision of God, for they belong together and must not be divided. He calls us and leads us through struggle and failure to see His face. As we learn this, we know that difficulties about time for prayer, costly decisions, and dark hours are as nothing compared with the amazing truth that when we pray we enter into the life eternal, which is to know Him.

Book List

The Quiet of Christ (A Talk about the Practice of Private Prayer). Crete Gray, B.A. (Epworth Press).

Prayer Circles I. E. C. Tanton (Epworth Press).

Prayer Circles II. E. C. Tanton (Epworth Press).

The Vigil with God. P. J. Fisher (Epworth Press).

A Time for Silence. E. Parsons, M.A., B.A., Ph.D. (Epworth Press).

2. *The Conduct of Public Prayer*

By the Rev. ARTHUR N. ROSE, M.A.

The Aim of Worship

BEFORE we can consider the planning of a service, we must try to define what we mean by worship. Worship may be described as the response of a soul meeting with God. Our task as leaders in congregational worship is to bring our people to that moment of encounter. Not only the prayers, but every part of the service, ought to be directed to this end. The spirit and purpose of worship must pervade the reading and the preaching of the Word, equally with the prayer and the praise. There must be this sense of meeting if worship is to be real, and no one can lead another to that point unless he has come there himself. We must be aware of God even before we are aware of the congregation.

The silent prayer which follows our entry into the pulpit is itself symbolic. We close our eyes to the congregation and lift our hearts to God.

The leading of congregational worship is very different from saying our own prayers in public. It may be moving to listen on occasions to someone praying who, forgetful of any audience, is himself rapt in the presence of God. It may inspire in others a desire to learn to pray, as when the disciples overheard their Master at prayer. But the leader of a worshipping company is not saying his own prayers; he is the voice of a congregation and must be sensitively conscious of their moods and needs. Anyone who leads others in worship is exercising a true priesthood. He is presenting God to his people and representing his people before God.

Common Prayer

Every service is a fellowship in worship. Its characteristic should be 'common prayer'. The congregation is not the preacher's audience, for all the while there is some definite part, whether audible or silent, which they should be taking in the service. The leader's business is to make their participation possible. This may be done in various ways. Congregational singing is one great traditional method by which Methodism has provided for community in worship. A Lesson may sometimes be used for the same purpose and read responsively by leader and congregation. Narrative or doctrinal passages are not suitable for such use, but Hebrew poetry in Psalms and prophetic writings by its very form lends itself to this. When the Lesson is read in the ordinary way, a brief explanatory introduction may help the hearer to penetrate the meaning and spirit of the passage, and to worship God with his mind as he listens.

There are many ways of securing the participation of the congregation in the prayers, but whatever method is used it can only afford a common framework into which the worshipper must bring his own personal confession or thankfulness or need. It is the more necessary, therefore, for the leader to study his people and to 'sit where they sit', and not merely to give expression to his own thoughts and petitions; hence the need for thoughtful preparation beforehand, with the congregation in mind.

Types of Prayer

There are three great traditions in the ordering of Christian worship preserved in the different branches of the Christian Church—the liturgical, characteristic of the Anglican, Roman, and Orthodox Communions; extempore prayer, used more generally in the Free Churches; and the silent worship which belongs to the Friends' Meeting. We may well learn from one another, for each method has its contribution to make to the conduct of Christian worship.

Silence enables us to recollect God's presence, to wait upon Him. It induces the 'listening' attitude which is proper to prayer. It enables us to dwell more thoughtfully upon some truth and its application to our own lives, or to use our imaginations to identify ourselves in understanding and sympathy with some human need. It is a challenge which demands the effort of personal prayer from each member of the congregation, and for that reason is, perhaps, difficult but none-the-less valuable for those unaccustomed to its use.

Rightly used, *responsive forms* of praise and prayer enable the worshippers to join more freely in the service than when they have to follow in silence the words of one man. Invitations to prayer or thanksgiving or confession, followed by a moment or two of silent response, and then, if necessary, gathered up in a brief spoken prayer, may break up a long prayer in a way which will make the continuous attention and participation of the congregation easier. A call to pray for some particular object, before the prayer is said, also enables those assembled to 'agree together' concerning that which they shall ask. Even the audible 'Amen' of the congregation at the end of each brief act of prayer or praise may draw the people together with a deepened sense of fellowship in worship.

It is not so easy to provide for responsive worship in a service where there is no printed order in the hands of the congregation, but it can be done successfully if the preacher leads clearly by some introductory word before each congregational response as, for instance:

LEADER: Let us pray for . . .
                      (*Silence*)

LEADER: Lord hear our prayer.

CONGREGATION: *And let our cry come unto Thee.*

Or:

LEADER: Let us give thanks for . . .
                      (*Silence*)

LEADER: Let us praise God.

CONGREGATION: *We give thanks unto Thee, O Father.*

The Leader should announce what the introduction and response are to be before commencing the prayer, and should not vary the response too often lest he burden the memory of the worshipper unnecessarily. The pause for recollection, between each petition or thanksgiving and the introduction and response, is helpful to thoughtful devotion.

There are hymns in the Methodist book, such as numbers 295 and 727, in the form of litanies, and passages at the end of the book ('Ancient Hymns and Canticles' numbers 11–14) which lend themselves to responsive use. Amongst these passages there are also some which can be used as prayers and thanksgiving spoken by the leader and congregation together, *e.g.* for confession (numbers 35 and 59), for adoration (numbers 9 and 60 or sections of the *Te Deum*), or for thanksgiving (numbers 51 and 52).

Discipline in Thought and Expression

In expressing the worship of the congregation, the leader should aim at simplicity and dignity of utterance; hackneyed phrases and pseudo-archaic language should be carefully avoided, but familiar and beautiful words have by association a gathered sacredness and may strike a responsive chord in the heart of the listener. Their very beauty will create an atmosphere of reverence, for beauty is one of the attributes of God. For thought and phrase, therefore, corporate worship may rightly draw upon its 'mother tongue', the language of Scripture, and upon the great heritage of devotion that has come to us from centuries of Christian prayer. These sources may be used to discipline expression, without hindering or replacing the freshness and spontaneity of the extempore prayer which is also part of our tradition.

One of the best preparations for *extempore prayer* is to pray privately before the service, with the special theme or aim of the service and the needs of the congregation in mind. It is also useful to have some general framework of subjects for prayer and thanksgiving to guide one's prayer and to avoid diffuseness and repetition.

The peril of formality can beset the use of extempore prayer as well as liturgy. If the leader is not careful to develop his range of thought and powers of devotional expression, he may easily become very limited in the scope of his prayers, and fall into the repetition of hackneyed phrases at least as stereotyped and far less beautiful than those of a set order. Another unconscious but easily acquired bad habit in public prayer is the too-frequent repetition of a particular form of address to God: it is not necessary to introduce 'O Lord' or 'Dear Father' or any other such phrase into every other sentence. We should try to avoid equally an undignified familiarity and formality of language. Public prayer has its conventions of speech, such as the use of 'Thee' and 'Thou', which, because of widely accepted custom are associated with worship, and, like the distinctive architecture of a church, help to create atmosphere. If these are lightly set aside, the unfamiliar may jar the minds of the congregation; but stilted and ecclesiastical language will create an atmosphere of unreality and remoteness from the ways of thought of ordinary folk. We can only escape these faults that lie in wait on either hand by going to school with the acknowledged masters of the art of prayer for help in the careful and deliberate discipline of preparation. Whether or not written prayers, prepared or borrowed from the library of Christian devotion, are used during the service, we do well to feed our own prayer life upon the thoughts and words of great souls at prayer, and to practise our own powers of orderly and worthy expression by writing down prayers and preparing schemes of prayer from time to time. If memorized or read prayers are used in the pulpit, we must remember that only the living spirit of worship, both in preparation and in use, can prevent them from becoming no more than the 'dry bones' of prayer.

The Full Chord of Worship

There are many varied notes in the full chord of worship—adoration and thanksgiving, penitence and confession, prayer for deliverance, the assurance of forgiveness, the petition for grace, the presentation of our personal needs, the commendation of loved ones to the divine care, intercession for all sorts and conditions of men. Each note should find its place somewhere in the service, but one or other may be dominant on one particular occasion and not every one need find its place in spoken prayer; it may be sufficiently voiced in hymns or in Scripture. This should be borne in mind in the selection of the hymns.

The service that is treated as a unity, in which each part leads up to some central memorable thought that is the keynote of the whole, will leave a more lasting impression than one which consists of unrelated fragments; yet the service should be varied enough to meet the needs of young and old, sinner and saint, the eager and happy, and also the tired and troubled. It should be challenging and disturbing, and yet have for burdened souls the gift of peace.

Adoration and Thanksgiving

One note should be the over-tone of all others—the note of *adoration*.

> *That stoop of the soul which in bending upraises it too—*
> *The submission of Man's nothing-perfect to God's All-Complete,*
> *As by each low obeisance in spirit I climb to His feet.*

No prayer should be a theological discourse or a disguised moral exhortation to the congregation, but it may well be preoccupied with God rather than with our human needs and desires. To help the congregation to dwell upon the beauty or majesty or holiness or love of God and to bow in wonder before Him, to say to them 'Behold your God!', to lead them to cry with angels and archangels, 'Holy, Holy, Holy, Lord God of Hosts, Heaven and Earth are full of Thy Glory,' is to lead them where wants and anxieties and all our little human concerns fall into a new perspective.

Thanksgiving gives a similar direction to our thought, and, as Paul reminds us in his letter to the Philippians, is a great antidote to anxiety. To take our life thoughtfully and thankfully from the hands of God is to lend an uncommon radiance to common things, and make even our daily bread the sacrament of His love. Thus one great aim of worship is the hallowing of ordinary life. Worship may be an escape from the world, but only for a time, and that we may return to it on a new level.

Confession and Intercession

In corporate *confession*, we are not only expressing our own contrition for remembered faults, but identifying ourselves with our world in its sin and strife, and bearing its burden on our hearts before God. In the same way, the Christian's *intercession* embraces the whole world for which Christ died, in all its varied needs; but such comprehensiveness is not effectively possible within the compass of one prayer or even one service. The selection of some one theme, perhaps some pressing concern which is present to the minds of those assembled at the moment and the concentration of intercession upon that, may be far more helpful than an attempt to compass too wide a range at one time. We cannot include all the needs of all the members of our congregation in any prayer that we make. An interval of silent intercession, in which each member is given an opportunity to add some prayer of his own, may provide for urgent needs and concerns which the leader has not gathered within the common prayer.

Our approach to intercession is important. We are not seeking to importune God. Intercession is first of all the simple, trustful presentation of His children's needs to the Father of all. It is also remembering before Him the world which is the object of His redeeming love, and sharing the longing and the burden of that love. It may have an intensity which amounts to agony when we are made great enough in heart to feel it, but this is not the intensity of anxiety: it is the intensity of the loving concern and compassion which we achieve only when we enter into the fellowship of His sufferings. Such intercession has upon it the stigmata—the marks of the wound-prints of Christ.

Introductory and Closing Prayer

If it does not become a formal introduction and conclusion, prayer immediately before or after the sermon is a goodly custom. It provides the right approach and the right climax, for every sermon should quite literally point men to God, else it is an irrelevance in the heart of worship.

Let the Benediction, too, be so pronounced that it is not a mere announcement that the service is now over and the folk may prepare to go home. Let it breathe the atmosphere of divine peace in which the congregation will naturally linger for the last moment of silence, and from which they will get up quietly and go thoughtfully.

We have continually stressed the need for a preparation of each part of the service as careful as our preparation of the sermon. The service must be 'ordered' throughout; that is not to say that its form need be rigidly determined or inflexible to unforeseen impulses of the Spirit; but the leader, in order to lead, must think himself beforehand into the heart of the congregation and into the presence of God, and he must study to give the worthiest possible expression on their behalf to the great acts of adoration and thanksgiving, of penitence and intercession. There must be nothing casual or little about any thought or word. Above all, the service must be begun, continued, and ended with the sense of an overshadowing Presence, for our whole business as leaders and preachers is to lead men to God.

Book List

Prayer. W. E. Sangster, M.A., Ph.D. (Epworth Press).
Healing Through Prayer. L. D. Weatherhead, M.A., D.D. (Epworth Press).
Women at Worship. A. C. Blain (Epworth Press).
The Service of Worship. Phil J. Fisher (Epworth Press).
Book of Family Worship. Issued by the Methodist Conference. (Epworth Press).

3. The Use of the Bible in Public Worship

By WINSHIP STOREY

Let the Bible Speak!

To realize that the reading of the Scriptures in Public Worship is not merely a time-honoured method of bringing in variety to the order of service, it is only necessary to hear them well read. It was the late F. Luke Wiseman who first electrified me by his intelligent, dramatic, and imaginative rendering of the lessons. As I listened to him I stepped into a new world. Here was language of superb quality to which justice had never been done in my hearing before. Its grandeur and its winsomeness; its sombre dignity and its light-hearted gaiety; its impressive argument and its fascinating descriptiveness; its thrilling narrative, told with an economy of words which is literary artistry of high order—all these facets of the Old Book suddenly became alive with a new light sparkling and flashing from them. I saw in a moment infinite possibilities for the enrichment of Public Worship, simply by giving the Bible a reasonable chance to speak for itself, so that it might make its own appeal through the preacher rather than in spite of him. Throughout the years, I have become more and more impressed with this truth. Indeed it is almost pathetic to notice with what a sudden quickening of interest a congregation becomes alive to the fact that the Word of God is being ably presented in the reading from its pages. The older folk who love its familiar sentences revel in the unexpected (alas the word is true!)—the unexpected status it has suddenly acquired; the younger folk, who have been bored with it often enough, wake up to the fact that this is great literature and, astonishing enough, quite gripping. The service becomes alive—nobody settles down to perfunctory decorum or preoccupied wool-gathering—something is happening. Something definitely is: the Book is speaking.

No preacher can afford to be blind to such a source of power; nor having once seen it, to neglect it.

He will realize too, that the Old Testament, as well as the New, still speaks, and speaks with power. It has not been superseded by the New but fulfilled by it. Jesus himself claimed, even when he was going beyond it in his teaching, that he had by no means come to destroy it. Paul quotes extensively from it, and, bearing in mind that in those days there were no pocket editions, it will be appreciated that this implies he had it largely in his head. If such a thinker as Paul placed such immense value upon the Old Scriptures, let us profit by his example and not neglect them. Most services, as I hope to show later in discussing the choice of the Lessons, can be enriched by selections from both the Old Testament and the New.

Well do I remember on 3rd September 1939 cutting out my sermon altogether, for my people on that tragic day needed a greater word than mine, and reading to them for an hour the great steadying reassuring promises of God, many of them from the Old Testament—to their infinite benefit as well as my own.

The Technique of Bible-Reading

It will readily be appreciated that before you can read well there is a technique to be mastered, and I know of few studies more rewarding than this. The limits of this brief article prevent anything like an exhaustive treatment of it, nor am I qualified for the task; but a few simple suggestions which I myself have proved helpful may be not without value.

First and foremost, learn to *look at your people* as you read. This will involve familiarizing yourself with the lesson beforehand. It is not necessary to memorize it, though if you can do so it will gain even more in effect; but if you have to refer to the book as you read, look back at your people before you resume speaking. There is something very compelling about a reader who *speaks to you*, just as there is something very soulless about a speaker who reads to you. Expression is given with the eye as well as with the voice. Do not neglect it. I have known people, devout enough to follow the reading in their own Bibles, lay them down and sit back enthralled. The reader had given personality to the printed word, and his own had been, in turn, illumined by it.

Remember that the essence of good reading is to give value to *pauses*. They can be most impressive. Be chary of gesture. Restraint is effective; extravagant movement distracting and melodramatic. It is always important to avoid diverting attention from the message to the messenger. The preacher is to be as a mirror reflecting the glory of the Lord, and it is only a faulty mirror that draws attention to itself.

The greatest medium of expression is, however, *the voice*. Wrong cadences can make the most beautiful language insipid and artificial to the ear. To speak *naturally* is the ideal to aim at, but one of the chief difficulties you will need to surmount is to speak naturally in phraseology which is not itself natural to you. Here is the real problem in reading the Scriptures well, for their language is more dignified, more impressive, more majestic than our normal free and easy conversation. It can, however, be done. Listen to a really gifted actor playing Shakespeare; he is meeting the same difficulty, but see how natural he can make it sound.

A very helpful method is to transpose Scripture into your own words and to note the cadences of your voice as you speak: it is easy to speak in a natural tone of voice when using your own words. Then, *preserving the same cadences*, restore the words of Scripture. The result will surprise you. Very little practice will enable you to improve your naturalness out of all recognition. For example, try this from the familiar Parable of the Prodigal Son.

'Lo, these many years do I serve thee, and I never transgressed a commandment of thine: and yet thou never gavest me a kid, that I might make merry with my friends: but when this thy son came, which hath devoured thy living with harlots, thou killedst for him the fatted calf' (Lk. 15 [29-30]).

'All these years I've pulled my weight on the farm here, and I've never let you down once. Yet you never gave *me* the chance to have any of my pals in—nothing but work, work, work. But as soon as this waster turns up again, after dragging the family name in the mire, you put up no end of a spread for *him*.'

Note your cadences—how indignation affects the timbre of your voice and the emphasis of your words: then transfer those cadences to the actual words of the Parable and see how it becomes alive.

You must, of course, practise this by speaking aloud. It is absurd to read the passage aloud for the first time when you are actually in the pulpit, and expect to do it well. The well-known instance of the preacher who read to an astonished congregation that the shepherds found 'Mary and Joseph and the babe lying in the manger' would never have happened had he taken the trouble to read it aloud first and to note the punctuation.

I use modern translations—Moffatt, Weymouth, Ronald Knox, and so on—to learn *what the Scripture means*, for you cannot possibly read with proper intonation and emphasis if you do not yourself understand what you are reading. My own view is, however, that they should be used sparingly in the actual conduct of Divine Worship. They lack the superb grandeur of the Authorized and Revised Versions, save in one or two inspired passages like Moffatt's 1 Corinthians, Chapter 13.

The Choice of Lessons

Of front-rank importance too, is the *choice* of the Lessons. How you read is important: what you read equally so. The use of the Connexional (or any other) Lectionary is, I feel, a matter for individual decision, for there are both advantages and disadvantages arising from it. It prevents your ringing the changes on a few favourite passages, but, more often than not, provides you with a Scripture-reading completely irrelevant to your subject. You can, however, use one with great advantage as a 'subject-finder', if you keep ahead of your appointment list and give yourself time to work up your subject when found. A good Lectionary can be of immense benefit in following out the Christian Year—a practice we Methodists have regrettably allowed to lapse to a large degree—and in this connexion one which will be found of great value is the *St. Andrew's Lectionary of Bible Lessons for use in Services of Public Worship* (Epworth Press, 2s.).

What seems to me the ideal method is to plan, not a sermon, but a whole service. Let Hymns, Lessons, Prayers, Children's Address and Sermon present a coherent and integral whole. By this method the choice of a Lesson will not only increase in importance, since it will have to have some connexion with the rest, but it will become as much part of your message as Prayers or Sermon or Hymns.

What, then, should govern the choice of the passage or passages to be read? The answer is, relevance to the subject. This does not mean that the Lesson should always be the context of the Text of the Sermon. Indeed, in my judgement, the opposite is nearer the ideal. For example—should the subject be 'Fellowship', a telling Lesson might be the story of Elijah on Horeb, fleeing

panic-stricken from Jezebel, believing himself the only one of
God's prophets left alive, and being reassured that God had
seven thousand in Israel which had not bowed the knee to Baal—
a great Fellowship of which Elijah had lost sight (1 Kings 19 1–18);
whilst the text of the sermon might be Phil. 1 3–5: 'I thank my
God . . . for your fellowship.'

It becomes immediately apparent, however, that you need to
know your Bible to be able to do this kind of thing effectively.
It is not so banal as it sounds to observe that one of the best ways
to get to know your Bible is to read it.

A striking effect may sometimes be obtained by reading, as
one lesson, passages from both Old and New Testaments. As
for example, the Battle at Rephidim between Israel and
Amalek (Exodus 17 8–13), together with Eph. 6 12–17. The
contrast and the similarity are both brought out more clearly
than if the two passages were read as separate lessons, divided
by an Anthem or a Hymn.

Or think of the moving story of Abraham's plea for the City of
Sodom (Gen. 18 20–33) placed alongside Christ's solemn words:
'Narrow is the gate, and straitened the way, that leadeth unto
life, and few be they that find it' (Mt. 7 14).

For Palm Sunday a fine sequence of passages on 'The Kingship
of Jesus' will be found in Lk. 19 29–40, Jn. 18 33–40 (using the
emphatic 'Certainly I am a King' in v. 37), Jn. 19 12–22, Rev.
19 11–16. These read without interruption, as one vital unit in the
service, can have a powerful effect.

I mention these merely as illustrations of a method. Let your
own individuality and imagination guide you. Do not copy
slavishly any other preacher, however great he may be. God has
given you your own message, and your use of the Word of God
can be a vivid part of it.

Use a *Marginal Reference Bible*. This is invaluable, for very
often it is possible to drop almost straight away on to a passage
wherein a similar subject is treated, and an appropriate lesson
is found to your very hand. Use a *Concordance* similarly—this is
only one of the uses of a good Concordance, but it is an important
one—selecting a key-word of your subject or a synonym of it
and tracing out related ideas.

If you are preaching from one of the Parables it will save time
in your sermon to read the Parable as a Lesson, provided you do
not go over the whole detail of the story again in your discourse.

The imaginative choice of Scripture passages is only possible to those who know what they have available to consider, and so we are driven back to the fundamental fact that familiarity with the Bible is the preacher's greatest asset. There are many aids to the exploration of this treasure-house (*see below*). Your own devotional life will be deepened by constant and regular study, your mind quickened, your vision clarified, your horizon widened, your preaching enriched and your soul reassured. Like the Master of whom it speaks, its touch hath still its ancient power, no word from it can fruitless fall.

Book List

Reading Your Bible (A New Lectionary). R. E. Davies, M.A., B.D. (Epworth Press).
The Making and Meaning of the Bible. G. Barclay (S.C.M. Press).
The Best Book in the World. P. T. R. Kirk (Epworth Press).
Helps to the Study of the Bible (O.U.P.).

4. The Gospel Message*

By the Rev. W. EDWIN SANGSTER, M.A., Ph.D.

WHAT is the Christian Gospel? What precise message is the evangelist commissioned to bring? It is news of God.

This news! That God has come to earth in Christ to give new life to everybody who will receive it. What He came to do, the evangelist affirms, He has done, and does still. It is life in all its fullness, abundant and eternal; it is, indeed, the very life of God Himself.

By faith—itself a gift of God—any poor, stained, and stunted sinner may be united to the life of God. His old self may die. He can say: 'To me to live is Christ.' He can, indeed, so have the life of God as *his* life, that it is not enough to call it the *power* of Christ, or the *help* of Christ, or even *Christ-likeness*. It is Christ Himself—not just saving him from without but actually living within; thinking, feeling, willing, in the life of His consenting servant. It is incredible—but true!

The offer is to persons, and can be accepted, therefore, only by persons; but as persons receive it, it transforms their related life and whole families may glow with the supernal life of God. Communities could be transformed. It could change the world.

The reception of this life does not depend on circumstances. Men who live heedless of God can be happy in a shallow way if their circumstances are kindly. That is why the multitude does not believe that religion is necessary to happiness and fullness of life. But an accident, a change of fortune, someone's death, and happiness is often finished for them; if they think ahead at all, they travel the rest of the road without peace or hope; they may simulate an outward gaiety, but the outlook is irredeemably dark.

This offer of new life in Christ is sometimes expressed in five 'universals'; certainly the chief leaders of the great eighteenth-

*This Article is a shortened version of a chapter headed 'The Substance of the Message' in Dr. W. E. Sangster's excellent book 'Let Me Commend' (Hodder & Stoughton, 5s.). I am most grateful to both the author and the publishers for permission to include this Article in our *Handbook*.— G. P. L.

century Evangelical Revival saw it that way, and held that the New Testament sustained their beliefs. An outline of the evangelist's task lies in these five 'universals'.

1. *All men need this life.*

The evangelist must convince heedless men, living (some of them) an animal life, drugging their conscience and believing a lie, that for all their talk of life they've never had it; that in the profoundest sense possible to human beings, they have never been born.

2. *All men may have this life.*

When desire awakens in them and their conscience condemns, the evangelist must convince them that the offer is for *them;* the most evil, sin-stained, blasphemous soul may come.

> *Pardon—from an offended God!*
> *Pardon—for sins of deepest dye!*
> *Pardon—bestowed through Jesu's blood!*
> *Pardon—that brings the rebel nigh!*
>
> *Who is a pardoning God like Thee?*
> *Or who has grace so rich and free?*

3. *All men who have this life, know that they have it.*

To have this quality of life, and not to know it, is impossible. Yet the evangelist must teach his convert not to live on fluctuating feeling, but to know his possession of this new life by the inward witness and moral power of God.

4. *All men must witness to its possession.*

The evangelist cannot allow a convert, even if it were possible, to carry this treasure about as though it were a guilty secret; something kept to the self and never mentioned to a soul. The plain duty and the high privilege of witnessing, he must impress on every one.

5. *All men must press on to perfection.*

The evangelist must make clear to those new-born in the life of God, that this life, like all life, involves growth; that no limit need be put to its development; that whatever decay marks the life of men, no decay mars the life of God. And *this* is the life of God! Therefore, it is 'nor wanting, nor wasting'.

But to these five 'universals', three other affirmations, rooted in the New Testament, have been happily stressed again by evangelists of recent years (*e.g.* by Dr. W. Russell Maltby).

1. *Once for All.*

However sure we may be that God has fresh light to break out of His Word, when The Word became flesh, God spoke for all time. All else is ancillary, comment, interpretation.

2. *All or Nothing.*

The response of a mortal to his God must, in the end, be utter. Though we know that our partial consecrations are not despised in heaven, and that we ourselves are not always aware of our own reservations, we know also that a dedication deliberately defective is dishonouring to God and limits the Holy One of Israel.

> *Love so amazing, so divine,*
> *Demands my soul, my life, my all.*

3. *Here and Now.*

There is nothing more glorious in the gospel offer than this. The evangelist can cry from the housetops that God will meet the sinner where he is. *Just* where he is! He can say 'Here'.

And 'Now'! It is no accident that gospel songs in all generations have had the note of urgency and of immediate offer. 'Make no delay.' 'Do not tarry.' 'Now, poor sinner.' 'Now to be Thine, yea, Thine alone.'

Charles Wesley's adoring soul had grasped the precious truth of it when he cried:

> *Father,* now *accept of mine,*
> *Which* now, *through Christ, I offer Thee;*
> *Tell me* now, *in love divine,*
> *That Thou hast pardoned me.*

But while the evangelical offer is gloriously the same in every age, because the herald is commissioned to bring the gospel 'once delivered to the saints', it remains true that the message has to be related to the particular need of each age, and expressed, to some extent, in its thought-forms. It cannot be denied, of course, that the deeper needs of men are the same in every age, but they cloak themselves differently and must be reached in different ways.

Relevant preaching cannot, in Phillips Brooks's phrase, simply be 'truth through personality'; it must be truth through personality in relation to the time of its utterance.

It is important, therefore, not only that the evangelist grasp the marrow of his message, but that he knows also the men and the age to which he speaks. The timelessness of the gospel does not mean that preachers can go on giving addresses made for men and women in the nineties, and expect them to be effective today.

What, then, are the characteristics of our age so far as they affect evangelism?

1. *There is a scepticism of all authority.*

We have lived in an age of propaganda and its plainest fruit is unbelief. Men have been treated as 'nit-wits' to be 'worked on', and some have believed that the only way to fight propaganda is more propaganda. Consequently, men do not believe what they are told on *any* authority. The only question in their minds as they listen is this : 'Why do you *want* me to believe that?' They suspect a soiled motive behind all advocacy, and they do not exempt the evangelist from their suspicions.

2. *There is a widespread and genuine social concern.*

It will always be true that the evangelical appeal must be addressed to individuals. Individuals are the unit of personality. To talk of 'group minds' is to talk in metaphor. Only a *person* can say 'Yes' or 'No' to God. In the nature of things, therefore, the evangelist makes his offer to persons, and would beat the air if he did anything else. He does well to remind people who use the prayer 'Thy Kingdom come' that there is only one place where God's Kingdom can come by their will alone, and that is in their own heart.

So he attacks the citadel of the individual heart and will, and in some ages he was not merely right, but felt wholly relevant.

He is still right, but does not feel so wholly relevant. He suspects that people listen to him now with their mind ranging over social and world problems. 'How much does it really matter what I do as an individual?' 'How is this going to influence, in any large way, the community and the world?'

Some nineteenth century evangelism is mildly satirized today, even in evangelical circles, because it was a simple 'Come to

Jesus' appeal, and folk as we know them now (if they can be won to interest in religion at all) are much more concerned with the rule of God over *all* life.

It is still to men and women that the evangelist must make his appeal, but it must be to persons in their relations rather than to individuals in their separateness.

3. *There is a scientific approach to most things and an excessive specialism.*

Tens of thousands of the thoughtful youth of the world (to whom the evangelist especially desires to appeal) approach truth on the assumption that what cannot be subjected to inquiry under scientific method is hardly a subject for knowledge at all. The business of truth today is regarded as the exclusive sphere of the scientist. Because the early expressions of religion were in human sacrifice and something bordering on necromancy, they wave all religion aside (even in its highest forms) as mythology. It seems not to occur to them that if they judged modern medical and surgical practice on the same basis, and recalled its origin in the 'medicine man' and the maker of 'charms,' they would have as little to do today with scientific healing as many of them do with the religion of Christ.

If these, then, are the chief characteristics of our age (as they affect evangelism), how may the herald of God approach his task? In what way (if any) can he wrest the difficulties to his advantage?

1. *He will remember that human nature still craves for happiness and inward peace.*

He knows in his own glowing experience that he has both to offer.

However happy a godless man in good health and easy circumstances may seem—and indeed *be*—if he thinks at all, he knows his happiness is transient. It is built on sand; sinking sand.

Hard questions gnaw in his mind—the old, hard, not-to-be-denied questions which have ever haunted our race: Why am I here? What is the meaning of life? Has it a meaning at all? What comes after this? Does love survive death?—Any man with a sure word from God concerning those questions can never be regarded as irrelevant. Mistaken, perhaps, but not irrelevant.

2. *The evangelist can also snatch opportunity from the prevalent world-despair*.

Surely, not even when Rome fell was fear as widespread, or as well founded, as it is today. Most of the scientists are scared men. Clearly, war does not end war. Science only gives more terrible weapons with which to wage it. Nor can science replace a lost moral authority, or fashion a new set of spiritual principles which will be universally accepted and observed.

Is it possible for the evangelist to relate his message to this world-despair?

Nobody is honestly content with things as they are. If men are less willing than once they were to admit personal sin, they are even eager to admit frustration and 'world sin'. Millions starve—and need not. Blind racial hate and ideological antagonisms swell, and fester, and threaten, at any time, to burst. Men batten on black markets, and are the direct cause of the slow death of innocent children.

Is this the brave new world? Is this the best that men can do with all their wit? Is it not plain that what is needed is the wide recovery and respect for spiritual authority and the whole moral counsel of God?

So the herald of the Kingdom demands to be heard. 'It isn't a new theory we want,' he says. 'No man, not smug in intellectual pride, believes that our ills can be cured by another mental formula. Man is sick inside. The disease is in the will more than in the mind. There *are* such things as external frustrations, but the chief frustration is sin in ourselves. When man *sees* what is wrong, he can't mend it. It is new life we need; the life of God. I offer it to you—in Christ. Here and now! It is potent. It can only enter the world through persons, but, so entering, the world itself can be transformed by its power.'

3. *The evangelist can also find opportunity in the acute personal futility people feel today*.

The ordinary man, when he thinks at all, is half-paralysed at the thought that he does not matter. The world is run, he believes (where it can be said to be 'run' at all) by 'high-ups'. For all the lip-service paid him by politicians, he feels that he is just 'one of the masses'. He suspects that he is planned-for, planned-on, and planned-over, but not enough treated as a person. He feels, at times, less than a pawn in a game played over his head by the people in authority, and he waits the next crisis, or the next depression, or the next war, powerless himself to put it off. He is 'mass-man', in an age of mass-production, with more than half his individuality ironed out.

The evangelist treats him as a person; assures him (incredible thought!) that he is dear to God—dear enough to shed the precious blood. He shows him the Cross. He is, so the preacher affirms, so intimately known to God that the hairs of his head are all numbered, and God has set such store on winning his love that He gives His own Son for the gift of a sinner's heart. If he will trust God for it, new life will flood into him—the life of God.

In an age of personal futility, the evangelist has a sovereign opportunity so to offer the life of God to people that futility will vanish in conscious effectiveness, and each new-born soul know himself a person in the sight of his Maker.

For the rest, the questions which evangelists discuss today concerning their message and its presentation are old questions, and new only in the sense that a new age might invite a new emphasis.

1. *Is the happiness motive in evangelism legitimate?*

It seems to me, quite emphatically, that it is. Even if some people have made the mistake, in time past, of supposing that God's chief purpose with us is to make us happy, when, of course, His chief aim is to make us good, it would be a pity if we forgot that the second fruit of the spirit is joy. In the Stoic world, virtue is its own reward, but Christianity includes more rewards for virtue than virtue itself. There is no need to over-refine our ethics. The New Testament is full of rewards. Indeed, the Beatitudes is a list of them.

The evangelist may justly invite people to Christ with the promise of unspeakable happiness from Him. Indeed, it is hard when one looks at people in trains, and sees how few of them look really happy when their faces are in repose, not to overleap all the conventions and accost them, though strangers, with the news of incredible happiness in Christ. To use the longing for happiness as a motive in others, and to illustrate its radiance in himself, is the privilege of every evangelist.

2. Is the fear motive in evangelism legitimate?

I don't see how it can honestly be left out, though it is the sounder strategy not so much to implant it as to find it there. It *is* there—and needs but to be awakened. If it is a plain and demonstrable fact that to say 'No' to the offer of new life in Christ brings the saddest consequences in this life, and consequences no less sad in any other life we can imagine, it seems to me more plainly our duty to warn people of the danger of this great refusal than to warn them—at which we are all busy—of risk in crossing the road.

Not all fear is evil. Fear is still the best policeman on our traffic-infested streets. Fear of a dread disease helped many a lad to keep the path of virtue when he was away at the War. One can call it craven and immature, if one wishes, but all of us, in our spiritual immaturity, have owed something to 'the fear of the consequences'. It may be that preachers, in other ages, have over-stressed the terrors of refusing God, and peopled the lower strata of children's minds with fearful images. But that is not a fault today.

In the past, all great preaching has been delivered on a background of impending judgement, and all true preaching must be.

3. Is the dread of emotion in evangelism legitimate?

Emotion cannot be cut out of life. To unpick human personality and remove all deep feeling is an impossible occupation, and, if it could succeed, would leave life sterile indeed. Imagine life without the warm overtones of love; conceive a family where everyone acted only from a cold sense of duty; suppose a youth to ask a maiden to marry him, having carefully explained to her first that he had no feelings for her—life cannot be filleted this way. It ends in vast absurdity.

And carry the same inquiry into religion. Require that the herald of God announce the offer of his King, freely to pardon and fully to bless, but firmly forbid that any transport of joy should accompany either the announcement of the news or its glad reception—and you ask the impossible.

The dread of emotion in religious expression has gone to extreme lengths, and some critics appear to suspect any conversion which does not take place in a refrigerator! No doubt there have been dangers in emotionalism. The evangelism which attacks the heart without any appeal to the mind, and snatches pathetic 'decisions' from folk gale-swept by feeling, but quite un-aware of what they are doing, is unworthy and dishonouring to God.

But that doesn't cut out emotion. The man who screams at a football match, but is distressed when he hears of a sinner weeping at the Cross, and murmurs something about 'the dangers of emotionalism', hardly merits intelligent respect.

4. Is the Gospel a demand or an offer?

It is an offer—an offer of pardon and new life in God. It is that which makes it good news. But it isn't hard to understand why men have discussed this question so long.

Preaching the gospel should always be preceded by preaching the moral law, whether the phrase is used or not. The moral law is what God *demands*, and what our consciences confirm as being due. Only people inwardly distressed by conscious failure are likely to hear the gospel as good news. To all the rest, it is perilously near to casting pearls to swine.

Hence John Wesley's evangelical strategy. He made no secret of the way he worked. He said that when he went first to a place, he preached 'the law *in the strongest, the closest, the most searching manner possible*'. Only as people became convinced of sin did he 'mix more and more of the gospel . . . to raise into spiritual life those whom the law had slain'.

It is true that the gospel is an offer and not a demand, but the demands of the law rightly precede the offer of the gospel, and if that precedence is borne in mind this old question can be laid to rest.

So the evangelist confronts a perishing world. So he stands—beneath the Cross of Jesus. So he calls—and, whosoever will, may come.

Book List

A Plain Account of Christian Experience. D. S. Ching (Epworth Press).

The Creed of a Christian. W. M. F. Scott, M.A., and H. Watkin-Jones, M.A., D.D. (Six Broadcast Talks) (Epworth Press).

The Comfort of the Creeds. R. E. Roberts, D.D. (Epworth Press).

Methodism, Her Unfinished Task. W. E. Sangster, M.A., Ph.D. (Epworth Press).

5. *The Christian Year*

By the Rev. FRED A. FARLEY, M.A., B.D.

WE often think that we live in a difficult age and in a society which is hostile to Christian evangelism. It is a mechanistic society, in which life is becoming more and more remote from Nature; and the works of man—his scientific achievements, for example, are appearing more and more important, and the works of God less and less significant. What point of entry has the Christian story into the mind of a child brought up in a home where Christian worship is not considered, educated in a secular school, and for whom the chief events which punctuate and brighten the year are football matches, school festivals, and political celebrations?

But then, what would we have thought of our task if we had been living in the first century A.D.? Our date would be reckoned from the year when the city of Rome was supposed to have been founded, and society would appear to revolve around a man, the Emperor, or his representative. How was the Christian message to find a place in the minds of the people of Corinth, Ephesus, or Rome? A few people only, those of the Jewish race, thought of a history in which God was active. For the rest—the Gentiles—time was punctuated by local festivals in honour of pagan gods—revels, junketings, carousals, in honour of Diana, Jupiter, Mars, or the Emperor. They could not take part in a social function without rejoicing in the power of some imagined deity. As the Corinthians once protested to St. Paul, if they were to avoid such pagan festivals they would have to go out of the world altogether. Some Christian leaders thought of a positive way of dealing with these hostile influences. Tertullian, toward the end of the second century, reminded Christians that they had their own feasts and celebrations. While others were indulging in an orgy in honour of some fabulous god, let the Christians remember some saint of their own church, one perhaps who suffered martyrdom for the name of Christ. Thus, each church gained its own saints' days.

This, however, was likely to separate the churches, each having its own calendar and its own occasions for rejoicing. Let their calendar unite them, rather than divide. The winter solstice was a time of general rejoicing. The shortest day of the year had been reached. Thereafter, there would be more daylight; the earth and its vegetation would begin to revive. What could be more fitting that to remember then the coming of the Sun of Righteousness and the revival of our life and hopes? Every year, at the Winter Solstice, thought was to be turned to the Nativity of our Lord. From that date, other festivals could be reckoned—our Lord's Presentation at the Temple, his Circumcision, the Massacre of the Children in Bethlehem (Innocents' Day), the Visit of the 'Wise Men' (the Epiphany). In fact the chief events in the life of our Lord could be associated with what had been pagan festivals. His Crucifixion took place at the time of the Passover, and from that could be reckoned Palm Sunday (his Triumphal Entry into Jerusalem), and Easter Day (his Resurrection), then his Ascension and the Coming of the Holy Spirit. His time of Testing or Temptation in the wilderness could be suitably associated with the Christian's preparation for solemnizing the Great Event at Calvary with its deliverance from sin. If, year after year, Christians regularly meditated upon these great themes, Man's Salvation would come to be regarded as worthily filling all their thought. Some of the local Church Festivals, especially those commemorating the Apostles, could also be retained, and these would fill out a distinctively Christian Year.

We are in danger today of encouraging the secularization of the year. We celebrate what *we* do, instead of what *God* has done. We pay more regard to our Guild Anniversary, Choir Anniversary, Women's Day, Men's Day, and so on, than to the celebration of the Conversion of St. Paul, or to the wonderful and terrible days of our Lord's last week on earth. There are children who hardly know why Easter Day or Whitsunday was instituted. The prevailing ignorance about the facts of our Lord's life and the Church's progress could be dispelled if the year was used for religious commemorations.

With the Christian Year as a guide to preachers, our pulpits could offer systematic instruction to all worshippers, old and young, and no important Christian theme need be neglected. On the Sundays in Advent we can preach on the Preparation for Christ's Coming. Christmas and Easter Day should be restored to their rightful position as the greatest days in our year. Pentecost was 'a time of refreshing from the presence of the Lord' when the Church expounded and 'signs and wonders accompanied the preaching of the Word', and in Methodist pulpits, Whitsuntide should be followed by preaching about the work of the Holy Spirit—The New Birth ('Power of the Spirit'), Christian Assurance (The Witness of the Spirit), Sanctification, and Holiness.

The Epistles and Gospels in the *Book of Common Prayer* suggest a syllabus of thought and prayer for Christian preachers. As we give attention to these suggestions, we may be delivered from the bane of Methodist preaching, which is the tendency to offer a congregation spiritual fare selected chiefly because the preacher for the occasion happens to have a sermon on a particular subject which can be used next Sunday. Thus our preaching gets stale. Our own minds must be kept stirred and active, our own thought about God's work must be kept moving. The Christian Year offers us a syllabus on which we can get busy at once.

One has known churches where no sermon on the Holy Spirit has been preached in living memory. This sad neglect was possible because it had become the custom to observe Whitsunday as Sunday-school Anniversary. Thus, the people were deprived of teaching upon a subject, vital and integral to the Christian Faith. We have one Bank Holiday (August) which has no religious significance whatever. Do not let us connive at the secularization of our Calendar.

PART TWO

Studies on the Christian Year

---

1. The Message of Advent

By the Rev. KENNETH GRAYSTON, M.A.

ADVENT means coming, arrival, or presence. To the Christian it means the coming of God Himself in Jesus Christ. It is the time of the year when we prepare ourselves to celebrate the Incarnation. On these four Sundays before Christmas we try to bear three things in mind: (1) the meaning of something that happened over 1,900 years ago in Palestine when God showed us His fullness in Jesus of Nazareth; (2) the experience of Christians —always startling and always new; and (3) the promise that Jesus will come again to fulfil the whole purpose of God. All these things are bound up in the message of Christmas—a past fact that gives us a present experience and a future hope. In other words, there is a great deal more to Christmas than gracious stories and the spirit of goodwill. It is the tremendous beginning of a life that was dedicated to our salvation. In its wonder and humility it is marked by the same grace that was shown in the Cross and Resurrection. So tremendous an ending was matched by a tremendous beginning. That is why we do well to devote the Sundays of Advent to preparing ourselves for these things. If we prepare as well as we can for God's coming, we shall not miss His arrival and we shall know His presence.

The three Advent studies suggest one way of preparing ourselves and our congregations.

The first study deals with God's coming to save His people.

The second study deals with God's coming to judge His people.

The third study deals with the beginning of God's salvation in Christ.

STUDY ONE. 'O COME, O COME, IMMANUEL'

Aim: To show the promise that God Himself will come to save
His people.

Readings:

Exodus 3–6: the first great deliverance of the people of God.

Psalms 42, 63, 84: the longing for God's help.

Isaiah 9, 11: prophecies of the Messiah.

Isaiah 40–66 (for chosen passages see end of Study 1): to a
people suffering in exile, salvation is promised from God
Himself and the character of God's servant is foretold.

Ezekiel 34: God Himself the Saviour of His people.

Matthew 3 and 4 [12–17]: the forerunner of God's coming in
Christ.

Luke 1: the longing of faithful people and God's promise.

Will Anyone Come?

Sooner or later most people find themselves in a situation
where they desperately need outside help. Recent years have given
us some vivid examples, but they can equally well be found in the
most ordinary human experience. Here are a few of them.

An elderly woman lives by herself in one room. She struggles
on gallantly against increasing tiredness, against loneliness,
against ill-health—and then she collapses. She can no longer
look after herself. She cannot be nurse, cook, and friend to herself.
Her one cry is: *will anyone come?*

A ship is wrecked on the high seas and the survivors take to
the boats; or an aircraft is blown off its course and crashes
in the frozen wastes of Canada; or any army truck breaks down in
the desert and the convoy goes on without noticing the casualty.
Hunger, thirst, injuries, and exhaustion at last bring those men
and women to the one thought: *will anyone come?*

A missionary in China has charge of a hospital to which
hundreds come every day—the wounded, the refugees, the sick,
and the dying. One pair of hands cannot begin to relieve this
mass of suffering. *Will anyone come?* Or an African village has
burnt its images and has placed an open Bible—which the villagers
cannot read—in a hut prepared for it. They have been promised
by an African evangelist that one day the white man will come
to tell them about Jesus and teach them to read that Bible.
And so for years they wait asking only one thing: *will anyone come?*

A nation stands alone against a powerful and ruthless enemy. It will withstand as long as it can, but then——. A group of guerrilla fighters, short of leaders and weapons, is being pushed back and back, capture is inevitable, and then——.

Common to all these situations (most of us can produce something of the kind from our own experience) is an urgent longing for help. Why do men add this last delusion to their present misery? What right have they even to hope that their longing will be answered? The answer to those questions depends on other questions. What grounds have they for expecting that someone will come where they are and see their desperate plight? If someone comes, how do they know he will be friend and not enemy? In other words, their longing and their expectation depend entirely on decisions they had made before their troubles began. If they can say: 'We know whose side we are on, we know who our friends are, we know they will search for us and reach us'—then their expectation is genuine. If they can say none of these things, if they have no firm past experience to guide them, their expectation is indeed a bitter mockery.

What is true of men longing for human help is true (in a deeper way) of men longing for God's help. In the Bible, expectancy is based firmly on past experience of what God has done. Time and again, prophets, psalmists, and lawgivers turn their thoughts to the great deliverance of the Exodus. 'And the Lord said, I have surely seen the affliction of my people which are in Egypt, and have heard their cry by reason of their taskmasters; for I know their sorrows; *and I am come down to deliver them*. . . . Come now therefore, and I will send thee unto Pharaoh, that thou mayest bring forth my people out of Egypt. And Moses said unto God, Who am I . . . that I should bring forth the children of Israel out of Egypt? And he said, Certainly *I will be with thee*' (Exod. 3 [7-12]). God has seen their distress and heard their cry. God Himself shall be with them to rescue them, and it is His gracious pleasure to work through Moses. This is by no means a casual act of kindness on God's part, like a sudden generous impulse in a man whose character is normally careless and self-centred. It is kindness that springs out of the very nature of God: that is what God is like. It is shown forth in His covenant, His freely given promise to people who have no claim on Him. 'I will take you to me for a people, and I will be to you a God' (Exod. 6 [2-8]).

As the people of Israel faced new terrors they often had a very uncertain grasp on that confidence. All too often they destroyed confidence within themselves by their wickedness and idolatry. But whenever the genuine note of longing and expectation is sounded, we find faithful men and women who know why they dare to hope. 'My soul, wait thou only upon God, for my expectation is from him' (Ps. 62 5). The Psalms are full of passionate entreaty for personal salvation (e.g. 42, 63, 84), and for national deliverance (e.g. 130). The cry goes up 'How long?' (e.g. Ps. 13 1-2, 35 17, Is. 6 11, Hab. 1 2). Underneath is the faith that 'he satisfieth the longing soul, and the hungry soul he filleth with good' (Ps. 107 9); and some Psalms give not only the entreaty but the thanksgiving when God has answered it (e.g. Ps. 22 1-21 entreaty; 22 22-31 thanksgiving). But however much God answered men's petitions for help, however frequently He saved Israel in their distress, there remains a note of unsatisfied longing, of unfulfilled expectation until the last page of the Old Testament (see Mal. 4 5-6). The people of Israel had possessed the promised land for so short a time. Most of their history had been a story of civil strife, warfare, and exile. The high hopes of the return from exile—the second exodus—had come to nothing. Where, then, were God's promises? And so, when we arrive at the New Testament, we find this sense of expectation aflame in faithful hearts. At least two found their heart's desire in the infant Jesus: Simeon who 'was righteous and devout, looking for the consolation of Israel'; and Anna who 'spake of him to all them that were looking for the redemption of Jerusalem' (Lk. 2 25, 38). The song of John the Baptist's father, Zacharias, has the same note of expectation being fulfilled: 'Blessed be the Lord God of Israel, for he has visited and redeemed his people,' and, to his son, he says 'thou, child, shalt be called the prophet of the Most High, for thou shalt go before the face of the Lord to *prepare his ways*, to give knowledge of salvation unto his people . . . because of the tender mercy of our God, whereby the dayspring from on high *shall visit us* (Lk. 1 68 and 76-78—see R.V.). Here then is the loveliest fruit of Jewish piety; and in different ways we find it reflected in John the Baptist himself (Mk. 1 7 and Mt. 11 3: 'Art thou he that cometh?') and in the popular expectations of the common people (Mt. 16 14).

This is the first pointer to the meaning of Christmas—the

sense of longing in the believer's heart. It is the privilege of preachers to strengthen that sense of longing, both by the sermon and the worship (see e.g. M.H.B. 242, 257, 261), and to bring it to life when it has been allowed to die. Indeed, we can go farther; it is the preacher's privilege to bring it to birth where before it has never existed. When the first Christian missionaries went out into the Gentile world they found longing hearts there also. Some Gentiles had been prepared by contact with Judaism (like Cornelius in Acts 10); some could reach no higher than pagan superstitions of gods who came down in the likeness of men (like the primitive inhabitants of Lycaonia, Acts 14 [8-18]); and even the cultured Athenians had their altar 'To an unknown god' (Acts 17 [22-33]). Men of many races were longing intently (though often in strange and pathetic ways) for the hope of deliverance. This is true today throughout the world, and it is therefore entirely right that the first Sunday in Advent should by custom be devoted to the world-wide mission of the Church. Charles Wesley expresses this theme in one of his hymns:

> Answer the universal: Come!
> The fullness of the Gentiles call,
>   And take Thine ancient people home—(M.H.B. 814;
>   and see 267).

If preachers in lands overseas dare to awaken the universal longing because they know it will not go unanswered, preachers in Britain may take courage to do the same.

God Himself Will Come

How can God answer that longing of the human heart? An obvious answer is that He will do again what He has done before and raise up for His people a great leader. The popular expectations at the time of Jesus have already been mentioned; and they are based on Old Testament promises. Deut. 18 [15] says: 'The Lord thy God will raise up unto thee a prophet from the midst of thee of thy brethren, like unto me (Moses)' and Mal. 4 [5] had promised the return of Elijah. In the disastrous days of defeat and exile, the reign of David seemed like a golden age and they remembered the words: 'If thy children take heed to their way, to walk before me in truth with all their heart and with all their soul, there shall not fail thee (said he) a man on the throne of Israel' (1 Kings 2 [4], and see the repetition of this in Jer. 33 [17],

23 [5, 6]). When Israel returned from Exile, the prophet Haggai proclaimed Zerubbabel, the governor of Judah, as the Messianic prince; but this hope ended in disappointment and men began to see that outstanding and remarkable qualities would be demanded of God's agent of salvation, the Messiah. There are three chief passages where his character is described: (i) Zech. 9 [9]: 'Behold, thy king cometh unto thee, righteous and granted victory, lowly and riding upon an ass'; *see* Zech. 4 [6]: 'not by might, nor by power, but by my spirit, saith the Lord of Hosts.' (ii) Is. 11 [1-5], followed by a description of the earth renewed (part of this passage is quoted in Is. 65 [25]). The family of Jesse, David's father, is by now merely a stump but it will flourish again, and the new representative will be so possessed by the spirit of God that he will be endowed with all the qualities and powers needed by the Messiah. (iii) Is. 9 [6-7], the most remarkable, and in some ways the most puzzling of all the Messianic prophecies. Light now shines upon the people that have been long in darkness and they rejoice before God with great joy; for the Lord has delivered the people from the yoke of a foreign oppressor and has made an end of war. Moreover, a child has been born, a native ruler in contrast to the foreign oppressor, who will exercise dominion, and is marked out as exceptional by the name which he receives. Like God Himself the Messiah will give counsel exceeding what has hitherto been known or heard (Wonderful Counsellor). He is to be more than mighty, more than a mighty man, more than a mighty king: he is to be a Mighty God (there is no parallel in the Old Testament to this astonishing prophecy). He is to be the loving guardian of God's people so long as he and they endure (Eternal Father), and the sovereign giver of all good (Prince of Peace). Thus the writer of this passage is convinced that God must bring about the restoration and exaltation of His people (like Ezekiel), and (like Haggai and Zechariah) he looks for a Davidic Messiah. Unlike Ezekiel, he gives to the prince a supreme place in the restored people; though (like the writer of Is. 40–66) he expects the restoration to be the direct act of God apart from the efforts of the Messiah. The Messiah reigns in the kingdom that God has already restored.

So, then we observe two things very carefully. First, the qualities demanded of God's human agent are steadily increasing. And second, the kingdom is always God's kingdom. However much men set their hopes on a human Messiah, it was in the mighty power of God Himself that they put their trust. Thus the full answer, and the only really satisfactory one, to the question: 'Will anyone come?', is to say: '*Yes, God Himself will come.*'

Those words can mean much or little: it depends on the God you serve and trust. The people of Canaan worshipped a multitude of Baals who were simply the forces of nature. For them 'God Himself will come' meant only that the harvest would be plentiful or that women would bear many children. Abundant food and flourishing families are indeed highly important; but men who make those things their gods are far short of the purpose for which men are created. When the people of Israel allowed their religion to become the same as that of the Canaanites, the prophets Amos and Hosea challenged them with the message: 'There is a God greater than these.' The great empires of Egypt, Assyria, and Babylonia worshipped their high gods and required conquered or allied countries to worship them also. Whenever Israel was tempted to accept the protection of a powerful neighbour, it meant worshipping the neighbour's god, who was simply the power of the state. To say 'God Himself will come' meant only that their country would be victorious and safe. A country's protection is indeed highly important, but men who make that their god at whatever cost are far short of the purpose for which men are created. Therefore Isaiah dared to say: 'There is a God greater than these.'

When the Old Testament talks about an *idol* it means an object of worship which is less than the living God, creator of the world, at work in the events, great and small, of human history. People today can be idol-worshippers—they may worship the forces of nature as controlled by science, they may worship the power of the state, they may worship themselves. But to the genuine cry 'Will anyone come?' an idol makes no reply. Two things must happen: (i) we must see that God is the holy God, who is not at our beck and call; (ii) we must see that our plight can be relieved by God Himself alone and by nothing less than God. The more clearly we see the holiness of God, the more certain we are that only God can save us. The more we fail, the more God must do for us.

One of the most moving expressions of this truth in the Old Testament is in Ezek. 34, where, faced by the plight of Israel and the corruptness of the rulers, God cries out: 'I myself, even I, will search for my sheep, and will seek them out. . . . I myself will feed my sheep, and will cause them to lie down, saith the Lord God' (vv. 11, 15). In v. 23 a Messiah of the line of David to reign over a renewed land is promised *when God has first rescued His flock*. There is no suspicion that the coming of the Messiah will itself be the salvation of God (as it is in the New Testament); but the possibility of it lies in the words 'I myself' for that expresses the amazing personal love of God.

The chief passages for understanding God's promise to come Himself have been kept till last. They are found in the second part of Isaiah (40–66); and it may help to have some of them collected in the following way:

(*a*) *The cry of longing*: 63 7–64 12, 'Oh that thou wouldest rend the heavens, that thou wouldest come down'—a cry based on what God had done in the past.

(*b*) *The majesty of God*: 40 12–31. It is this God, the Creator and King of Kings, who gives power to the faint. 44 6–28. Not an idol, but the Lord beside whom there is no god. 45 9–13, 45 18–25. 'Only in the Lord is righteousness and strength.'

(*c*) *The good news of salvation*: (to the writer it meant return from exile) 40 1–2, 41 8–20, 46 8–13 'my salvation shall not tarry', 51 4–6, 52 7–12.

(*d*) *God Himself shall save*: 40 3–8 'Prepare ye the way of the Lord', 40 9–11 'behold your God', 43 1–13 'when thou passest through the waters I will be with thee'. 45 1–7, 51 12–16 'I, even I, am he that comforteth you'; 57 15–21 'I dwell in the high and holy place, with him also that is of a contrite and humble spirit'; 60, no need of sun or moon because God Himself is the everlasting light.

(*e*) *The servant of God*: 42 1–9, 49 1–13 50 4–9, 52 13–53 12. Perhaps to the writer these passages meant an individual man or the faithful people of God regarded as a person, or perhaps no clear distinction was possible. But when, in the fullness of time, the cry of longing was answered and the good news of salvation was proclaimed by an angel (Lk. 2 10) the glorious majesty of God Himself was made flesh in Jesus who took the form of a servant (Phil. 2 7).

STUDY TWO. 'SO TERRIBLY GLORIOUS HIS COMING SHALL BE'

Aim: To show that the coming of God to save His people brings judgement.

Readings:

Amos 5 [1–24]: God's judgement on His people.

Isaiah 6: sinful man in the presence of the holy God.

Matthew 18 [23–35], 25: parables of judgement and responsibility.

Mark 13: dark sayings on the future prospect.

Luke 13 [22–30], 14 [15–24]: the sternness and blessedness of Christ's coming again to sum up all things.

John 3 [16–20], 5 [19–47], 9 [1–41], 12 [20–50], 16 [7–11]: the judgement that Christ brings in his words and actions.

Romans 7, 8: the confidence of the Christian.

When God Comes to Save, He Judges

Our need is so great that only God Himself can save us. But are we really prepared for God Himself to come? 'Behold, I send my messenger, and he shall prepare the way before me: and the Lord, whom ye seek shall suddenly come to his Temple; and the messenger of the covenant whom ye delight in, saith the Lord of hosts. But who may abide the day of his coming? and who shall stand when he appeareth? for he is like a refiner's fire, and like fuller's soap' (Mal. 3 [1–2]). If it is really the coming of God we plead for we must remember the word of Heb. 10 [31]: 'It is a fearful thing to fall into the hands of the living God.' When Isaiah saw the Lord high and lifted up in His temple (in the famous passage, chapter 6) he was forced to cry out: 'I am a man of unclean lips, and I dwell in the midst of a people of unclean lips.' When Peter saw the glory of God in Christ, he could only say: 'Depart from me; for I am a sinful man, O Lord' (Lk. 5 [8]). Whenever we are confronted with the majesty of God here before us, we know that we are in the presence of judgement.

If we look back over the Old Testament passages used in the first study, we can see that when God comes to save, He judges.

(i) The very fact that He *saves* His people means that He judges their enemies. He vindicates the faithful and condemns the proud and disobedient. 'Behold, all they that are incensed against thee shall be ashamed and confounded' (Is. 41 [11]). Of the faithless and cruel rulers of Israel, God says: 'Behold, I am against the shepherds' (Ezek. 34 [10]). Therefore part of the Messiah's work is to 'set judgement in the earth' (Is. 42 [4]), to uphold the kingdom 'with judgement and with righteousness from henceforth even for ever' (Is. 9 [7]; see also 11 [4]). (ii) But God also must judge the faithful. It is all too easy to assume that we are both saved *and safe;* and the people of Israel often did take it as a matter of course. With shallow cheerfulness they said: 'Come, and let us return unto the Lord: for he hath torn, and he will heal us; he hath smitten, and he will bind us up' (Hosea 6 [1]). God will forgive: that's what He's there for. They looked eagerly for the Day of the Lord when their enemies would be judged and they themselves set free; and they had no thought for their own injustice and idolatry. Therefore Amos was compelled to say: 'Woe unto you that desire the day of the Lord! Wherefore would you have the day of the Lord? it is darkness and not light' (Amos 5 [18], see also vv. 11–15). The truth of the matter is given in 1 Pet. 4 [17]: 'The time is come for judgement to begin at the house of God: and if it begin first at us, what shall be the end of them that obey not the Gospel of God?' You cannot rescue people who insist on clinging to the very things that have brought them into danger. A man ruined by gambling cannot be saved if he will continue to gamble: a drunkard cannot be saved if he will go on drinking. Salvation involves judgement, forgiveness, and purification. 'Seek ye the Lord while he may be found, call ye upon him while he is near: let the wicked forsake his way, and the unrighteous man his thoughts; and let him return unto the Lord, and he will have mercy upon him; and to our God, for he will abundantly pardon' (Is. 55 [6–7], see also e.g. 43 [25], 44 [22] and 53 [4–12], where the Servant bears our iniquity).

It may seem that the thought of judgement is a very grim preparation for Christmas; but if there is no repentance at Christmastime there is no joy. The glorious liberty of the children of God comes when we have been delivered from the bondage of corruption (Rom. 8 [21]). In speaking of judgement, the preacher can therefore be confident that he is preparing hearts to receive Christ. He does *not* say that Christ will only come to hearts that have already been purified (from the Gospels themselves that is obviously untrue); he does say that when Christ comes we are thereby judged. The preacher is like John the Baptist: he prepares the way of the Lord by a call to repentance and a proclamation that the Kingdom of God is at hand (Mt. 3 [1-12], Lk. 3 [1-20]).

Judgement is one of the great dominating themes of St. John's Gospel.

(a) 3 [16-21]: the divine purpose of the coming of Jesus is salvation not judgement, eternal life not destruction. But His coming inevitably brings into the open the distinction between those who do and those who do not believe. The primary purpose of the sun's shining is not to cast shadows, but it does cast them nevertheless. 'This is the judgement, that the light is come into the world, and men loved the darkness rather than the light, for their works were evil' (v. 19).

(b) 5 [19-47]: after a cripple had been cured in Jerusalem on the Sabbath, the Jews sought to kill Jesus 'because he not only brake the sabbath, but also called God his own Father, making himself equal with God' (v. 18). But in condemning the disease that had enslaved the cripple for thirty-eight years, Jesus had shown forth God's judgement on all evil. Jesus has full authority now to separate believers from unbelievers. The action that men take when they hear His words decided the judgement that will be passed in the final reckoning (see also 8 [12-20]).

(c) 9 [1-41]: 'And as he passed by, he saw a man blind from his birth.' The disciples at once invite Jesus to pass judgement either on the man or on his parents for the sin which (they assume) had made him blind. But Jesus refuses: instead, he gives him his sight. 'I am the light of the world.' When the Pharisees get hold of the man they require him (and his parents) to pass judgement against Jesus. 'He therefore answered, Whether he be a sinner, I know not: one thing I know, that, whereas I was blind, now I see.' The Pharisees therefore condemn him, and thereby are themselves condemned. 'For judgement came I into this world, that they which see not may see; and that they which see may become blind' (v. 39). Judgement can be salvation.

(d) 12 [20-50]: as an ancient writer said: 'Seeing therefore that the Gentiles are hastening in eager desire to see him and to turn toward him, on this account he says: The hour is come.' That he may answer the longing of all men, Jesus turns resolutely to the cross, the decisive act of judgement on the power of evil. 'Now is the judgement of this world: now shall the prince of this world be cast out.' Jesus now moves to complete the purpose for which he came into the world when his own received him not, the purpose for which the Word became flesh (1^{9-14}).

(*e*) 16^{7-11}: The Spirit continues and enforces the work of Jesus: 'He, when he is come will convict the world in respect of sin, and of righteousness, and of judgement; of sin, because they believe not on me; of righteousness, because I go to the Father; of judgement, because the prince of this world hath been judged.' The word *convict* really means *expose*, i.e. both 'hold up for all to see' and 'hold up to rebuke'. The preacher, by virtue of his own gift of the Spirit, has every right to expose the sin which comes from unbelief in the Son of God who came in the flesh, to expose the righteousness of God which is made manifest by the departure of Jesus to the Father through the Resurrection and Ascension, and to expose the judgement on that powerful evil which crucified Jesus.

In the first three Gospels there are a number of sayings of Jesus which begin with the words 'I came' or the like. They give us our most important clues for understanding why God was made man in the Incarnation. Here again we find both salvation and judgement.

(i) 'I came not to call the righteous, but sinners' (Mk. 2^{17} and Mt. 9^{13}, R.V.), i.e. Jesus is justifying his practice of associating with people of doubtful character. He says that the very reason He came was to call them, to give them the divine invitation into the Kingdom of God. This is the amazing paradox of the Gospel:

> *If you tarry till you're better,*
> *You will never come at all:*
> *Not the righteous—*
> *Sinners Jesus came to call*—(M.H.B. 324).

But Luke, writing his Gospel for the different situation of the pagan world, adds the words 'to repentance' (and the Authorized Version, translated from less ancient manuscripts than those on which the R.V. is based, adds the words to Matthew and Mark). It was a true instinct on his part: Jesus came to offer the free grace of God to undeserving sinners, but the offer carried with it a call to repentance.

(ii) 'Think not that I came to destroy the law or the prophets: I came not to destroy but to fulfil' (Mt. 5^{17})—both the commandments and the promises, as the whole chapter shows.

(iii) 'The Son of Man came to seek and to save that which was lost' (Lk. 19 [10]). Zacchaeus had already passed judgement on himself.

(iv) 'The Son of Man came not to be ministered unto, but to minister, and to give his life a ransom for many' (Mk. 10 [45])—which is a judgement on the request of James and John.

(v) 'I came to cast fire upon the earth, and would that it were already kindled' (Lk. 12 [49]—this translation, from the American Revised Standard Version, seems to be the right one). Fire means the cleansing fire of judgement.

(vi) 'Think not that I came to send peace on the earth: I came not to send peace but a sword' (Mt. 10 [34]), i.e., the sword which divides and shows which side people are on.

If we now turn to the stories of the birth of Jesus we find that judgement is at work even there. The character of Joseph is displayed in all its gentleness, the character of Mary in her faithful obedience. The shepherds are shown as men of simple faith, Herod as a cruel and cunning hypocrite. Strangest of all are the wise men from the East, experts in the magic arts, popular astrologers of the day, who claimed to know the secret of a man's luck or destiny (see Simon, the sorcerer, in Acts 8 [9-24] and Elymas in Acts 13 [4-12]; and also Acts 19 [17-20]—the ancient world was full of these people, and the modern world can provide many parallels). When these Magi fell down before Jesus and worshipped him, they knew they were in the presence of judgement, and forthwith they renounced the wealth they had gained by their profession, and the frankincense and myrrh which accompanied their spells. All these they surrendered to Jesus.

So then, at Christmas are we willing for the Christ-child to show us up for what we are? Are we willing to renounce unholy things for his sake?

The Christian Looks for God's Coming Again

If the Christian is willing to be judged by Christ in every part of daily life, then the message of Christmas will come home with power and great gladness. He will be able to say with the psalmist: 'The Lord is nigh unto all them that call upon him' (Ps. 145 [18]). That indeed may be one meaning of the words in Phil. 4 [5]: 'The Lord is at hand'; but there is surely another meaning also: the Lord is at hand in His coming again. We must build our faith firmly on the coming of Christ at the first Christmas, on his life, and death, and rising again. We do not deny that, or the present work of the Holy Spirit, if we believe that the Christian still looks forward to the completion of God's promises. It is true that Jesus established the Kingdom of God in the midst of us (Lk. 17[20], translation of Revised Standard Version), and judgement is already taking place by the way in which we respond to that fact. But it is very clear that the purposes of God are not yet completed, and in these days it is not easy to see that we are steadily (or even unsteadily) moving toward the glorious fulfilment.

> *And now we watch and struggle,*
> *And now we live in hope,*
> *And Zion in her anguish*
> *With Babylon must cope;*
> *But He whom now we trust in*
> *Shall then be seen and known,*
> *And they that know and see Him*
> *Shall have Him for their own*—(M.H.B. 652; see also 502).

'Now are we children of God, and it is not yet made manifest what we shall be. We know that if he shall be manifested we shall be like him; for we shall see him even as he is' (1 Jn. 3[2]).

We are children of God *now*. One of St. Paul's favourite ways of expressing the Christian's salvation is to use the language of the law-court and to bring in the picture of a judgement being made. In Romans, for instance, the first two chapters are a scathing exposure of sin both among Jews and Gentiles (and at the end of all his letters he has some pointed warnings against sin among Christians). In chapter 7 he lays himself bare, and shows how with the best will in the world he is quite unable to appear as an innocent man before God. But when by faith he dares to stand before Him, he finds One who justifies the ungodly (Rom. 4[5])—instead of the fully justified sentence of condemnation, he is set free (the reason is given in 3[21-26]). 'There is therefore now no condemnation to them that are in Christ Jesus (8[1]). It is inconceivable that we should be condemned when the judge is Christ Jesus who died for us, rose again for us, and intercedes for us at the right hand of God (8[34]).

All that is true; but it is also true that we are encouraged to look for a fulfilment of God's purposes, a final act of reckoning when Christ shall be all in all. St. Paul is quite clear about it (see e.g. Rom. 8 ¹⁸⁻²⁵) and we have authority in Christ's own teaching. The parable of the talents (Mt. 25 ¹⁴⁻³⁰) is a favourite theme of preachers, though we usually seem to spend far too much time on the imagined characters of the three men, and we confine ourselves to urging our hearers to use their gifts, whatever they may be. That is harmless enough, but the important points of the parable are these. (i) Three men stand before their master and the accounts are made up : there is to be a reckoning (*see also* Mt. 18 ²³⁻³⁵, where Jesus shows the need for mercy in the day of reckoning; and the judgement scene of Mt. 25 ³¹⁻⁴⁶). When we look out on our world today and see so much that looks cruel and meaningless, it is a marvellous thing to know that a reckoning can and will be made. The master left *his* property to *his* servants and it still belongs to *him;* thank God that he does return and say: What have you done with my property? (ii) Two men accept this responsibility; one does not and he is condemned. We cannot escape responsibility for others—we all have it. The fact that we have different capacities for it simply means that we are not solitary individuals, but members one of another. An animal cannot accept responsibility: a human being can. A man who refuses it is sacrificing the glory of his manhood. It is a joyful thing, therefore, to look forward to God's coming again in judgement. In the words of a hymn that appeared in Wesley's hymnbook, now no longer sung:

> *He comes! He comes! the Judge severe,*
> *The seventh trumpet speaks Him near;*
> *His lightnings flash, His thunders roll,*
> *How welcome to the faithful soul.*

'And his lord said unto him, well done, good and faithful servant: thou hast been faithful over a few things, I will set thee over many things: enter thou into the *joy* of thy lord.'

This theme—the coming again of God in judgement—has lent itself in the past to the wildest extravagances. All the same, it is a genuine part of the Christian hope, and many New Testament passages help us to understand it (e.g. Mt. 13 ⁴⁷⁻⁵⁰, Lk. 13 ²²⁻³⁰, 14 ¹⁵⁻²⁴). Chapter 13 of Mark is one of the strangest in all the Gospels (the parallel chapters in the other Gospels are:

Mt. 24 and Lk. 21). It seems to be a mixture of sayings of Jesus about the fate of Jerusalem on the one hand, and of vivid pictures of the day of reckoning. It is not at all easy to discover which is which; but one sentence of Luke's (21 ^{28}) brings it all on to the solid ground of Christian faith: 'Look up, and lift up your heads, because your redemption draws nigh' (see M.H.B. 264).

The final word of this study therefore must be: Watch! We have heard it already in Mt. 24 and Mk. 13. It is the theme of the parable of the wise and foolish virgins (Mt. 25 $^{1-13}$); it comes again in 1 Thess. 5 ^{6}, Eph. 6 ^{18}, 2 Tim. 4 $^{1-5}$, 1 Pet. 4 ^{7}, and Rev. 16 ^{15}. To be on the watch is the right attitude for Christmas. There were shepherds, doing their ordinary work, keeping watch by night. The wise men would not have seen the star if they had not been watching (see M.H.B. 255).

Almost the last words of the Bible are: 'Amen: come, Lord Jesus' (Rev. 22 ^{20}).

STUDY THREE. 'VEILED IN FLESH THE GODHEAD SEE'

Aim: To show the fulfilment of God's promises in the birth of Christ.

Readings:

Genesis 1 ^{1}–2 ^{3}: God's Word and the first creation.

Isaiah 7 $^{1-17}$: The sign of Immanuel.

Hosea 11 $^{1-4}$: God's love in rescuing His people, the first exodus.

Micah 5 $^{2-4}$: the promise of the Messiah.

Matthew 1 ^{18}–2 ^{23} }
Luke 1 ^{1}–2 ^{39} } the birth of Jesus.

John 1 $^{1-18}$: God's Word and the new creation.

John 6 $^{41-59}$: the flesh and blood of Jesus, the bread of Heaven.

Romans 1 $^{1-7}$: an early Christian confession of faith.

2 Corinthians 4 $^{1-6}$: Christ Jesus is Lord.

2 Corinthians 8 $^{1-15}$: the grace of Christ and Christian conduct.

Philippians 2 $^{1-11}$: the grace of Christ and Christian worship.

Colossians 1 $^{9-23}$: Christ at the centre of the universe.

Hebrews 1 $^{1-4}$ and 2 $^{5-18}$: why He became man.

1 John 1, 4: the Incarnation proclaimed in word and conduct.

The Beginning of the Gospel

Every preacher knows that St. Mark's Gospel has no story of the birth of Jesus. With that breathless urgency so characteristic of him (in the first chapter alone, he uses 'straightway' nine times), he goes straight to the ministry of John the Baptist with only two introductory verses from Mal. 3 [1] and Is. 40 [3] (*see* two previous studies). But his very first words are: 'The beginning of the gospel of Jesus Christ, the Son of God'; and there is a wealth of meaning hidden in that word *gospel*. We can fill out its meaning if we carefully study every passage in the New Testament where it is used; but what is its original meaning? Supposing a Jew, knowing his Old Testament, had read those opening words of St. Mark's story: what meaning would 'gospel' have for him *before* he had read the words and deeds of Jesus? What *good news* would he be expecting to hear about?

'Gospel' goes back to a Hebrew word that had two quite everyday meanings: (*a*) tidings of victory (2 Sam. 18 [19]); and it is characteristic of Hebrew ways of thinking that the messenger is identified with the message. This explains David's apparently savage act (2 Sam. 4 [10]) when he slew the messenger who brought good tidings (as he thought) of the death of Saul. In fact, that was bad news for David and so the messenger was given the same reception as the news itself. We shall return to this thought later on, and we may not find it so strange as it first appears. (*b*) Tidings of the birth of a son (Jer. 20 [15])—a very joyful event to every Israelite. Now later writers of the time of the Exile built upon these everyday meanings and gave the word a thoroughly religious sense. 'O thou that tellest *good tidings* to Zion, get thee up into a high mountain; O thou that tellest *good tidings* to Jerusalem, lift up thy voice with strength . . . say unto the cities of Judah, *Behold your God!*' (Is. 40 [9]). 'How beautiful upon the mountains are the feet of him that bringeth *good tidings*, that publisheth peace, that bringeth *good tidings* of good, that publisheth salvation; that saith unto Zion: *Thy God reigneth*' (or 'hath ascended His throne,' Is. 52 [7]—*see* Study 1). This good news is the report of God's victories. God Himself is returning with the procession of the exiles going back home. He has ascended His throne, He gives peace (i.e. every kind of well-being) and salvation, and His final purpose for mankind (for this salvation is for the Gentiles as well as Israelites, Is. 42 [6, 10], 45 [22], 49 [6]) begins to be fulfilled.

Therefore, when a Jew in first-century Palestine read St. Mark's opening sentence, he would know that this particular good tidings was meant—for every Jew knew only too well that Isaiah's prophecy had not yet been fulfilled. And if we imagine a Gentile reading the same words, he would probably have in mind something like these words which belong to pagan worship of the Roman emperor: 'The birthday of the god (i.e. the emperor Augustus) was for the world the beginning of *tidings of joy* on his account' (an inscription made about 9 B.C.)

This message of God's Kingship, victory, and salvation is all bound up in the word 'gospel'; and behind it all is a thought which controls everything else: the messenger and the message are one and the same. Jesus *is* the Gospel. Let us take two examples from our own experience to explain this statement. During the war many families had a telegram which said in effect: 'Your son is missing.' How anxiously they waited for some good news, even if it meant that the boy had been taken prisoner! With what hopes and fears they waited for another telegram! And then supposing a knock came at the door one morning— and there on the doorstep was the missing soldier. No need of a telegram then: he himself was the good news. Or again, imagine that you have a friend who has undergone a serious operation. From time to time you hear news of a slow and hesitating recovery, but after a time you lose touch with him. And then, suddenly you meet him in the street, healthy, vigorous, fully recovered. You need no longer wonder whether he is better— there he is, himself the good news.

Jesus Himself is the Gospel. Jesus did not come on earth merely to be a great teacher. The birth of a teacher however great is no more interesting (except to his parents) than the birth of any other baby. Jesus came to earth to do and to die, to *be* Himself.

> *Pleased as man with men to dwell,*
> *Jesus, our Immanuel*—(M.H.B. 117).

And the angel said unto them, Be not afraid; for behold, I bring you *good tidings* of great joy which shall be to all the people: for there is born to you this day in the city of David a Saviour, which is Christ the Lord' (Lk. 2 10). 'On earth peace among men in whom he is well pleased' (Lk. 2 14). Here is the Messiah of the line of David, bringing peace and salvation, but not merely an agent of God's purpose. He is the Lord Himself.

St. Augustine, in his *Confessions*, has a passage where he speaks of the things he learnt in the books of the non-Christian Greek philosophers. 'And therein I read, not indeed in the very words, but to the very same purpose, enforced by many and divers reasons, that In the beginning was the Word . . . (and he goes on to quote Jn. 1 [1-5], [9-11]). But, that He came unto His own, and His own received Him not; but as many as received Him, to them gave He power to become sons of God, as many as believed in His name; *this I read not there*. Again I read there, that God the Word was born not of flesh nor of blood, nor of the will of man, but of God. But that the Word became flesh, and dwelt among us *I read not there*.' In other words, here is something new and wonderful. God's Word, His message, became man—the message and the messenger are one.

> *Knees and hearts to Him we bow;*
> *Of our flesh and of our bone,*
> *Jesus is our Brother now,*
> *And God is all our own*—(M.H.B. 134).

Behind the opening words of St. John's Gospel lie the first chapters of Genesis where God made all things by His Word, i.e. when He spoke. If we examine the accounts in Genesis we see that God spoke eight decisive words of preparation: light, water, and earth—the fundamental things by which life as we know it is built up. He made matter and energy. The other five were words of increasing accomplishment: plant life, the stars and planets, birds and fishes, animal life, and finally human life. When St. John says 'In the beginning was the Word' he means the same Word that made the universe, the real world, and saw that it was very good. It is the same Word that made us and cares for us.

God's Word is therefore a Word of creative power. Even a human word can have immense power. Think what one kind or cruel word can do to people. Think what a broadcast word can set in train. And a spoken word demands a response—if once we hear it, we can accept it or refuse it, we are free to do that, but we inevitably respond in some way. It is true of the words of Jesus. It is true of Jesus Himself. For in Him is the power behind the ordered world, the power that made it good to live in, the power that sustains its life, the power that *cares* for men and women. All *that* was living out a human existence in Jesus.

> *Ah, Lord, who hast created all,*
> *How hast Thou made Thee weak and small,*
> *That Thou must choose Thy infant bed*
> *Where ass and ox but lately fed?*—(M.H.B. 126).

The theme of St. John is therefore the *new creation*. Jesus was full of grace and truth. The *truth* is the truth that lies behind the whole wide universe, the truth of our human nature and destiny, the truth of God's way for man in the world. *Grace* is the overwhelming love of God, freely given to mankind, without thought of our deserving.

> *Stupendous height of heavenly love,*
> *Of pitying tenderness divine*—(M.H.B. 135).

> *We need not now go up to heaven*
> *To bring the long-sought Saviour down;*
> *Thou art to all already given*—(M.H.B. 771).

'We beheld his glory, glory as of the only begotten from the Father.' There, on the one hand, is the undoubted fact of the birth of Christ; here, on the other, is the Christian witness. The Incarnation is not a theory, an interesting speculation; it is woven into Christian experience. We cannot get away from the words 'We beheld' (Jn. 1 [14], 1 Jn. 1 [1–3]). Jesus himself drove this home with startling words (Jn. 6 [41–59]). The Jews imagined that they knew all about him—born to Joseph, quite an ordinary child; but Jesus says at one and the same time that he is both the bread that comes down from heaven and a real being of flesh and blood. In later times there were men who were willing to believe in a purely spiritual Saviour but not a flesh and blood Christ. In our own day, there are people who unhappily stumble at the same point; but the real mark of the full Christian faith is to believe that Jesus Christ is God made man (1 Jn. 4 [2–3], 2 Jn. [7]). The reason for insisting on this is not an obstinate prejudice; the reason lies in the Christian experience of Christ as the *new man*, the new creation.

But this thought of the new creation does not exhaust the richness of Christ's birth. The stories in Matthew and Luke are packed with Old Testament quotations and echoes.

(1) Mt. 1 [23] quotes Is. 7 [14]. The prophet had gone to meet Ahaz, King of Judah, whose country had been attacked by an alliance of Israel and Syria. The King and his people had lost faith in God and were afraid to ask of Him a sign. And so a sign

is given by God; a young woman, not yet a mother (which is the meaning of the original Hebrew), will shortly bear a son. Though everyone else is faithless, she will call her son 'God with us'. It is a sign of faith; and in the birth of Christ that faith was demonstrated in strange and marvellous ways. But the essential thing is: God with us.

(2) Mt. 2 [6] fulfilling the promise of a Messiah from David's own town of Bethlehem (Micah 5 [2]; and *see* Ezek. 34 [23f] and Lk. 1 [32]).

(3) Mt. 2 [11] referring to Ps. 72 [10, 15], Is. 60 [6]—the promise of salvation to the nations.

(4) Mt. 2 [15] quoting Hosea 11 [1–3], one of the tenderest and loveliest of all Old Testament passages, picturing the exodus from Egypt with God, like a loving father, teaching His son to walk, carrying him in His arms, healing his injuries—even though Israel was a rebellious and ungrateful child. St. Matthew means that the birth of Jesus was the *new exodus*—the great salvation of God.

(5) Mt. 2 [18] quoting Jer. 31 [15]—the world of tragedy into which the Saviour came.

People have sometimes thought that the Gospel writers were rather simple-minded in supposing that prophecies (originally spoken for a different situation) would be fulfilled literally in the life of Christ. But that is to misunderstand them. They were writing as Christians who knew the difference Christ had made to their own lives, to the people of God, and to the pagan world. They were writing to explain it to other people; and they tried to help them to see the truth by giving them some pointers. In the Old Testament they found places where understanding might begin. If their readers began there, they would certainly have to go far beyond the strangest hopes of the Old Testament, but at least they would be on the right road.

A Truth to Worship, Preach and Live By

The truth of the Incarnation is full of riches for every side of Christian life. Anyone reading the New Testament will see at once that the event in Christ's life most spoken about is the Cross; but the Cross takes its whole meaning from the firm belief that '*God* was in Christ reconciling the world to himself' (2 Cor. 5 [19]). Only so could Wesley say:

Now discern the Deity,
Now His heavenly birth declare!
Faith cries out: 'Tis He, 'tis He,
My God, that suffers there!—(M.H.B. 191).

The birth of Christ is the necessary foundation of our salvation.

And so we find his birth as part of the earliest preaching of the new-born Christians. In Rom. 1 [3], St. Paul (probably quoting a common confession of faith) tells how Jesus was born into all the weakness of human 'flesh' and was declared to be Son of God by the mighty power of the Holy Spirit. The same thought is expressed in one of the earliest Christian hymns in 1 Tim. 3 [16]. Although St. Paul became a follower of Jesus only when the earthly ministry had ended, he knows that the coming of Christ in the flesh is the rock on which all his preaching is founded. (The apparent contradiction of this statement by 2 Cor. 5 [16] arises from a poor translation of the original Greek which makes it clear that what St. Paul is talking about is 'fleshly knowledge,' i.e. imperfect knowledge that judges by purely human standards.)

The theme of the new creation appears once more when St. Paul calls Christ 'the image of God' (2 Cor. 4 [4]) for it calls to mind the first creation when God created man in His own image (Gen. 1 [27]). The consequences of this are worked out with splendid discernment in Colossians: 'the image of the invisible God, the firstborn of all creation, for in him were all things created' (1 [15]).

The Invisible appears in sight,
And God is seen by mortal eye—(M.H.B. 362;
and see 141).

And once again this is not theory and speculation: it is based on our needs and our experience. The Epistle to the Hebrews, after its magnificent opening verses, goes on to explain, in most moving words, why God should manifest Himself in the flesh. 'Since then the children are sharers in flesh and blood, he also himself in like manner partook of the same; that through death he might bring to nought him that had the power of death . . . wherefore, it behoved him in all things to be made like unto his brethren, that he might be a merciful and faithful high priest in things pertaining to God, to make propitiation for the sins of the people. For in that he himself hath suffered being tempted, he is able to succour them that are tempted' (2 $^{14-18}$). This is a truth to preach.

All the great Christmas carols are songs about the divine grace—the amazing love of God that freely stoops to us; and this is a genuine response to the Christmas story. A word about the Virgin Birth falls into place here. This belief is to many a sacred certainty: to others it causes puzzlement and uneasiness of mind. No preacher will wish at Christmas time to divide men, but to bid all men 'rise to adore the mystery of love' (M.H.B. 120). It would be wrong here to enter into controversy; though it is worth saying that (a) there can be no greater miracle than God 'in flesh appearing' (M.H.B. 118), in whatever way it happened; and (b) that there is a solid core of actual history in the nativity stories that obstinately refuses to be removed. However, the important point is the *meaning* of the Virgin Birth tradition. What central fact of the Christian faith does it express? The answer is: *grace*. Mary could have expressed her joy in the words: I, and yet not I but the grace of God in me. God asks everything from us and yet does it all Himself—that is the miracle of grace.

Grace is the foundation of Christian living. St. Paul, in a passage where he is appealing for a generous collection for the needy saints at Jerusalem, says: 'Ye know the grace of our Lord Jesus Christ, that, though he was rich, yet for your sakes he became poor, that ye through his poverty might become rich' (2 Cor. 8 ^{9}). He left the perfection of love, of joy, of understanding, of fellowship and of power and entered a world of hatred, sorrow, perplexities, strife, frustration. That is the pattern of Christian life; and the cause of Christian worship also. Although Jesus was 'in the form of God' (i.e. he really did express God in His fullness, or 'was divine by nature' as Moffatt has it), he regarded his equality with God as something to be manifested by making himself of no account and really becoming a servant. It is when men contemplate this grace that every knee shall bow and every tongue confess that Jesus Christ is Lord (Phil. 2$^{5-11}$).

'When the fullness of time came, God sent forth His Son, born of a woman, born under the law' (Gal. 4 ^{4}). The time is God's own choosing: it is His decree, His word is law. The decree of Caesar Augustus in Lk. 2 ^{1} reminds us that we also are very familiar with laws and decrees; and we are grateful for them for they help to make life just and bearable. But over and above them is the law and decree of God; and it is stronger than Caesar's.

In that faith, it is possible to rejoice at Christmas and not to forget the misery and conflict of our world. We know that God chooses the time to send forth His Son; we know that the whole vast panorama of time is in His hands. Every moment is His— this moment when we are preparing to preach, the very moment when we face our congregations. For the first word God speaks to us is not: 'Look back 1,900 years', or 'Some time in the future'; but NOW. We cannot do better at Christmas than say:

> *Cast out our sin, and enter in;*
> *Be born in us today*—(M.H.B. 125).

Book List

The Second Advent. Dr. T. F. Glasson (Epworth Press.) Should be read because of its rather different viewpoint from the article above by Kenneth Grayston.

The Person of Jesus Christ. H. R. Mackintosh (T. & T. Clark).

The Person of Christ. Sydney Cave (Duckworth).

Jesus, Divine and Human. J. A. Findlay (Epworth Press).

A Saviour in Sight. L. C. Horwood (Epworth Press).

2. Covenant Sunday

By Prof. H. Cecil Pawson, M.B.E., M.Sc.

Aim: To lead those who are Christians, through remembrance to rededication; and those who are not yet fully committed to Christ, through resolution to reconciliation with God.

Bible Readings:

Genesis 8 [15-22]. Note, in v. 20, what Noah did when he first looked out upon a new world; also the promise in v. 22.

Genesis 9 [8-17]. God's remembrance in v. 15, and the covenant which the centuries have confirmed.

Deuteronomy 8. The challenge of God's past dealings. Note v. 2, 'the way which the Lord thy God *led* thee . . .'

Psalm 90. The argument which culminates in v. 12, and the climax which is one of the greatest prayers in the Bible in v. 17.

Psalm 116. Vv. 17 and 18 are suggestive of the purpose of Covenant Sunday. To gather up our thinking, feeling and aspiration into vows or promises made to God, and to pray that we may be kept loyal to them by God's help, are the only worthy New Year resolutions.

Romans 12. Opportunities for the expression of the kind of life described in this chapter are sure to come to everyone as we travel through the year ahead. Vv. 1 and 2, rightly interpreted and applied, should provide an excellent prelude to participation in the Covenant Service.

Hebrews 8. The fuller revelation of the Divine Purpose makes possible a richer knowledge and experience of the eternal promises of God, even as the Old Testament finds its fullest development and expression in the New.

Hebrews 12 [18-29]. God's final promise or covenant is in Jesus. Note in v. 28 the abiding security of the Kingdom of God in a world where so little seems secure and where so many things have been shaken. We receive the Kingdom when we enthrone the King.

Introduction

'Covenant Sunday is full of sacred memories in our Church.'
It has a rich tradition, for 'on this day we meet expressly as
generations of our fathers have met'.

Although, in Wesley's time, this service was introduced at
Bristol in October, at Dublin in April, and in another place in
August, in his *Journal* for 25th December 1747 he wrote:
'Both this and the following days I strongly urged the giving up
ourselves to God, and renewing in every point our Covenant
that the Lord should be our God.' It is now generally associated
with the first Sunday in the New Year. Our aim at this milestone
in the Calendar of His Grace should be, through challenge, to
bring comfort (in the N.T. meaning of 'strength') to both young
and older Christians, as well as to provide the opportunity for
those who have not been won for Christ, in the fullest sense,
to yield themselves in conscious, intelligent, unqualified surrender
to His will. The aim, therefore, should be the conversion and
consecration of souls. To this end, the service should be impressive, heart-searching and challenging, because the preacher
himself, consciously dependent on the power and guidance of
the Holy Spirit, and by prayerful dedication, is 'ready for all
Thy perfect will'.

Remembrance, Resolution and Rededication

It is often helpful to bring two passages of the Bible together,
for Scripture confirms and illustrates Scripture. Here is an
example:
'I stir up your pure minds by way of remembrance . . .' *or* 'by
way of reminder, to have you recollect . . .' (Moffatt): 2 Pet. 3 [1].
'What manner of persons ought ye to be?': 2 Pet. 3 [11].

Memory and Hope are two of God's greatest gifts; memory,
or rather the power of recollection, which takes us back over the
years, and 'hope that sends a shining ray far down the future's
broadening way' (M.H.B. 600). We need to pray for a quickening
but sanctified *recollection*. A much-needed prayer is to ask God
to help us to forget (sometimes to remember to forget) the things
we ought to leave behind; e.g. resentments, all trace of the
unforgiving spirit, needless regrets, injuries and disappointments
experienced at the hands of others. Equally we ought to pray for

the remembrance (the power to recall or rediscover in the files of memory—to 'stir up' our minds) of the things we ought to ponder, e.g. the Providence of God, and His manifold mercies and acts on our behalf. Do you remember the section in the Covenant Service which is headed 'Thanksgiving'? 'O God our Father, the fountain of all goodness, who hast been gracious to us, not only in the year that is past but through all the years of our lives; we give Thee thanks for Thy loving-kindness, which has filled our days and brought us to this time and place.'

Peter, in this chapter (2 Pet. 3) and in both his epistles, appeals to these early Christians to *remember*—'that ye may be mindful'—and suggests how memory may be a challenge and comfort to the soul. The friends to whom he writes are counselled to remember the teaching and commandments of God through prophets and apostles (the Old and New Testaments or Covenants). To remember that God rules, but on the scale of eternity (vv. 8–10). The great affirmation of the Psalmist rings down the centuries: 'Even from everlasting to everlasting Thou art God' (Ps. 90 [2]). Men may flout the righteous laws of God, but they do not suspend their operation; and to defy them is simply to illustrate them. (This may be illustrated from the physical, mental, and spiritual realms of life.)

The challenge of Peter's words in this chapter is *personal*, for it is surely clear that the most important thing he seeks to emphasize is not what is going to happen next, catastrophic as such happenings may be, but what kind of persons we ought to be. Persons are more important than events. What line of action I shall take, what kind of person I shall be, are more important than what outward events will take place in the year before me. Some possible developments of this theme are suggested in the following paragraphs, which are capable of much greater expansion and illustration.

(a) *Remembering our Christian inheritance*, what manner of persons ought we (not *you*) to be? Think of that inheritance! Citizenship in a Christian country, the Church, the Bible, Sunday, Y.M.C.A., Hospitals, and a host of other institutions, owing their origin and, in most cases, their continuance to the direct contribution of those who belong to the Christian faith. In social reform, the witness of the Tolpuddle Martyrs, Lord Shaftesbury, Charles Kingsley, and many others. Our Methodist inheritance: 'Methodism is Christianity in earnest.' So many of us, too, can and should remember with gratitude our Christian parenthood and homes. Our privileges are our responsibilities. 'Other men laboured, and ye are entered into their labour' (Jn. 4 [38]). Wherefore, 'seeing we also are compassed about with so great a cloud of witnesses,' what manner of persons ought we to be? The Divine promises made to our fathers are made to us. 'We come unto our fathers' God, their rock is our salvation' (M.H.B. 71).

(b) *Remembering the service and sacrifice of others on our behalf.* 'Freely ye have received, freely give' (Mt. 10 [8]). Because of those who died that we might live, we should be constrained to consecrate our remaining years, whether few or many, to the highest service. All we enjoy has on it the mark of sacrificial service. Our homes, our food, our freedom have been won for us at great price. Not the *price*, but the *cost* in life and blood should be remembered, and to realize this ought to rid our soul of selfishness, and challenge us afresh to sacrifice, that others may share.

(c) *Remembering the need of the great world* in its chaos and confusion, its sin and its distress. Are we helping to solve its problems or adding to them? Are we stumbling-blocks or stepping-stones to better things? Are we showing the way to the realization of that Kingdom which is joy and peace and real brotherhood, in the Fellowship of Him who alone can make all men one in God? The Christian hope is the only hope for the world, and *our lives* should be the revelation of the Gospel, the good news that in Christ we gain the victory over *all* sin.

(d) *Remembering Him, who gave His life* to save us and all men. 'Remember . . . Jesus Christ . . .' (2 Tim. 2 [8]). His life, his death, his risen living Presence with us. Let us measure our life by the standard of his example, if we would know how shabby and sinful our lives are in his Light. 'Thou judgest us, Thy purity doth all our lusts condemn' (M.H.B. 103). Remember Calvary. 'Bearing shame and scoffing rude, In my place condemned He stood' (M.H.B. 176). What manner of persons ought we to be, redeemed by him 'at such tremendous cost'? When John remembered the atoning sacrifice of Christ, he wrote 'Beloved, if God so loved us, we *ought* also to love one another' (1 Jn. 4 [11]). We ought and we *can*, in Him, whose promise is, 'If we confess our sins, He is faithful and just to forgive us our sins, and to cleanse us from all unrighteousness' (1 Jn. 1 [9]). He can resolve the conflict between the-person-I-know-I-am and the-person-I-know-I-ought-to-be. 'The wish is there, but not the power of doing what is right.' 'Who will rescue me . . . ?' 'God will' (Rom. 7 [18-24], Moffatt). And when this act of God, this work of grace, has been wrought in my heart, I shall know the motive of all worth-while Christian service, as expressed in M.H.B. 388.

Many resignations would never be written and more volunteers for service would be forthcoming, if this experience were more common: 'O to grace how great a debtor, Daily I'm constrained to be!' (M.H.B. 417).

Remember His power and grace so freely available to us all in the offer of His living, loving Presence, 'that Christ may dwell in your hearts by faith' (Eph. 3 [17]). There is no sin which cannot be cleansed, no wrong habit which cannot be broken, no temptation which cannot be mastered, if we are willing to receive Him and the promise of the New Covenant. 'And I saw more than ever that the Gospel is, in truth, but one great promise from the beginning of it to the end' (John Wesley's *Journal*, 4th June, 1738). The question is: 'Wilt thou be made whole?' (Jn. 5 [6]). We can be free to become the converted and consecrated children of God He wants us to be, if we are willing to accept Christ as Saviour (conversion) and follow Him as Lord (consecration). Dora Greenwell writes: 'The curse of religion is the habit of translating into a vague future tense what Christ offers us now.' Hear His own word: 'If thou canst believe, all things are possible to him that believeth' (Mk. 9 [23]).

Remember the promises of God in Christ. Have we taken them seriously, we who call ourselves Christians? How deeply do we believe them to be true? Are they really of effect in all our daily concerns? And to those of us who have no recollection of having answered for ourselves His call to personal surrender, and no real assurance that 'I am His and He is mine, for ever' (M.H.B. 423), there comes here another opportunity in the mercy of God for us to believe the promise: 'But as many as received him, to them gave he power to become the sons of God, even to them that believe on his Name' (Jn. 1 [12]), 'and him that cometh to me I will in no wise cast out' (Jn. 6 [37]).

The promises of God never fail, and in a world where opinions change overnight, and treaties are often mere scraps of paper, it is good to be able to trust the unchanging truth of the covenant-keeping God. 'Blessed be the Lord . . . there hath not failed one word of all his good promise . . .' (1 Kings 8 ⁵⁶). 'But as God is true, our word to you was not yea and nay . . . for all the promises of God in him are yea . . .' (2 Cor. 1 ¹⁸⁻²⁰). This is well expressed in M.H.B. 495, v. 1.

Is our trust fixed on Christ? Do we rely on Him? How much easier it is to drift than to decide; but drifting hardens into the wrong kind of decision, and no man knows when the last opportunity to decide has come. Someone wrote across the face of his clock: 'It's always later than you think,' on which statement Ethel Mannin, the writer, comments: 'It is, God help us, it is'. The calendar reminds us of its truth.

The Gospel challenge is expressed in the simple, short words 'here' and 'now', but the offer of God in Christ cannot be realized without our personal assent. He speaks, but we must make our personal response. 'I will *arise* and go to my father'. 'I will pay my vows unto the Lord *now* . . .' 'I will accept His offer *now* . . .' 'He wills that I should holy be.' 'Wilt thou?' Let my heart say: 'I will.'

> *I will accept His offer now,*
> *From every sin depart,*
> *Perform my oft-repeated vow,*
> *And render Him my heart—*
>
> (M.H.B. Verses, No. 26).

Note for the preacher. Read through the words of the Covenant Service before Covenant Sunday, and the final section at least twice, and then ask yourself the question: 'Does my message for the congregation to which I am called to preach really lead up to this vow?' Let me remind you of the words of that vow.

I am no longer my own, but Thine. Put me to what Thou wilt, rank me with whom Thou wilt; put me to doing, put me to suffering; let me be employed for Thee or laid aside for Thee, exalted for Thee or brought low for Thee; let me be full, let me be empty; let me have all things, let me have nothing; I freely and heartily yield all things to Thy pleasure and disposal.

And now, O glorious and blessed God, Father, Son and Holy Spirit, Thou art mine, and I am Thine. So be it. And the Covenant which I have made on earth, let it be ratified in heaven.

Now unto Him that is able to keep you from falling, and to present you faultless before the presence of His glory with exceeding joy, to the only wise God our Saviour, be glory and majesty, dominion and power, now and ever. Amen.

Book List

1. *Public Prayers and Services for the Use of the People called Methodists* (early editions). Note the heading, 'Direction to Penitents and Believers' for the section dealing with 'Making and Renewing their Covenant with God'. Also the separate section on 'Directions to Penitents for making their Covenant with God' (alternative service approved by the Conference of 1897).

2. *A Service for such as would make or renew their Covenant with God*. A beautiful, though abbreviated, form of the earlier services, and, when used, should not be read through without periods for silent meditation on what is read (Epworth Press).

3. *The Methodist Hymn Book;* especially the sections headed 'Dedication', 382–405, and 'Lovefeast and Covenant Services', 744–750, though many other hymns are very suitable for the day.

4. *Methodism can be Born Again*. W. E. Sangster, M.A., Ph.D. (Hodder & Stoughton).

5. *The Methodist*. A survey of the Christian Way in Two Centuries, including 'The Rules of the Society of the People called Methodists', by Henry Carter, C.B.E. (Epworth Press).

6. *The Pattern of Methodism*. S. B. Frost, M.Th., Ph.D. (M.Y.D.)

7. *In the Secret Place of the Most High*. A. J. Gossip, D.D., LL.D. (Independent Press). Studies in Prayer. Prayer is the secret of power on Covenant Sunday and all other occasions.

3. The Gospel of the Cross

By the Rev. S. B. FROST, M.Th., Ph.D.

Introduction

THE *aim* of these six studies is to show that the Message of the
Christian Preacher is in this, as in every age, an offer of Jesus
Christ as Saviour of men.

Some of us may straightway protest that this is to circumscribe
the content of Christian preaching far too narrowly, but that
is not so. Every aspect of life and thought is within the province
of the Christian preacher provided that it is recognized as being
a feature of, or a fact related to, that Salvation which Christ has
procured for all mankind. As in a painting, various articles of
greater or less importance in relation to the theme of the whole
work may be individual studies, and yet each one is so treated
as to bring out its relationship to that theme, contributing it
maybe by its own dulled surfaces to the general soberness of
the background, in order to heighten the vivacity and eagerness
of the young face that seems to lean forward expectantly out
of the gloom, toward the light; so, too, the whole range of human
interest is proper material for the Christian Preacher, if he can
see and communicate the significance of that interest as it stands
in relationship to God's redemptive activity throughout the
whole of time. We have too often made of the Cross of Jesus a
little and impoverished thing and then declared it too narrow a
field to confine our preaching. Seen as the expression in time of
the eternal purpose of God, it embraces both time and eternity,
and our thought can propose no subject that does not fall within
its scope. The whole and only message of the Christian preacher
is the Gospel of the Cross.

One of the characteristics of Paul's writing so often remarked
upon, is the way small issues lead him back to the basic convictions of the Christian. He urges the Philippians to be humble:
yes, to be humble as was Jesus Christ, who though He was in
the form of God—and he is launched on one of the most profound
Christological statements in the whole of Scripture (Phil. 2 $^{5-11}$).

An appeal for a Poor Fund offering leads him to proclaim the grace of the Lord Jesus, who though He was rich yet for our sakes became poor—and Paul is led on to declare the merciful injustice of the Gospel as the paradox it is, whereby His poverty enriches us (2 Cor. 8 ⁹). So, too, we can safely preach on the relationship of science and religion or the need for the political parties to compose their differences, or on whatever else we think God has given us to say, if our sermon bases itself firmly upon our great and abiding convictions, and if what we have to say is itself an expression of, or related to, the Gospel of the Cross. We cannot preach the whole Gospel every time—in some sermons we may not mention perhaps the words salvation or redemption—but the relationship must be there, *and it must be clear in the preacher's mind.* If we cannot see that relationship, then it is no Christian sermon that we preach, and it is our word we speak, not God's.

In my present pulpit, the book-rest was carved by a former minister of the Church. It reminds each preacher: 'We preach Christ crucified.' Yes, either Him crucified, or we do not preach.

STUDY ONE. THE ETERNAL PURPOSE

Bible Readings:

God as Creator, Man as Created: Gen. 1–3, Is. 45 ¹⁻¹³, Rom. 9 ¹⁻²⁴.

God's Purpose as Eternal. Eph: 1 ³⁻¹⁴.

Where, then, shall we begin to contemplate the Cross of Jesus Christ, but *at the beginning?* 'In the beginning, God created the heavens and the earth . . .' Why? Why should God create a world? The Bible allows the question and gives the answer.

Love the Motive of Creation and Redemption

'Let us make man in our image, after our likeness . . .' (Gen. 1 ²⁶). Why must man be made in God's image? Obviously because God intended man to have fellowship with Himself. Fellowship can exist only between beings sufficiently alike for them to have interests in common; hence the need for man to be made in God's likeness.* Wisdom (almost God's 'Other Self' in this passage), speaking of the joy of the first beginnings of creation, says: 'And

---

*cf. The prisoner's affection for the mouse in his cell; the shepherd's companionship with his dog; the fellowship of a David with his Jonathan.

my delight was in the sons of men' (Prov. 8 31). When John tells us that God's whole nature is love (1 Jn. 4 7-8) we know straightway why He created men and women—because it is the nature of love to give itself to a beloved and to desire the self-giving of the beloved in return. When we read (in Eph. 1 4-5, 11) that in Christ we were fore-ordained to be a heritage to which God Himself is to be heir at the end of time, we see that the reaching forth of God's love toward man is an eternal purpose—prior to time and seeking its goal where time has died for ever. Only as part of that purpose did the Spirit of God brood upon the waters, and it was to this end that God said: 'Let there be light.' It was for this that Adam was formed, and Noah entered the ark; it was for this that Abram was called from Ur of the Chaldees, and Joseph went down into Egypt, and Moses fled to the land of Midian; for this was the Red Sea and Sinai, Jordan and Jericho; for this, Gideon and David, Elijah, Isaiah, Jeremiah, and Ezekiel; for this was Exile and Return, and the years of patient hope, and the voice crying in the wilderness; for this, the Birth, the Baptism, the Temptation, and the Teaching; for this Gethsemane; for this the Trial and Scourging, the Via Dolorosa and the crown of thorns, the nails, and *Eli, Eli, lama sabachthani;* for this the Empty Tomb; for this His 'Peace be unto you'; for this Pentecost, the Church, the Second Coming, and the Last Judgement, for this—that God having made trial of mankind should find some worthy of Himself (Wisdom 3 5). (The significance of that word 'worthy' is one of the things we shall have to study.) Down through all the ages runs God's Word: 'I will be their God, and they shall be my people' (Jer. 31 33; Gen. 17 8; Lev. 26 12; Hosea 2 23; Mk. 1 15; 1 Pet. 2 9; etc.). God needs man. This is His one need, a need deliberately chosen, undertaken, planned-for and embraced. In the Kingdom of God, man will love God, as God even now loves man. It was for this that he was made in God's image.

But what is it to be made in God's Image?* Obviously, it is to be a person, because God is Personal (He is more; He is 'Super-personal,' but that includes while it transcends Personal); that is, He is a free, moral Being, who makes His own choices, and the one that is supremely important in His eyes is the choice between Good and Evil. Now we are relatively persons (not fully personal as He is) and therefore our freedom of moral

*See later studies on *The Doctrine of Man* (page 139 *infra*).

choice is a relative and circumscribed freedom. I am not free always to choose between the ideal Good and absolute Evil; sometimes my decision is limited, by the circumstances of my situation, to a choice of a less or a greater evil, as when I must either resist a brutal man by force or stand aside and allow him to ill-treat a defenceless child. That was the situation of Nicholas Nickleby with Wackford Squeers in Dickens's novel. But each of us has* a sufficient area of freedom in life wherein he can exercise his moral choice for good or evil, and in so doing 'exercise himself unto godliness' (or piety, reverence: 1 Tim. 4 [7]), and increase day by day the strength of his choice, that finally it may become as uncompromising in its intention as is the choice of God Himself.

> There we shall see His face,
> And never, never sin;
> There, from the rivers of His grace,
> Drink endless pleasures in—(M.H.B. 410).

Of our own free choice, we are to be holy because He is holy (Lev. 11 [44], 1 Pet. 1 [16]).

But the same remarkable parable that so clearly sets the scene, not only for the Biblical histories, but for the whole life of mankind on earth, is not content to set forth God as Creator, and Man as made in His Image. It also sets forth *Man as a fallen creature*. 'The serpent beguiled me, and I did eat' (Gen. 3 [13]). Here, the most important thing to be said is that we Christians do not believe man to have a bias to evil merely because the story of the Fall is in the Bible. We believe it to be so, because it is also a fact of experience which none can deny: 'For the good which I would, I do not: but the evil which I would not, that I practise' (Rom. 7 [19]). The story came in to explain the fact; the fact has not been invented to bolster up the tale.† Man had free-will; he has used it to choose selfishly in life and has thrown God's love, expressed in creation and in providence, back in His face.

But just as to choose rightly is to grow firmer and more uncompromising in the choice of good, so to choose wrongly is to make it harder and harder, indeed impossible to choose rightly.

*Here we are discussing man as being no more than *relatively* free, even as the ideal creature of God in a fallen world. Actually, it is a false situation, because he is himself a fallen creature and in reality his relative freedom is further limited by his sinful nature. *See* the next section.

†N. P. Williams, *The Ideas of the Fall and of Original Sin*, Chapter 2.

Man cannot find his own way back. 'For my thoughts are not your thoughts, neither are your ways my ways, saith the Lord. For as the heavens are higher than the earth, so are my ways higher than your ways, and my thoughts than your thoughts.' (Is. 55 8-9). Many theologians go so far as to say that man has wholly lost his freedom to do good and retains only a freedom to do evil. That is open to serious attack, but nevertheless it is one aspect of the truth, for here we come upon the great antimony of free-will and prevenient grace. What is undeniable is that man pays a terrible penalty for his wrong choice. In attempting to gratify himself, instead of serving and loving God, as he was made to do, he let loose on the earth two terrible powers, by which every generation of mankind is hag-ridden, and none worse than the men of today—the powers of Fear and Greed. Greed is the child of his own self-assertiveness, and Fear that of his neighbour's. Hence come wars and oppressions, injustice, bribery, cruelty of all kinds. But there comes also a ghastly perversion of his own nature, whereby he delights in evil and loves cruelty—there's a streak of it in all of us. Hence comes Belsen and hence comes Dachau. No beast tortures another, least of all its own kind, as man has tortured man. Moreover, even when the evil nature of man is restrained by good influences, such as Christian traditions, home-life, education, he is left a restless and dissatisfied creature. 'Thou madest us for Thyself and our heart is restless, until it repose in Thee.'*

Creation and Redemption One Plan

Why then did God ever allow so awful a state of affairs to come into being? Is this the nature of love, to create a situation in which things might go—have gone—so disastrously wrong? Could not He foresee? Or has the situation passed beyond His control? Can it be that God like Frankenstein has created a monster which finally will destroy Him?

If this were all we had to tell of God and His purposes, we should have no answer to these questions. But He did foresee and He did foreprovide. He gave the freedom, and the possibility of all this world's misery and sin, and therefore the moral responsibility for this world's affairs lies at His door; but He meets it gloriously. For the act of creation itself is but the completion of His plan. Incarnation and Atonement are part of the same plan.

*Augustine, *Confessions*, i.i.

Before time was, God saw the Cross and did not flinch. If He was to create a being morally free, then He must be prepared also to forgive and to redeem. Such a creature would need rescuing from himself. Thus the Cross is planted in the heart of the universe, as it is implanted in the heart of God. When the Seer gazed into Heaven, he saw upon God's throne a Lamb standing, as though it had been slain, and later he speaks of the Lamb that hath been slain from the foundation of the world.* Creation without Atonement had been an immoral act—and God is holy in all His ways.

Moreover, that offer of atonement, reconciliation, and deliverance, is *an offer to all*. Some have found in Romans Ch. 9, the terrible doctrine of 'double election'—some men are predestined to salvation and some to damnation. It was this great error which lay like a shackle on eighteenth century Christianity, until Wesley smote it hard and long and finally succeeded in loosening Christian thought, Anglican and Nonconformist, from its grip.† We Methodists believe that God's offer of Himself is to all.

> *O for a trumpet voice,*
> *On all the world to call!*
> *To bid their hearts rejoice*
> *In Him Who died for all;*
> *For all my Lord was crucified,*
> *For all, for all my Saviour died*—(M.H.B. 114).

But *do* we so believe? When you preach, do you believe that the people *not* in the Chapel, the cultured Third Programme listeners, the dog-track addict, the hard-bargain business man, the prostitute and the rake—do you believe that *they* would find anything in what you have to say to interest *them*? We may need to learn to speak a new language and put our message into their own dialect or even slang, *but the message of the Cross holds good in every language under the sun and can be relied upon to make its appeal to all*. Are our modern crowds less likely material for the Christian preacher than the gin-sodden, bull-baiting, cock-fighting savages of eighteenth-century Wednesbury or Kingswood? When 'at a loss for a subject', and faced with a 'difficult' congregation (whether the difficulty arises from sophistication or

---

*Rev. 5 6, 13 8 (but cf. R.V. margin and Commentaries); cf. Acts 2 23 and 1 Pet. 2 19-20.

†*See* Wesley's 'Notes on the New Testament,' Rom. 8 29-30 and 9-11. Also an excellent exposition in 'Sermons,' LVIII, On Predestination.

sheer ignorance of the Christian Faith), follow Paul's example (1 Cor. 2 $^{1-2}$) and that of Wesley's *Journal* for January 2nd, 7th, 13th, 1738, and preach Jesus Christ and Him crucified. Our Gospel is the Gospel of the Cross. It was designed for all, and has its appeal for all.

Here, then, we may pause and sum up what we have said so far. God created man that He might love him, and be loved by him. It was necessary that man should be like Him, and in particular possess freewill. Man uses that freewill to turn from God, and so involves himself in perversion and disaster; therefore God sets out to save him from that disaster and to win him back to Himself. He does this by means of the Cross. To preach about the Cross, then, is to preach on the meaning of life, and to preach about that which concerns and appeals to all mankind.

STUDY TWO. IS SALVATION NECESSARY?

Bible Readings:

Man under sentence of death: Gen. 3, Is. 38 $^{10-20}$, Mt. 22 $^{1-13}$, Lk. 13 $^{22-30}$, Rom. 5, 1 Cor. 15 $^{50-58}$, Eph. 2$^{1-10}$.

One day, before the war, we sat on a beach in the Isle of Wight. Before us lay the Solent, rippling contentedly in the sunshine of a glorious summer day. The beach was pleasantly filled with holiday-makers, and the sea dotted with the bathers. Lazily we watched the *Europa*, the German rival to our own *Queen Mary*, steaming toward Southampton and the docks. Suddenly a commotion arose. Fishermen came running along the beach, snatching up deck chairs and urging people off the beach on to the sea wall and promenade. Many protested; it was not time for lunch yet; they did not want to move; they were comfortable; when the fishermen tried to convince them of danger near at hand they laughed. A blue sky, a perfect English summer day, a dancing sea—what danger could there possibly be? But the fishermen had their way and we stood on the promenade and watched. Across the placid sea we now saw advancing a great wave, some four feet high, which dashed on to the beach and broke on the sea wall with the fury of a wild beast. In the backward surge went magazines, rowing-boats, deck chairs, and a dog. On the other side of the Solent, the wave hit Southsea beach and carried away a little girl. The fishermen, you see, had noticed that the *Europa* was going too fast for those restricted waters. Her great bow-wave ran across the placid sea like a living thing and scoured the pleasure beaches of the Solent as if the hungry ocean had risen to find its prey.

The Urgency of the Gospel

Is that a legitimate illustration of the present religious situation? We are hardly the careless and indifferent generation we were in the inter-war years, but our anxieties are political and economic, not religious. As Christian preachers, like Bunyan's Christian and the Early Methodists, we warn men to flee 'from the wrath to come'; but our generation no more believes in divine wrath than the holiday makers believed in the sea's power. This morning's newspaper, as I write this, reports a speaker at the National Road Safety Congress urging that road-safety lessons should take the place of religious instruction in schools, at least for younger children. That is, we are to be taught to fear physical disaster, but to ignore the possibility of spiritual disaster. That presumably is negligible in comparison with the danger of the roads. It follows, if that is true, that we do not need a Saviour and that the Christian Gospel is designed to meet a need which never existed—and therefore is not merely valueless but positively false.

That pleasant man for instance, who lives next door and does his gardening on Sunday morning and his entertaining and visiting Sunday tea-time, but never goes to Church—he is not an atheist, or a Marxist, or anything violent. He is just an ordinary fellow, who has plenty to worry him, but not God. There are his main-crop potatoes and his wife's health, and all the forms he has to fill in at work, and there are memories of the last war and fears of a next, but he never loses a moment's sleep about God. He presumes there is one, and no doubt He is a decent sort; but your neighbour has got enough to bother with, without worrying his head about *that*. Why, look at the price of tobacco—

Now that fellow is the hard case of our problem. We have to ask ourselves two questions:

(a) Is he really in any danger?

(b) If he is, how can I get him to see it?

Until we have answered those questions rightly and have an unshakable conviction that our answer *is* right, we have no cause to preach the Gospel of the Cross,

Is he really in any danger?

To answer this first one we turn to the Bible once more, and to the Genesis story for a first beginning. If we believe that it correctly emphasizes the Creatorship of God, His purpose in making man, the nature of man as personally free, and as wrongfully self-assertive, what has it to say about the consequences of man's rebellion against God? Man is forced to leave the Garden of Eden, where he formerly met God face to face, and is told that drudgery is to be his lot, until the day that he returns to the earth he came from. For his sinning, then, he receives a sentence of death (Gen. 3 [19]; cf. Rom. 5 [12] and I Cor. 15 [21–22]).

But '*death*' can mean so many things. To those Greeks, who believed that the body was the prison-cell of the spirit, death was a joyous release. So apparently the Druids thought too. The Buddha saw death as merely the obverse of life, and the inexorable wheel of existence carried you through the one experience as through the other; but both alike were existence, and it is existence which is evil. The scientist sees death as merely the dissolution of a complex organism into its component elements, the first sign being the cessation of that intangible by-product of its complexity which we call 'life'. The lamp disintegrates, so the light inevitably goes out. But for the Bible, death is something different from all these. Death is something to be feared. Death is man's last and final and implacable foe. Death is in itself something horrible. Something fundamentally foreign to his true nature. It cuts a man off from life and from God.

Thus in the earliest days, the feeling was that the dead soul might seek to cling tenaciously to life and so haunt his relatives. The earliest mourning rites were an attempt both to satisfy the dead and speed his departure, while disguising the relatives so that he should not know them. The classical expression of the fear of death is the so-called Sheol doctrine: Sheol is the abode of the dead, wherein they do indeed have an existence, but their existence is so shadowy that it can hardly be called existence. It is a place of infinite weariness and boredom. Above all, it is an existence cut off from God (Isaiah 38 [11], [18–19], Ps. 6 [5], 88 [10–12], 115 [17], 30 [9]). The fact that Job actually longs to go there is indeed the measure of his wretchedness; life must be a terrible thing before a man longs for Sheol! (Job 3).

The astonishing thing about the Old Testament is that this is held to be *the lot of all men*. Possibly some kind of exception was made for the Ideal Hebrews, the patriarchs, Abraham, Isaac, and Jacob, for Elijah and perhaps Moses; we cannot tell. But the Book of Psalms is effective witness for the fear of the experience and state of death for the generality of men in Old Testament times. Only in the very last of its writings, Daniel and Isaiah 24–27 (i.e. 'Pseudo-Isaiah', an apocalyptic work of the Greek period) do we get any dependable assertion of a 'life' after death, as distinct from mere Sheol existence. Dan. 12 [1–3] and Is. 25 [8] and 26 [19] bring hope into man's contemplation of the future life for the first time in Scriptural writings.*

But they do not overthrow the Sheol doctrine. They supplement it by a doctrine of Resurrection from Sheol to life. But for those who do not partake of that Resurrection, Sheol presumably still remains their unenviable lot.

When we come to the New Testament, we enter upon a glorious certainty of Resurrection, demonstrated in Jesus Christ and made available to all who by their fellowship, through faith in him, in his death and sufferings, are also identified with him in his Resurrection. 'If we died with him, we shall also live with him' (2 Tim. 2 [10]). 'For if we become united with him by the likeness of his death we shall be also by the likeness of his resurrection. . . . But if we died with Christ, we believe that we shall also live with him' (Rom 6 [5, 8]). But there is no suggestion anywhere in the whole of the New Testament, that the unbeliever shares in the Resurrection. For those who do not enter in with the Bridegroom, there is only the shut door and the outer darkness, the weeping and the gnashing of teeth (Mt. 25 [12]; cf. 22 [1–13], the Man without a Wedding Garment, and 7 [11–12]). Jesus affirms

---

*Many readers may feel that a note of further explanation is necessary here. Ps. 16 [10–11] and Ps. 72 [24] express a confidence that Jehovah cannot leave His beloved uncared for in Sheol, but produce no thought-form to express the alternative. They are, however, first signs of a dissatisfaction with the Sheol doctrine. Is. 53 [8] and Ps. 139 [13–16] have been interpreted as implying resurrection but the evidence is extremely uncertain. Hosea 13 [14] should be read as a threat, not a promise: 'Shall I ransom them from the hand of Sheol? Shall I redeem them from death?' (these are questions expecting the answer 'No'). 'Where are thy plagues, O Death? Where is thy destruction, Sheol? (i.e. bring them forth). Pity shall be hid from my eyes.' (*See* Horton, *Century Bible*, and G. A. Smith, *Expositor's Bible*.) Job 19 [25–27] is notoriously difficult, owing to a damaged text, but Oesterley and Robinson decide against the attempt to find in it a doctrine of resurrection. On the whole subject, see their book, *Hebrew Religion*, Chapters 8, 9, 21, 36.

the fact of a Resurrection to the Sadducees, but on that occasion says nothing of the way of attainment (Mk. 12 [18–27]); but the parable of the Sheep and Goats (Mt. 25 [31–46]) and the saying which closes the series of sweeping claims for himself as the Custodian of Eternal Life, following upon Peter's Confession at Caesarea Philippi* leave us no room to doubt that the Epistles rightly interpret the mind of Jesus, when they assert that Resurrection is by Him and Him alone: 'For if by the trespass of the one death reigned through the one; much more shall they that receive the abundance of grace and of the gift of righteousness reign in life through the one even Jesus Christ' (cf. 1 Cor. 15[20–26], 1 Pet. 1 [3–4], 1 Jn. 5 [11], also Jn. 11 [25–26]).

But is that the *true* account of death? Or were the Druids right? Or was Buddha? Or is it the scientist who has the accurate and factual view of death? As Christians, we believe the Biblical view is the true account of death. It *includes* the scientific, but goes beyond it, in saying that death is not only the dissolution of the physical organism, *but is also a spiritual state of separation from God*. As Christians we can hold no other view. Either we think Biblically, that is, we look on life as the Bible does, on man as the Bible does, on death as the Bible does, and therefore on Salvation as the Bible does, or we have neither a Gospel nor a need for it. If we preachers are to be able to say, 'Thus saith the Lord,' we must learn to speak the Lord's language—so that when we say 'salvation' we mean what He means; and when we say 'death' we do not mean merely what the scientist means, or the pseudo-Christianity which leaves the word 'judgement' out of its vocabulary; but rather, we mean an entering into a state of existence which is not properly to be called 'living' at all, which is indeed alien to life, wherein one is aware of that light from which he is shut out and of the door that is closed against him, and of the primal, elemental horror that possesses him. It is a fearful thing to be cut off from God.

If, however, we are prepared to think Biblically in this modern age, the question about your pleasant pagan neighbour answers itself. He needs salvation because he and all the human race are under sentence of death. There is but one road of escape, and

* 'For whosoever shall be ashamed of me and of my words in this adulterous and sinful generation, the Son of Man also shall be ashamed of him, when he cometh in the glory of his Father with the holy angels' (Mk. 8 [38]).

that road is by the true and living way, Christ Jesus. 'And in none other is there salvation: for neither is there any other name under heaven that is given among men, wherein we must be saved' (Acts 4 [12]). 'Made like Him, like Him we rise' or we do not rise at all. But if your neighbour stands in need of the Gospel, he is an awful responsibility to have upon your conscience, is he not? There are some of us who have 'pleasant-pagan' relatives, friendly men and women, likeable and kindly, folk who are of our own flesh and blood, and bound to us by ties of gratitude and affection and love. Are we to believe that *they* are under this universal sentence of death? But how much easier to preach to a multitude than to speak to one of our own family! And yet is it not true that you cannot preach in the pulpit if you do not preach out of it? And, of course, this raises in its acutest form the question as to the fate of those who die apart from the salvation offered in Jesus Christ. Are we to be sundered from them by the very life which we have received and they have not? Luke 12 [51-53] takes on a fresh and significant meaning. Is there then no hope for those who have died apart from Christ? We have no authority to say anything; we can only leave them to God's mercy and wisdom. But we *have* authority to proclaim that salvation is by Christ the Lord!

If he is, how can I get him to see it?

Our other question was how can we persuade that decent non-Churchgoing neighbour of yours that he needs Jesus Christ? What convinces one man, means nothing to another. But we may suggest three possible lines of approach, among others, to this, the outstanding problem before the Church today:

1. We must seek a revival of conviction *inside* the Church of the paramount need for Jesus Christ as Saviour. There is a lot of dormant faith in Christian hearts, and the clear and reiterated enunciation of Christian beliefs will remind our congregations that these *are* the things they sing in their hymns, that these *are* the things they read in their Bibles, that these *are* the things they believe in their heart of hearts, and will remind them that they have always known John Three-Sixteen as the epitome of the Gospel. And wherever you have a believing community, its belief is infectious. We have to revive the Christian Faith in our villages and towns and cities, so that insensibly it becomes once again the basic assumption of English politics, arts and letters, and

social life. Your neighbour will not be saved on his own, his whole factory and Trade Union and social group must come in too. But the place to begin is *your* appointment next Sunday.

2. We can be ready to discuss these things directly with him, or anyone else who joins in. On a Commando Campaign, this story was told, by one of the 'home' team: 'My Society Steward tells me that in his workshop is a Communist, who is always trying to pick an argument with him, and when I asked him what he did about it, he said he "just walked away and left him to it, because it is no good arguing with that sort of person".' Oh the pity of it! The shame and defeat of it! We Christians have twice as good a case as the Marxists, if we will only use it—because ours is truth and theirs is at best but half-truth. (And, by the way, do not always fight on *their* ground; make them fight on yours. They will want to drag you off into politics—you see that they have to stay and face the questions they like to avoid; *religious* questions of man's nature and destiny, his deepest satisfactions, his sense of spiritual need, his moral standards, and his attitude to death!) But you will need to read as widely as you can.

3. By holding fast to our belief in Jesus Christ as Saviour, we shall ourselves be better able to face the personal sorrow, the occurrence of death in our homes, the threat of war, and the strain of modern life. T. R. Glover's famous dictum was that the Christian out-lived, out-thought, out-died his contemporaries of the Ancient World. We, too, must move more sure-footed in life than our pagan neighbours, with a more conscious sense of security and satisfaction, with the unassumed joy and the sturdy serenity, which are the proper fruits of our faith in Jesus Christ. Christian character counts every time, inside the pulpit and out. And it is the gift of Jesus Christ through the indwelling of His Holy Spirit.

We may sum up our whole study by saying that salvation is no mere speculation, nor a luxury 'extra' on the bill of life. It is a vital practical necessity for every man, woman and child on the face of the globe.

If we seem to have made salvation almost wholly salvation from death rather from sin that is because we were discussing the *necessity* of it: had it been our *need* of salvation we should have stressed that salvation is from sin. But that salvation is not only salvation from death but also the gift of eternal life here and now, the next study will attempt to bring out.

STUDY THREE.   WHAT IS SALVATION?

Bible Readings:

Salvation as the offer and acceptance of life: Deut. 30, Is. 55, Ps. 116, Lk. 4 [16-30], 10 [17-24], Jn. 5 [19-29], Rom. 8 [1-12], Col. 1 [9-23].

The three great names of the evangelical tradition are those of Paul, Luther, and Wesley. The outstanding feature common to all three is not their theological training (though it is well to notice each would have been the last to repudiate the value of education), nor is it their ability to expound and to convince (though it is well to notice that each spared no pains to be an effective preacher), nor was it even their personal holiness and mystic Christian experiences (though it is essential to notice that each was a man deeply versed in the intimacies of the Spirit). The outstanding feature common to all three, which sets them apart as 'The Three', even as men distinguished above all the 'Thirty' of the King's most glorious Host,[*] is the intensity of their conviction that they had something to offer, something they *must* offer to the men of their day.

As preachers, then, we need to read all we can and constantly to further our theological education; we need to train our voice, prune our gestures, prepare our sermons with meticulous care—and then know that what matters supremely is whether we have anything to *offer*.

What Have We to Offer?

The days when our doorsteps were besieged by hawkers, pedlars, and vacuum-cleaner men seem like a bygone dream. Now it is we who hunt for goods in short supply. Firms maintain their connexions, but the travellers who call can only keep personal contacts in repair and describe in glowing terms the commodities of which they have not even samples. The shopkeeper, patient as he is interrupts at last—'But what can you offer me for immediate delivery?' All too often the reply has to be: 'Well, nothing for immediate delivery, but we have every hope that when the export drive——' and his voice tails off in pitiable confusion. What a position to be in—a traveller with nothing to sell! Calling on shops crying out for goods, to commend commodi-

[*]2 Sam. 23 [22-23].

ties he cannot produce! All his fluency and expert salesmanship only go to reveal more clearly the emptiness of his bag!

Is there a parable here? When you hear your brethren preach, is it a case of the more able they are, the more they reveal that they have nothing to offer? When *you* are preaching and your brethren are listening to you, do they hear the confident voice of one who has much to offer, *everything* to offer? Is it not true that the Methodist pulpit of the present century has been increasingly characterized by its readiness to argue, deliberate, advise, and by its reluctance to *offer*? A recent Commando Campaign was prefaced by study of a pamphlet entitled: '*What have we to offer?*' Every preacher needs periodically to face the same question: 'What have I to offer?'

Our studies so far have led us to find the purpose of God's love to be the ground of creation, the meaning of history, the significance of our own being. As men and women, made for fellowship with God, but in revolt against Him, we have seen our neighbours, our families, ourselves under a sentence of death. God's Salvation is, then, first an offer of reconciliation, then the restoration of our ravaged nature, and then the gift of eternal life with Him. 'I came,' said Jesus, 'that they may have life, and may have it abundantly' (Jn. 10 10). It is only life with God that is abundant life (M.H.B. 416).

There is a line in one of Wesley's hymns which Charles repeats entire in another—a not infrequent practice, of course, but a significant one, in that such lines reveal his 'watchwords'. A repeated phrase is a significant phrase. Twice, then, he describes what Christ has to give in the same words: 'Pardon and holiness and heaven.'

> *Thy mighty name salvation is,*
> *And keeps my happy soul above;*
> *Comfort it brings, and power, and peace,*
> *And joy, and everlasting love:*
> *To me, with Thy dear name, are given*
> Pardon, and holiness, and heaven—(M.H.B. 98).

The other verse is equally forceful:

> *To him that in Thy name believes,*
> *Eternal life with Thee is given;*
> *Into himself he all receives,*
> Pardon, and holiness, and heaven—(M.H.B. 362).

What, then, is Salvation? Pardon, and holiness, and heaven! What, then, have we to offer? Pardon, and holiness, and heaven!

Pardon

One of the most enigmatic texts in the whole of Scripture is Ps. 130 [4]: 'For there is forgiveness with Thee, that Thou mayest be feared.' But the enigma quickly resolves when we consider the wealth of ideas that the Hebrew crams into the verb which we translate as 'to fear': guilty fear, the sense of overwhelming awe at God's presence, reverence or respect. God's power to forgive gives rise not to guilty fear (though it *does* increase our sense of sinfulness), but rather to a profound reverence and respect for Him—which is also not without its sense of awe at the unsurpassable love of Him who can forgive without stint. Thus the main light of the verse falls on the meaning 'to reverence', but in the peripheral half-lights we are aware of the wider ranges of the word's significance on either side.

The fact, then, that God forgives is a claim upon our reverence; not in this instance our love, but our *reverence*. The commentary we need here is the story of Jesus and the Pharisees in Mk. 2. Jesus said to the man 'borne of four': 'Son, thy sins are forgiven.' The scribes said: 'Why doth this man thus speak? he blasphemeth: who can forgive sins but one, even God?' Now, whichever way you interpret Jesus' answer, 'The Son of man hath power to forgive sins' (i.e. 'I, the Son of man, have power . . .' or simply 'A man has power . . .'[*]), he obviously means 'I have power' and the complementary comment is Matthew's 'the multitudes . . . glorified God which had given such power unto men'. The whole incident turns on the fact that the power to forgive sins resides in God's hands alone. That is why—one of the reasons and one of the most profound—we reverence Him; not only as Creator and King, but as the One in whom alone the power to forgive resides. As Ps. 51 [5] testifies, the full effect of our sins is not directed against those we harm among our fellow-men, but against God; even as in the Parable of the Sheep and Goats, Jesus claims that the real heinousness of the crime of those who neglected 'one of these my brethren, even these least' is revealed in the fact that in its direst effect their selfishness was aimed at Him. Sin is always sin against God; thus it is God alone who can forgive sin.

[*] So Manson, *Teaching of Jesus*, 2, p. 215; Lake-Jackson, *Beginnings of Christianity*,' 1. 379.

What we proclaim, then, is something unique, when in God's name we proclaim the forgiveness of sins. Our many debts have been contracted with this one, that one and another, but God in Christ has under-written them, and we have but one Creditor with whom we must come to terms—God Himself. But if that one Creditor should freely forgive—then we are free of *all* debts!

I have spoken of it as a release from debt; Bunyan's metaphor was that of a burden rolling off a man's back; Paul's great word was 'justification'—a verdict of acquittal in a court of law. Whatever the metaphor, the experience is a genuine one of inner release, of a new-found freedom and joyousness of spirit, an experience which finds its expression in Paul's shout of triumph in answer to his own despairing cry: 'Who shall deliver me from the body of this death?—Thanks be to God, through Jesus Christ our Lord!' Between that question and its answer stands the experience of forgiveness—not the theory, nor the doctrine, but the experience of forgiveness. It was the *experience* of forgiveness which enabled the palsied man to rise up and carry out the bed that carried him in. For the sense of sin clings and hampers, confuses, and betrays a man (Heb. 12 [1]), and is often the cause of physical illness, very often the cause of mental illness, and is always the aggravating circumstance of the diseases of the soul. But to be forgiven, that is to be released; to be released as surely as if the great gate of Wormwood Scrubs had opened up to let you through into the sunlight and open air, and then swung to with a mighty clang as if to say: 'Now you are out, stay out!' A man *knows* when his sins have been forgiven! We offer to men and women the experience of forgiveness, cleansing, releasing forgiveness, as something they can accept *now*.

It is what thousands are hungry for—that word of forgiveness. They may not realize it; but they know it when the offer is made to them! It is our task as Christian preachers to offer to all the forgiveness of sins!

Holiness

Yet there is a greater thing than pardon, *to outgrow the need of pardon*. When the Prodigal Son first came home, there was so much to remind him of his shame; he had forgotten where things were kept and had to ask; he was not aware that a new byre had been built by his brother, while he was away, and found himself lost in his own farmyard in the dark of his first night! There were the distant sounds of drunken revelry from the village inn, that made his mouth go dry and his skin clammy with desire; but as the days passed he lost interest in his old friends and made himself new ones. Unconsciously he imitated his father's speech, gesture, and outlook, until, when the memory of his former escapade was faint and dim, the village was shaking its head playfully and saying with kindly satisfaction: 'Ah, he's a true son of his father!' *Now* there was no need for the father to see him while yet he was a great way off—the young man was already at home, both physically and mentally. He lived the life of home naturally and instinctively; he was truly a part of it.

The Christian believes—no, more than that, he *knows*—that to live day by day in love and loyalty with Jesus Christ works great changes in his character. He too becomes a true son of his Father. In Jeremiah's day* the Covenant was enshrined in a book, perhaps for the first time, and men said, 'Now we shall be all right; the law isn't just vague tradition in men's minds, or the conflicting traditions of the priests at different shrines. It is in a Book; we can all read it and keep God's law now.' Whatever Jeremiah may have thought of this new Book of the Law in his early days, he certainly saw through the vain hope in his more mature years. 'The Covenant', he said, 'which we will be able to keep is not one written on tablets of stone, or in folklore, or in a written Scripture; it is heart-religion, not book-religion, that transforms a man. It is the covenant written in the heart, in the man's desires and affections which is the only covenant he will keep.' And Jesus adds: 'Yes, and I have come to establish that new Covenant: My death will seal its inauguration by its spilt blood as surely as did the sacrificial victim's blood at Sinai in Moses' day' (Mk. 14 ²²⁻²⁵).

Thus, then, we are called into a new covenant—the covenant of the changed nature. Not changed by our effort, not disciplined into new habits by our strength of will, but rather brought to birth within us by the Holy Spirit of God. Ezekiel has the same hope: 'A new heart also will I give you, and a new spirit will I put within you: and I will take away the stony heart out of your flesh, and I will give you an heart of flesh. And I will put my spirit within you, and cause you to walk in my statutes and ye shall keep my judgements, and do them' (Ezek. 36 ²⁶⁻²⁷). Jeremiah and Ezekiel have the vision. Paul has the realization: 'If any man

*2 Kings 22; Jer. 11 ¹⁻⁸; 8 ¹⁻⁸; 31 ³¹⁻³⁴.

be in Christ, he is a new creature' (2 Cor. 5 ^{17}). We offer men and women, not new lamps for old, but new selves for old!

Holiness is a concept which has a long history. The connecting thread seems to be that it expresses the wonder, the awe, the moral purity, the 'otherness' of God's nature. But we are called to be holy, after the order of His holiness (1 Pet. 1 ^{16}). This was, as we have emphasized, the very principle of our creation. We were to be created in the image of God; holy because He is holy. Thus, that we should seek after holiness, that we should receive it afresh from Jesus, is only to say that salvation *is* salvation. Salvation either means the re-creation of man's fallen nature, the restoration of his true nature, or it is not salvation. Pardon cancels the sin of the past, as only full forgiveness can; but we must also deal with present and future sin. That, too, must be cast out. 'He breaks the power of cancelled sin,' cries Charles Wesley (M.H.B. 1), and we know that he means that hard on the heels of pardon, indeed, simultaneously with it, the gift of holiness comes pressing in.

In many, many chapels we have loyal companies of hard-working Methodists who have lost sight of the word 'holiness'. They remember that being a Christian means 'being good', and they try their best; but holiness as a joyous participation in God's own nature, holiness as a gift which He wants to bestow, holiness as something to be *accepted*, this they have forgotten—and the pulpit seldom attempts to remind them! Our people are so often people without hope; they have got out of the habit of looking forward. The eschatological hope of the Kingdom of God is removed for them to an infinitely-distant culmination of mission-ary endeavour overseas (but not at home, for some reason), while the individual hope of holiness has been transmuted into the uninspiring business of moral effort in an immoral world. Our folk are so often spiritually middle-aged, unenterprising, unex-pectant, and settling down to a complacent acquiescence in themselves as they are. We have to arouse them to hope and spiritual ambition once again! It is our generation of preachers who must awaken them from that sleep and revive the hope and expectation of our people! They are referring to us when they sing: 'Then loud be their trump, and stirring their sound, To rouse us, O Lord, from slumber of sin'—(M.H.B. 788). We need then, to insist again and again that not only Pardon but Holiness is the very essence of Salvation.

Heaven

The third of Charles Wesley's great words is Heaven. What shall we say of Heaven? Has it *any* significance among us in these modern and practical days?

For far too long we have allowed cheap jibes like 'Pie in the sky when you die' and 'dope for the masses' to inhibit us from even the most decorous references to Heaven. But there can be no preaching of the Gospel without it. For man's situation is that, because he has sinned and turned away from God, he has chosen death rather than life. But in Christ, God meets his sin by the gift of pardon and holiness; and He meets the sentence of death by the gift of eternal life. Now Heaven and Eternal Life are one and the same thing. Salvation is pardon and holiness *and heaven*.

When Jesus died upon the Cross, his death was truly death. Not just a 'suspension of animation', nor a temporary withdrawing into Heaven, as an actor withdraws into the wings to be ready for his next appearance. No, it was death as human beings know death, the spiritual experience of death.* When he rose from the dead it was out of the experience of death into the experience of life—and life is being with God, as death is separation from Him. But when Jesus rises, he is our fore-runner; our Pioneer.† He goes before that we may follow. 'Made like Him, like Him we rise.' Thus when he 'reascends His native heaven' (M.H.B. 221), it is to be with the Father; but where He is, we shall be (Jn. 14 ³). Heaven is being with God in Christ, as death is being apart from Him.

That is why as Christians we are profoundly disinterested in the psychic 'proofs' of man's immortality. That spiritualists are so jubilant at receiving 'messages' from the dead means nothing to us as far as our future hope is concerned, whatever we may think of its value as a piece of scientific research. That this life continues, we believe, but this is life-in-death; this side of the tomb is apart from Christ; to continue in it beyond the tomb is no thrill, but may well be horror. What we want to learn is not of human survival, but of resurrection—not 'do we continue to exist?' but 'can we share in His return to His heaven?' Can *we* go in, and be with God?

---

*The clause in the Creed, 'He descended into Hell,' explained in our *Book of Offices* as 'Hades, or the World of Spirits', was intended to safe-guard that truth. Jesus passed into the experience of death, in the Biblical sense of that word (*see* previous study).

†Heb. 12 ² (Moffatt).

'Come, ye blessed of my Father, inherit the Kingdom prepared for you from the foundation of the world' (Mt. 25 [34]). It will be those gracious words that shall greet us as we pass through the valley of the shadow of death. We shall escape the spiritual horror of death because united with Him by our faith and love in this world, and possessing already that quality of life which we call eternal, we shall rise out of and beyond death into Heaven, that where He is, we may be also. Thus comes the full circle round and we arrive at the point of departure: God's need of fellowship, God's desire for those whom He could love and by whom He should be loved. We shall be those of whom God has made trial and 'found them worthy of Himself' (Wisdom 3 [5]. *See* p. 64 *supra*). That 'worthiness' is not inherent, it is conferred; it is holiness given to us by, and accepted in, the Holy Spirit. But it *is* holiness. We shall not be the fearful, unbelieving, and abominable; the unclean or he that maketh a lie. We shall not be those who may not enter God's city (Rev. 21 [8, 27]); we shall not be he who put his hand to the plough and looked back, but he who endured to the end (Mk. 13 [13]; Lk. 9 [62]). We shall be those who have been transformed by the renewing of their mind (Rom. 12 [1]). Therefore, we shall be those who are written in the Lamb's book of life (Rev. 21 [27]), for we shall be what God desires. We shall be received into Heaven to be with Him.

But what about the streets of gold and the white robes, the palms and the crowns? They are John the Seer's imagery, the rich and precious imagery of an eastern mind. Moreover, when we see how it becomes the inspiration for so delightful a hymn as 'Jerusalem my happy home' (M.H.B. 655), when the Fourteenth Olympiad reminds us that the 'crown' is really the victor's wreath, and the palm is the palm of victory accorded to the conqueror in the games, then we recognize afresh how significant that imagery is. You must have your pictures of Heaven, and John has provided the setting and models for the compositions of all the ages that follow. But when we seek to press beyond the imagery to the reality we come up against Paul's great misquotation (he often seems at his best when he misquotes someone else!):

> *Things which eye saw not and ear heard not,*
> *And which entered not into the heart of man,*
> *Whatsoever things God prepared for them that love Him.*
>
> (1 Cor. 2 [9]).

As A. E. Whitham said, if we saw too clearly into Heaven we should forget our duties here in our longing to be there. What we do know is that Heaven is life with God, the completion of God's plan, and the satisfaction of man's nature. Moreover, it is assured to us in Jesus Christ. Salvation is the gift of pardon and holiness *and heaven*.

What have we to offer? Not vague promises, but pardon now, holiness as the years pass, and hereafter heaven. We have *everything* to offer, who offer Christ!

STUDY FOUR. SALVATION IS OF CHRIST ALONE

Bible Readings:

Jesus, Pre-existent, Divine, Unique, Alone able to save: Jn. 1 1-18, Heb. 1 1-2 18.

Reconciliation is through Christ alone: 2 Cor. 5 11-6 2, Gal. 2 11-3 14.

Jesus' own view of his role: Lk. 4 1-12, Mt. 11 20-30, Mk. 8 27-9 1, Lk. 9 51-62, Mk. 14 27-43.

The Unique Claim

So far we have attempted to establish three conclusions—that the doctrine of salvation is the clue to the meaning of life; that, on the Biblical account of this world, all men are in desperate need of salvation; and that salvation is a present as well as a future experience. But why do we attach this salvation to the name of Jesus, and why not, for example, to that of Jeremiah or of Paul? The question may sound foolish, put like that; yet there are very many within the Church, yes, within the pulpit, who would maintain that it is not the death of Jesus, or the Person of Jesus, but the teaching of Jesus which saves a man. But there have been other teachers than Jesus; to speak thus *is* to class him with Paul and Jeremiah and all the other great names of the Biblical tradition. His teaching is not unique in its ethical aspects; the Sermon on the Mount is in the true Biblical tradition and is of a texture with the Ten Commandments, the Book of the Covenant, Deuteronomy, Leviticus; its outlook is the outlook of Isaiah 1, Amos 5, and Micah 6. Jesus becomes unique, not when he tells us that the true manner of man's life is to love the Lord our God with all our powers, and our neighbours as ourselves (both sayings are, of course, direct quotations from the Old Testament), but rather when he adds to the ethical teaching of the Sermon the Parable of the Houses (Mt. 7 24–27); or when he accepts Peter's recognition of him as Messiah, and straightway adds that his role is to suffer, be killed, and return again to life, and that whoever joins him in that vocation shall be saved and whosoever refuses will discover that he has lost his life (Mk. 9 27f). The unique character of Jesus' teaching shines out clearly as he makes the Gracious Invitation: 'Come unto me, all ye that labour and are heavy laden (the prophets said: 'Return unto *the Lord*) and I will give you rest (the scribe knew the promise: 'God's presence shall go with thee and *He* will give thee rest'). Take my yoke upon you (the rabbis talked about 'the yoke of *the Kingdom*') and learn of me (the Wise Men said 'Learn of *Wisdom*') for I am meek and lowly of heart and ye shall find rest for your souls. For my yoke is easy and my burden is light' (the Psalmist said: 'Cast thy burden upon the Lord and *He* shall sustain thee'). Jeremiah or Paul, Prophet or Rabbi, all other Jewish teachers point away from themselves to God: Jesus alone calls men and women to himself. Jesus is unique, not in his teaching of what man ought to be and do, but in his proclamation of himself as the true and living Way, by which alone men come to God. 'No man cometh unto the Father, but by me' (Jn. 14 6).

This was indeed the lesson that the first disciples learnt in their discipleship, and this was the grand new truth that the Early Church was concerned to proclaim. When Peter first confesses Jesus to be the Messiah (Mk. 8 27f) his mind is leaping out to a daring speculation, the full significance of which he does not yet realize. But after the shattering experience of the crucifixion and the resurrection, his belief in Jesus as Messiah has become a profound, unshakable conviction. Indeed, one might say that he has passed from faith to knowledge. In the great Pentecost speech (Acts 2) Peter speaks as uncompromisingly of Jesus, as had Jesus of himself: 'Let all the house of Israel therefore know assuredly that God hath made him both Lord and Christ, this Jesus whom ye crucified.' Before the Sanhedrin he flings down the challenge of the new Gospel before the old Judaism: 'In none other is there salvation, for neither is there any other name under heaven that is given among men, wherein we might be saved' (Acts 4 12). When Paul is converted, he straightway begins to preach his new faith, and it is nothing other than that Jesus is the Son of God (Acts 9 [20]). When we are given a typical sermon of Paul's to a Jewish audience (Acts 13 [16f]) the whole aim of the discourse is to prove that Jesus is the fulfilment of Old Testament predictions, that he is Messiah and Saviour: 'Be it known unto you therefore, brethren, that through this man is proclaimed unto you remission of sins: and by him every one that believeth is justified from all things, *from which ye could not be justified by the law of Moses.*' Ah, that is the point! To be told what we ought to be and do (which the Law very effectively does, as is recognized by Jews and Christians alike), is in itself of no avail. We need release from sin, forgiveness for the past, new life for the future. This the Law cannot give—but Jesus can! And that Luke has not misrepresented Paul is undeniably established, when in *Romans* we find it put even more forcibly: 'For what the law could not do, in that it was weak through the flesh, God, sending His own Son, in the likeness of sinful flesh, and for sin, condemned sin in the flesh: that the requirement of the Law might be fulfilled in us, who walk not after the flesh, but after the spirit' (Rom. 8 [3] R.V. margin).

This explains one feature of the apostolic preaching that many find so puzzling. Why is so little said about the life, the ministry, the good works and healings of Jesus, either in the epistles or in *Acts?* The answer is, because the ethical teaching of the Christian Church does not differ from that of the Jews, and even the example of a perfect life was not the necessary thing to be stressed: what was important was the relationship of that teaching (whether as expounded in the Law or as exemplified in the life of Jesus) to the Person of Jesus himself. Only once in Acts (twice if we include the slight reference in 2 [22]) is the earthly ministry referred to, and that is for the benefit of a Gentile, a 'devout person' (Cornelius, Acts 10 [38]). In his two typical speeches to pagan Gentile audiences, Paul naturally spends much time on the existence of God, His creatorship and goodness; but then moves unswervingly forward to the proclamation of Jesus as World-Ruler and Judge (Acts 14 [8–18] and 17 [22–31]). That the Teaching and Healing Ministry was, of course, esteemed and lovingly recalled, yes, and treasured in a thousand hearts, the very fact of the existence of the Four Gospels bears witness; but it was not the burden of Apostolic preaching.* The Apostles were

*See further *The Apostolic Preaching* by C. H. Dodd, esp. pp. 28 f. (Ed. 1944.)

primarily concerned to proclaim, not the Sermon on the Mount, but Jesus Christ as the sole Saviour of mankind.

The Permanence of the Law

At this point, we may divert from our main subject to notice two further matters in passing. The first is the essential character of the Old Testament. The Old Testament scriptures are not simply to be explained as the record of God's preparation of a people for the coming of His Son amongst them. They are themselves God's Word, and have a permanent significance. They set out the situation of man: his creatureliness, his relationship to God, what God expects of him. The Ten Commandments stand firm as the temporal expression of God's eternal demands. We have to give their full significance to Jesus' words, that he came not to destroy, but to fulfil.

The other flows out of this. The Gospel of Jesus Christ has no meaning apart from the Law.* Jesus preached to men and women who acknowledged, even if they did not fulfil, the Law of God. His offer of salvation is the offer of ability to keep the Law, that is, the offer of holiness 'without which none may see the Lord' (Heb. 12 [14]). Thus the meaning of the Good News is lost where there is not first a recognition of the inexorable demands of God's holiness. Therefore, in order that he may preach the Gospel the Christian preacher must also preach the Law.† John Wesley's *Letter on Preaching Christ* (*Works*, XI, p. 480, 3rd Ed., 1830), is insistent on this very point:

> I think, the right method of preaching is this: At our first beginning to preach at any place, after a general declaration of the love of God to sinners, and His willingness that they should be saved, to preach the law, in the strongest, the closest, the most searching manner possible; only intermixing the gospel here and there, and showing it, as it were, afar off.

> After more and more persons are convinced of sin, we may mix more and more of the Gospel, in order to 'beget faith,'

*The law is *permanent* as God's requirement laid upon man: *impermanent* as a means of salvation (Rom. 8 [3]; Gal. 3 [19-26]).

†Rightly understood, the exposition of Christ's Teaching Ministry and Healing Ministry is, of course, itself a preaching of the Law. Nor do we need less preaching of the Sermon on the Mount and of Christ's Example. On the contrary, we need more of it, so long as it is made clear that the Sermon and Christ's Example are Law and not Gospel.

to raise into spiritual life those whom the law hath slain; but this is not to be done too hastily neither. Therefore, it is not expedient wholly to omit the law; not only because we may well suppose that many of our hearers are still unconvinced; but because otherwise there is danger, that many who are convinced will heal their own wounds slightly; therefore, it is only in private converse with a thoroughly convinced sinner, that we should preach nothing but the Gospel.

Later he says:

According to this model, I should advise every Preacher continually to preach the law; the law grafted upon, tempered by, and animated with, the spirit of the Gospel.

It is to be wished that every Local Preacher and every Preachers' Meeting could be persuaded to study that *Letter* most carefully. It has so much to say to us to whom the continuance of John Wesley's preaching has been committed—and we are James Wheatleys, almost to a man!*

But that is by way of digression. Our concern in this study is to remind ourselves that the offer of salvation cannot be divorced from the personal challenge of Jesus Christ. Whether or not you accept that salvation is wholly determined by your attitude to Him. Accept Him and you accept salvation: refuse Him and you refuse life and choose death. This was the belief and message of the Apostles, and they had learnt their new point of view from Jesus himself. It was a point of view which stood opposed as we have seen, to all Jewish thought and practice. Was there *anything* in Jesus' life which might lead him so to think of himself? We can discern two things: his sense of destiny and his reading of the Old Testament.

Jesus' Vocation

First, Jesus grew up under a strong sense of vocation. Like Jeremiah, Jesus believed that his role was foreordained (Jer. 1 [5]). The choice of his name is indicative of his mother's belief, and if Jesus knew of that belief (mothers naturally do make their hopes known to their children, very often at the earliest age) it may well have been the first factor in his consideration of his future. Names mean much to the Hebrew: their ability to express

*James Wheatley was the preacher whose wrong method of preaching Christ (the Gospel without the Law) occasioned Wesley's *Letter*.

character was fully recognized:* 'Jesus' is the Hebrew Joshua—
'Jehovah is Salvation' (Mt. 1 21). To bear that honoured and
pregnant name would set a thoughtful Jewish lad asking many
questions of his mother and of himself. At the age of twelve,
he has already a deep sense that he must be concerned with
'the things of his Father' (Lk. 2 49, R.V. margin). But it is not
until he is thirty or so years old that he emerges from the
obscurity of a Galilean village.

But let us acknowledge that there is a sense in which Jesus
never does emerge from obscurity. We know what he did and
what he said, but always through the eyes of a third person—
Mark, or Luke, Matthew or the Early Church—never through
his own. Jesus did not speak about himself: about his work,
his vocation, his coming ordeal, yes, but not of himself. That
is why any attempt to penetrate to the 'self-consciousness' of
Jesus is not only in danger of being irreverent, but is also in the
result irrelevant, in that it tells us nothing certain about Jesus,
but reveals very clearly the imaginative ingenuity and spiritual
poverty of the investigator. There are, however, brief moments
in the life of Jesus when the veil of reserve does drop—and on
each occasion Jesus is revealed as a man conscious of his destiny
and that it is a destiny of suffering and death.

Thus after his Baptism, wherein a voice had spoken to him,
confirming his awareness of an especial relationship to the
Father (Mk. 1 11), Jesus went alone into the desert. He was
confirmed in his belief that he was a 'Designated One',† and
that to him was committed the supreme task of history. He was
to make God's bid for man's love. But how? And when? With
what means? It was to answer these questions that Jesus went
away to think and pray. No one was with him. What happened
there was known to none save Jesus only: here, and here alone
in all the Gospels, we have the one touch of certain autobiography.

Yet even so, the story of his inner struggles is curiously
objectivized, and is given to us in a narrative which externalizes
the mental conflict. Does it mean that the inner story is only to
be discerned by the spiritually minded? That as the enigmatic

*e.g. Abram, Abraham; Jacob, Israel; Is. 9 7, etc.

†So it is best to understand at this stage the term 'Messiah': the
Davidic Prince was not the only one to be called a 'Messiah', or 'Anointed
One', and the particular interpretation which Jesus himself gave to the
term is elucidated in the paragraphs which follow.

form of the parables was sometimes intended apparently to puzzle men into thought, so here the story yields its true meaning only to that sympathetic insight which is the gift of the Holy Spirit?

Our task, then, is to say what must be said, and leave each one to expound for himself. Suffice it to say, that Jesus tells how he envisaged three possible methods, and dismissed them all as temptations to choose an easier road than the one he must travel. Those methods were that he should gain adherents by satisfying their material needs, or by overwhelming their intellectual judgements with dazzling miracles, or by the use of power, political and military. He reviewed them and rejected them as of the Devil.

What we are *not* told is what road he recognized as the right road. Of that we are left at this stage in ignorance—but not he. If I were an artist, depicting Christ in the wilderness, I would make it a desolate scene of crags and rocks and a harsh, glaring sun, and Jesus seated, oblivious of the heat, staring into the haze, his back set against the foot of a huge wooden Cross that is too big to be wholly contained in the limits of the scene. Anachronism? No, it *was* there, in the desert: as it was every hour of every day, of every week, in the mind of Jesus; until it became not more real but only more external, so that others could see it, too, and they could nail him to it. It was there, but for the time it was his secret. Our first glimpse is of his firm conviction that no road will suffice, but one—and later we learn that that one road is the road of the Cross. He knew it from the beginning.

When Peter came to see, at Caesarea Philippi (Mk. 8 27f) that Jesus was the Davidic Messiah, he began to disclose his secret to his disciples. There are some things which words just cannot convey, nor minds appreciate without long and slow preparation. The disciples were not ready: their ears heard, their minds could not receive. But the second lifting of the veil comes through their obtuseness. John and James, believing him now to be the Messiah, want to be one on each side of him in his glory. The innocence, the tragic irony of it! To ask to share *that!* 'Are ye able to drink the cup that I drink? or to be baptized with the baptism that I am baptized with?' (Mk. 10 38). But it is Luke who has the revealing verse: 'I have a baptism to be baptized with: and how I am held fast till it be accomplished.'* It is the cry of one

*Lk. 12 49: R.V. 'straitened': the word is used of a prisoner 'held in charge.'

whose iron composure deserts him for a fleeting moment and reveals a man who is in the grip of a destiny—*and who knows it daily, hourly, moment by moment.*

The third glimpse is the most revealing of all. Was John Mark the unseen watcher, the young man who fled from Gethsemane naked? (Mk. 14 $^{51-2}$). Someone, not the sleep-drugged Galileans, shared that lonely watch, seeing, feeling, not fully understanding but, thank God, remembering. Here is Jesus with all his defences lowered: alone, he need not preserve the composure which he must maintain in the presence of men. God in heaven, is there *no* other way? 'Father, Father, if it be possible ... if it be possible ...' But he needs no divine voice: while his flesh shrinks and nauseates with horror, his spirit triumphantly calm above the tumult of his own soul is aware that he is still 'held fast' in the grip of God's Eternal Purpose. His way is a way of destiny, his way is the way of the Cross. John's Gospel, that superb commentary on the life of Jesus, records a last shout of triumph from the Cross. The physical voice was too silent in the throes of death, it may be, for the ears of the Synoptists to hear it; but John, who listens to the over- and under-tones of Jesus' spirit, hears it ringing forth and writes it down that we may all hear it for ever more: *tetelestai!*—'Finished!' It is the same word that we had in Lk. 12 ^{49}: '... until it be accomplished.' Now it *is* accomplished: the guards release their grip, the fetters slip to the floor: and the very walls fall back: the Prisoner is free.

Jesus, then, believed from the beginning of his Ministry, at least, that his was a role of destiny, and that it was a destiny of suffering and death. 'Behoved it not the Christ to suffer these things and enter into his glory?' (Lk. 24 ^{26}). Moreover, it was a role which was of a decisive character for the whole race: 'Every one therefore who shall confess me before men, him will I also confess before my Father which is in heaven. But whosoever shall deny me before men, him will I also deny before my Father which is in heaven' (Mt. 10 $^{32-33}$). Jesus believed that: the Early Church believed it (1 Tim. 2 $^{5-6}$). Do *we* believe it? Or do we think that education, or politics or science, are the real hope of mankind? Do we, *can* we, preach Christ as the only Saviour? When we preach God's Word, we both can and do.

The other thing in Jesus' life which led him to call men to himself and to believe that he was himself God's offer of salvation to mankind was his understanding of the Old Testament. That is the subject of our next study.

STUDY FIVE. THE CROSS AS GOD'S WILL

Bible Readings:

The Messiah: Is. 8 [19]–9 [7]; Mk. 11 [1–10].
Covenant: Exod. 24; Jer. 31 [31–40]; Ezek. 36 [17–38]; 1 Cor. 11 [17–34].
Suffering Servant: Is. 52 [12]–53 [13]; Acts 8 [26–40]; 1 Pet. 2 [18–25].
Atonement: Lev. 16; Ps. 51; Heb. 9.
Jesus, Consummator of O.T.: Acts 2 [11–26].

Jesus, then, was a man who knew his destiny, and that destiny was the Cross. It was his destiny because it was God's will for him. Can we attempt any further explanation of the Cross as God's will? Why did Jesus believe God was calling him to traverse that road and no other? We have already suggested that he found the direction, not only in the intimacies of his own experience of God, but also in his reading of the Old Testament.

Jesus and the Old Testament

Jesus was a Jew whose mind was steeped in the Old Testament. He found in them a Pattern which delineated the role he was to play. None had found that Pattern before him, and the Early Church was curiously slow to recognize it when he had given them the clue. But Luke tells us that Jesus after the Resurrection makes that the supreme matter of his discourses to the disciples (Lk. 24 [26f, 44–47]).

Running through the Old Testament are a number of apparently unrelated strands. The hope of the *Messiah* is one. Isaiah looks for a perfect King because in his days, when no one had conceived of any alternative to monarchical government, only by means of a perfect King could Israel become a perfect people. The old destiny promised to Abraham was that his descendants should live in peace and prosperity with Jehovah as their God. That ideal could not be fulfilled until the perfect King should come. But the hope of that ideal was a certain hope: therefore the King was a certain King: 'Unto us a child is born, unto us a Son is given, and His name shall be called Wonderful Counsellor, Mighty God, Everlasting Father, Prince of Peace' (Is. 9 [6]).*

*cf. Is. 11 [1–9], 32 [1–8]; Jer. 23 [5–6], 30 [8–9]; Ezek. 34 [23–24]; Zech. 3 [9], 6 [12] (*see* Commentaries), 9 [9], etc.

A second strand is that of the *Son of Man*. Here the trail is rather more difficult to follow, but there can be no doubt that it is there. The phrase itself is born of Hebrew poetry and idiom. In order to say that a man possessed a particular characteristic in good measure, the Hebrew said that he was a son of that quality—a son of Belial (worthlessness) is a thoroughly worthless fellow, a 'son of might' is a mighty man, and men worthy of death are even 'sons of death'. (Compare our sayings 'Like father, like son' and 'a chip off the old block'.) 'Son of man,' then, is a designation of man in his frailty—'very human man,' as it were (Ps. 8 [4], Ezek. 2 [1], etc.). The next stage is where it is taken into the vocabulary of the apocalyptists, those strange men who delighted in the use of symbolic language, and especially that of describing various nations as animals—the Hebrews as sheep, the patriarchs as bulls, the Gentiles as asses, hyaenas, wolves, eagles, and so on. Then how are you to describe angels? By describing them under the symbolism of, not animal but *human* representation—i.e. as 'a son of man'. Thus a phrase which starts off by stressing the weakness and mortal nature of man, ends by acquiring a technical sense in which it denotes, not a man but a heavenly being.

This last process was closely connected with two particular passages: *Daniel* 7, where 'one like unto a son of man' obviously means a Fifth World-empire, designated not like the previous four by animal-symbolism, but by a human form. After the four beasts, the Seer sees a human figure and knows that he represents the reign of God's saints. (It is important to notice the element of judgement in the chapter.) The other passage consists of those chapters in the non-canonical *Book of Enoch*, known as 'the Parables', in which a mysterious figure, designated as the 'Elect One', or 'the Son of Man', takes his seat on God's throne to judge all mankind. Thus *Enoch* lent colour to an interpretation of *Daniel* 7, whereby 'a son of man' was taken to be an angelic being, conserved in Heaven by God until the times were ripe for world-judgement, when 'the Son of Man' would be revealed in glory to pass God's judgement on all mankind. That that judgement was inevitable had been borne in upon the Jewish mind by centuries of Gentile domination. The nations were so wicked, so idolatrous, so determined to destroy God's people, that only His cataclysmic intervention could be a fitting commentary on the whole of human history. Judgement was necessary for the vindication of

God's character. That judgement was to be pronounced by 'the Son of Man'.

Yet another strand is concerned with the mystery of *pain* and *sin*. Why do men suffer? The old answer was because men are wicked and so are punished. But what of the *good* man who suffers the blows of life? (cf. Ps. 73). That is the problem of the book of Job. The question was asked not merely with regard to individuals, but also concerning the nation: Israel, removed from her own country because of her sinfulness, found herself in the midst of foreigners whose lives were dissolute in the extreme. Then why should Israel suffer so terribly and these other nations go scot-free? In comparison with them, the Hebrews were a righteous people. Why then is Israel made to suffer? The problem, either in its individual or national form, receives its finest answer in the Servant Songs of Deutero-Isaiah: 'God's Servant suffers to serve?'*

Allied to this line of development is that of the 'suffering righteous man' who so often appears in the Psalms. The experience of the nation is envisaged as that of David the persecuted outlaw, David the Righteous Man, cruelly opposed and hunted for his life. Ps. 22 is a notable example. Here the answer is in the portrayal of 'David's' loyalty and trust in God and the underlying confidence that God will step in to save and deliver him, i.e. Israel.

A further element in the Old Testament is the teaching on *moral responsibility*. Does a man suffer for his own sins alone, or does he suffer for his father's, and others'? Is Ezekiel right when he says that not even Noah, Daniel, and Job could save a wicked city from destruction (Ezek 14 [14]), and that each man suffers or is rewarded strictly for his own sins (Ezek. 18, especially verse 4: 'The soul that sinneth, it [alone] shall die'), or is Gen. 18 [16f] right, when it says that ten righteous men might avail to save a whole city? Can a man bear another's fault? Can the goodness of one avail for his brother? Do we suffer for the sins of our fathers, to the third and fourth generation (Exod. 20 [5]), or is each one punished for his own sins only?

We have already been led on to another vast subject, *the Old Testament view of sin*, its punishment and expiation. The experience of the Exile had brought with it a new consciousness of sin, and a need for cleansing and forgiveness (e.g. Ps. 51). To meet

*Is. 42 [1-7], 49 [1-7], 50 [4-9], 52 [13]-53 [12].

that need, the ritual and mystery of the age-old institution of sacrifice was pressed afresh into the service of man's soul (e.g. Lev. 16). The ritual might grow more ornate and the ceremonial more gorgeous and costly, but the underlying convictions recording the value of the surrendered life, the provision of common ground by an altar where God and man might meet, and the efficacy of sacrifice to 'atone' for sin, were never obscured.

Such were some of the various strands in the Old Testament that Jesus found to guide him as he reviewed his sense of vocation. He was a man with a destiny and he looked to the Old Testament to discover its method and its purpose.

Let us pause here, to remark that taken alone, apart from the later development of the New Testament, the Old Testament is like a glorious symphony that loses its sense of direction in its third movement and peters out in the fourth from lack of inspiration. The more closely we investigate the vast hopes and fears, speculations and convictions, practices and prophecies of the Old Testament, the less we are able to find any one meaning, any order or over-riding significance in its complexity. Lines of thought cross and re-cross, influence and are influenced, but by the time you reach *Malachi* (or even more *Daniel* and *Pseudo-Isaiah*, 24-27) the more aware you are that the Old Testament has become like Abanah and Pharpar, rivers of Damascus—mighty in their full flood, but baffled in their final suffocation by the unquenchable sands of the desert. The streams of thought and hope have petered out, the wells of deep truth, like Isaiah 53, have been abandoned and deserted, and only the fatalistic, despairing hope (or the fanatically hopeful despair, call it which you will) of the oasis of apocalyptic remains.

Here, then, is where the religious genius of Jesus, if we may use that term, comes in. It is he, who, surveying that immense inheritance of his people, the Old Testament scriptures, brings to them a new dominating conception which gathers into itself all the discoveries, foreshadowings, dreams, and revelations of the Old Testament, and gives them unity and purpose, direction and goal. Messiah, Son of Man, Son of God, Rule of God, Suffering Servant, World-Judgement, Sacrifice, Atonement, Wisdom, Covenant, Law, Chosen Nation, World Mission—all now fall into place (Acts 8 [26f], esp. v. 35). They fall into place because he *gives* them their place; he shows their relation to himself and so gives them a relevance to each other. He constituted himself a focal point for the whole of the religious development of his people. Each prophecy has its purpose, each conception its significance, each age-old longing its part to play in the blended fullness of the final whole.* In a Yorkshire mill I have watched bewildered the thousands of threads running from the 'cheeses' or reels of yarn, each suspended on its own peg, disappear into the working machinery of the loom, and have marvelled to see them reappear in planned sequence, so that the shuttle may catch and miss them in due and ordered regularity, and the patterned cloth appear as if by magic under the minder's hands. The secret, I am told, lies in the 'cards' through which the threads pass: each different design necessitates the cutting of new cards or patterns and it is they which order the threads in the required sequence and repetition, and thus they which decide the design. Change your cards and you change the pattern. So Jesus Christ receives into himself the complex and tangled skein of the Old Testament and gives it the unity of pattern and ordered sequence it had lacked.

What, then, is this new, this decisive idea? 'Peter answereth and saith: Thou art the Christ. And he began to teach them that the Son of Man must suffer many things . . . and be killed and after three days rise again' (Mk. 8 $^{29-31}$). There lies the key to the Old Testament and there the clue to God's Eternal Purpose. The Messiah, says Jesus, *is* the Suffering Servant of God, and *therefore* Son of Man†. He judges because he rules, and he rules because he suffers, and because he suffers therefore is he judge. Through him, God is Himself stretching out His arms in His appeal to His creature. This is the meaning of the Old Testament and therein are all its speculations grounded and all its hopes fulfilled. Jesus knew himself to be a man of royal destiny, but it was in the Old Testament that he learnt that that destiny was the way of suffering and death, and that this was and

---

*We have not space to draw out the meaning of these strands as applied to the life and mission of Jesus. In a sense, they are the commonplaces of Christian teaching. But an excellent piece of work for a study-group would be to take them one by one and determine the significance each has for Jesus.

†Notice how Messiah, Son of God and Son of Man are all together again in the High Priest's question at the Trial, Mk. 14 $^{61-62}$ The phrase Son of Man as applied to Jesus is to be understood in the apocalyptic sense as one who comes in God's Name as Judge: if we want to stress his humanity the phrase 'Son of Mary', or some such phrase as 'the Carpenter of Nazareth' is appropriate. 'Son of man' is not.

had been through all eternity the plan of God. To this, the whole history and calling of the Hebrew people pointed; in this, God's initiative in history culminated. The Cross was God's Master-stroke. When Jesus cried *Tetelestai*, it was not his task alone that was accomplished, but also God's Will.

The Cross as God's Will

Can we press a little farther and ask *why* was the Cross God's Will? It is a question the Bible never asks, Old Testament or New. It was enough for Mark, that when Jesus died, the veil of the Temple was rent in twain—the barrier between man and God was broken down (15 38). For Paul, it was enough that God was in Christ, reconciling the world to Himself (2 Cor. 5 19). For John, it was enough that if Jesus be lifted up, he would draw all men unto him (12 32). For the writer of the Hebrews, it was enough that when he had made purifications of sins, he sat down at the right hand of the majesty on high (1 3); for Peter, that Jesus had begotten us again unto living hope (1 Peter 1 3). Because the Suffering Messiah is Son of Man, the Keys of the Kingdom are his (Jn. 5 27); the gift of salvation was in his hands to bestow on those he loved. This they knew and it sufficed. But further than this they did not press.

We may, however, say three things as a bare minimum. They are not all, they are hardly a beginning, but these three things are the ABC of the Cross, the alphabet in which all its horror and its glory are proclaimed.

(*a*) The Cross of Christ was intended to reveal God's love. How far, then, *would* God go for men's sake? The answer the Cross gives is 'all the way!' His love would give wholly and without reserve, paying the supreme price. Had Jesus been saved from the Cross, we should have known that God loves us, but only so far, and no farther. For Jesus to stop short of the Cross would have been to set a limit to God's love—and there is no limit.

(*b*) Again, the Cross was to show us once and for all the wicked-ness, the downright sinfulness, of ordinary men and women. The men who crucified Jesus were not bandits and robbers, but responsible officials, highly moral priests, well-intentioned scribes; people like us, in fact. But their pride and obstinacy, their love of wealth and power, bring him to a cruel death, and in death they gloat over him. The Cross placards for ever before our eyes, not only Jesus Christ, openly set forth crucified (Gal. 3 1), but also man as weak and vicious, man as perverted and sinful. If Jesus had been spared, we should have been spared the final degradation of man's pride: we should never have known what man can and does do in his wickedness.

(c) The third thing is the vicarious nature, the sacrificial character of the dying of Jesus. Let us again begin at the beginning. God made man in His own Image. He was looking for one who could in some sense be His fellow: as He loved and undertook for man, so man should love and serve Him. But no man ever gave to Him that full and untrammelled response, except Jesus of Nazareth. But because it is the nature of bad men to hate good men, since they themselves are aware of the inevitable comparison, it became apparent to Jesus that they would seek to destroy him. Should he obey God or fear men, persist in his life of holy obedience, or compromise with his enemies? The answer was never in doubt. He was loyal to God, in obedience and self-surrender to the end: through the long silence in the Judgement Hall, through the scourging, through the hatred and bloodlust of an Eastern crowd, through the final torture of the nails and thirst and delirious pain. Here was a self-giving of a Beloved to a Lover that had no reserve or limitation. One man at last loved God with all his heart, and with all his soul, and with all his mind. It was what God had ever willed, when He first said 'Let there be light!' in the dawn of creation. God's Eternal Purpose had been fulfilled.

But that self-giving is not of himself or for himself alone. Jesus on the Cross becomes Representative Man, Second Adam of the Race. What he offers there is himself *and all who acknowledge him as Lord*. Thus it is a sacrifice into which you and I can enter, by placing our faith in Jesus Christ as Saviour and acknowledging him as Lord. I cannot give myself to God, but he gives himself, and in so doing offers me to God in that same act of obedience and love. In *his* death God's Will for me is fulfilled, for me and for all who receive Jesus as Lord by faith. We enter by our faith into his dying and are made one with him on the Cross and thus become one with him in his triumph. When God receives *him* joyfully, *we* are received joyfully. *His death, then, is a saving death*. That is why it was God's Will.

The Cross, then, was God's will. It was His will, in that it was the crown and apex of all that had gone before and He chose that way in order that He might show forth His love, and reveal man's sin for all to see: it was further God's will in that there the second Adam gave himself to God, pure and holy without spot or blemish, with nothing to mar his sacrifice. But the significance of Christ's death as a saving death leads us on to a study of the Resurrection, as only in the light of that glorious triumph can the full significance be glimpsed.

STUDY SIX. RESURRECTION AND SALVATION

Bible Readings:

The Easter Stories: Mk. 16; Mt. 28; Lk. 24; Jn. 20, 21; Acts 1; I Cor. 15 [1-8].

The Easter Faith: Acts 4 [1-11]; I Cor. 15 [35-38]; 2 Cor. 4 [16]-5 [10].

The Story of the Resurrection is remarkably confused, largely because Mark, at this crucial point, fails us. Quite evidently he is only just beginning his story when his Gospel finishes abruptly with the remark 'for they were afraid' (16 [8]. *See* R.V. margin to v. 9). Equally evidently, the end of Mark's Gospel has been lost. If it should yet be discovered in some crumbling manuscript, what would it contain? We do not know, and it is idle to guess. But no discovery relating to the past would mean so much as that one precious document! It is one of the mysteries of God's providence that so serious a loss could befall the Scriptures. Or was it that there never was an ending? It is possible Mark meant to end in that enigmatic way at 16 [8], or that he died at just that point, and left his Gospel incomplete.

The Evidence

The fact remains that Mark merely relates that the two Marys and Salome came to the tomb and found the stone rolled away. In the tomb, there was a young man who announced the resurrection and gave them a message for the disciples that Jesus would precede them into Galilee, where they should see him. The women flee, and say nothing to anyone because of fear.

Matthew has substantially the same story, with heightened effects, but adds to the fear 'and great joy' and then says that as they ran to the disciples they met Jesus himself, who repeated the injunction to meet him in Galilee. The scene then changes to the mountains of Galilee, where Jesus appears to the disciples, 'but some doubted' (28 [17]—surely the most fearlessly candid remark in all Scripture!).

Luke tells the story differently. Several women met two men at the tomb: the message was that they were to remain in Jerusalem: they told the disciples, but they disbelieved them: verse 12 we must leave out of account, since its authenticity is more than doubtful (*see* Commentaries). Thus, for Luke, the first Easter Sunday is a day not of rejoicing but of fear and bewilderment. Only in the evening does Jesus appear to two relatively unimportant disciples on the way to Emmaus, then to Peter, then to 'the eleven and all that were with them'. He talks with them, leads them out to Bethany and ascends into heaven, apparently that same day.

John tells of Mary Magdalene coming alone to the empty tomb, and fetching Peter and the Beloved Disciple, who straightway believes before he sees the Risen Lord; then the incomparable story of Mary meeting her Lord in the garden; the eventide appearance to the cloistered disciples; the appearance a week later to Thomas, and an obvious appendix which relates the sea-side appearance and Peter's commission.

Acts claims, in strange contrast to Luke's other work, that Jesus' appearances occurred over a period of forty days. Paul lists the appearances in 1 Cor. 15 [5-8], and begins with Peter, then the Twelve, then above five hundred disciples at once, then to James, then to all the apostles and last of all to himself (Acts 9 [5]). The women are noticeably absent from the list.

How, then, can we reconcile the foregoing accounts one with another? Here we can only briefly indicate the lines of arguments which need to be taken much farther:

(*a*) The Resurrection was a shattering event, following on a week of tension, terror, and other disaster. It is not surprising that the various accounts do not tally. Even more than in an ordinary case, identity of evidence would be highly suspect.

(*b*) John tells of Jerusalem appearances, but does not in any way rule out Galilean appearances also. Since (as Acts shows) Luke's account is so severely telescoped that he appears to limit the appearances to Easter Sunday without intending to do so, the command to stay in Jerusalem may either have been of a temporary nature, and was followed by a command to return to Galilee where further appearances occurred, or, more likely, the disciples were not all in one place: some, like the Eleven, were in Jerusalem, others were at home in Galilee. Jesus appeared in both places and hence the two traditions arose.

(c) If Jesus did not rise, why did not the authorities produce the body? Or can you believe that the disciples had stolen it, they knew he was not risen and spent their lives publishing a lie? If two facts in all history can be accepted, one is that the early apostles were sincere in their belief and the other is that the authorities who would have been delighted to disprove them *were not able*.

(d) Easter Day seems to have opened with the bewilderment caused by the empty tomb. The appearances to the women may either have been too much for them or others to grasp, until further appearances brought joyful confirmation; or the stories in Matthew and John may be due to a later tendency to ante-date the first realization and assurance of the greatest wonder of all time.

Further arguments will be found in *Who Moved the Stone?*, by Frank Morison (Faber, 5*s*.). We can sum them all up by saying that, as Christians, we can be reassured that the most searching criticism of the historical records has not made any less credible the fact of the Resurrection. We may also add that to believe that Christ rose 'spiritually', but not 'physically', solves no problem but creates many more: it is especially unscientific in that it abstracts certain facts from the records as dependable and denies others as false, on the question-begging principle 'that dead bodies do not come to life again' and that a 'spiritual' resurrection is 'easier' to believe. Moreover it cuts across the Biblical doctrine of man's nature as Body-soul (cf. esp. 2 Cor. 5 $^{1-4}$).

Its Meaning

We accept, then, the *fact* of the Resurrection. What is its *significance*? If we accept the Biblical doctrine of death, it is a life-less separation from God. Because men are sinful it is the common lot of mankind. Jesus was made in all things like us, that he might offer that perfect obedience and loving response which man could not offer, and so be man as God intended. He therefore, though he enters into death for man's sake, cannot be holden of it, and so as one of us he dies, but as sinless and perfect he is not alienated from God as we are, and therefore escapes from death into life. But his purpose in all this was redemptive, and so far we have no gospel of redemption. For Jesus to demonstrate his perfection is no help to you and me: indeed, it condemns us. It is preaching the Law in all its austerity, but it is no Gospel. But at this point we see a further principle involved. He demonstrated that perfection *as a man amongst men, as one of us;* flesh of our flesh and bone of our bone, part and parcel of the human race, he demonstrated the possibility of perfect sonship in order that we might learn of him, and be inspired to do likewise.

Still, however, we have no Gospel. That the life of Jesus is not merely a demonstration of perfection, but an inducement that I should attempt perfection—that is better, but it is not Gospel. But what if it is not only demonstration and inducement but also the communication of *power* to become like him? That is indeed Gospel! But how can his death and resurrection communicate power?

We believe that Jesus died and took upon himself the calamity of death. He suffered not only the physical effects of death, but also he entered into the spiritual experience. But having, in order to be one of us, surrendered to death, he then began to fight back again, to the light and sunshine and air of God's presence. (Here language must be metaphor—for who can penetrate the reality?) Out of that experience of death, Jesus emerged intact and triumphant, and in so doing pioneered (Heb. 12 [2], Moffatt) for us a way by which we too might follow, out of death into life. He becomes the first born from the dead (Col. 1 [18]), the first fruits of them that are asleep (1 Cor. 15 [20]; *see also* Rom. 8 [29]).

Thus the great principle of our relationship with Jesus Christ is made abundantly clear: He became like us, *that we might become like him.* He became man, like us, lived our life and died our death, in order that we might become perfect like him, and rise like him out of death into life for ever more. That identity of disciple and Lord is occasioned by faith in him, and faith is first believing, secondly trust, and thirdly self-committal, the identifying of all your being with his. You are identified with him in his death, in your utter penitence for sin, and in your determination to be as dead to all your old ways and outlook and desires. You are identified with him in his resurrection, that is, in the accession of new life, that comes flooding in when you receive him into your life as Lord.[*]

That new life is nothing more or less than a renewed fellowship

[*]This, of course, is the imagery underlying the Sacrament of Holy Baptism—*see* Rom. 6 [1-11].

with the Source of Life, God Himself. His presence in your heart is a new distinctive presence of God, which we know as the Holy Spirit. This then is that communication of power of which we spoke: it is the communication of the Holy Spirit. The immediate fruit of our Lord's Resurrection is the gift of the Holy Spirit, both originally at Pentecost and also every time a humble penitent, identified with his death, enters into the joy of new life by identification with his resurrection. (*See* M.H.B. 280 $^{vv. 1-2}$).

Somewhere recently I met with the following illustration: Jesus' coming into our world for man's salvation, his death and resurrection, his ascension into Heaven, is to be likened to a youth who stands poised on a great rock above a deep tarn in the hills. He launches himself out and down in a gleaming curve, through the sun-drenched air to the water below. He strikes the water, and descends rapidly to the depths of the pool, down through the clear, light-filled water, down to its grey bottom, foul and slimy, the home of life divorced from light. There he gropes in the mud and rottenness, seeking the jewel he has lost. When his lungs are bursting, and the blood is singing in his ears, his fingers at last close upon it, and with a desperate leap he begins to rise again, out of the slime into the murky waters above, through the grey depths into the limpid upper freshness, until he bursts triumphantly through the surface of the lake, and climbs into the sunlight, clutching his recovered possession. So Christ descends and so he rises, but takes with him what he came for—you and me.

What a great parable lies in a Christian interpretation of Psalm 24!

> *The earth is the Lord's and the fullness thereof;*
> *The world and they that dwell therein.*
> *For He hath founded it upon the seas*
> *And established it upon the floods.*

It opens with the proclamation of God's majesty and creatorship, of man's dependence upon God and his belonging to Him. But he has disgraced himself from before God's presence. Who dare appear before Him?

> *Who shall ascend into the hill of the Lord?*
> *Or who shall stand in His holy place?*
> *He that hath clean hands and a pure heart;*

> *Who hath not lifted up his soul unto vanity,*
> *And hath not sworn deceitfully.*

Are your hands clean? Mine are not. My heart is not pure, and the one thing I know about you who read this book is that your heart is not pure. 'There is none righteous, no, not one' (Rom. 3 [10]; Psalm 14 [1]). We are for ever barred from God's presence: we must stand without the gates, and look with bitter despair where we may not enter. But suddenly there rings out a bold challenge to the sentries, who have heard no summons since they first took up their flaming swords at the entrance to Eden:

> *Lift up your heads, O ye gates;*
> *And be ye lift up, ye everlasting doors:*
> *And the King of Glory shall come in!*

Affronted and suspicious they demand credentials:

> *Who is the King of Glory?*

Straightway they are given:

> *The Lord strong and mighty,*
> *The Lord mighty in battle.*

Mighty indeed! For has He not striven with death, the last enemy, and has He not overcome? Is it not flushed with victory and radiant from the tomb that He stands there? But this is news in heaven! The sentinels are confused: they hesitate and while they delay, the cry rings out again, more insistently than ever:

> *Lift up your heads, O ye gates;*
> *Yea, lift them up, ye everlasting doors:*
> *And the King of Glory shall come in!*

Still they temporize and want to know further:

> *Who is this 'King of Glory'?*

And the answer does indeed tell them much, much more:

> *The Lord of Hosts,*
> *He is the King of Glory!*

Ah, that is the point! The Lord *of hosts:* He does not come alone. The great gates fold back and the heralds' trumpets sound a welcome and He advances in His Kingly State—but He is not alone! With Him are Peter, James, and John, Paul and Apollos, Augustine and Francis, Luther and Loyola, Wesley and William Booth—and hundreds, hundreds, thousands more, a great host that no man can number. Crusader's armour, Franciscan habit, preaching-gown and lounge-suit, Salvationist jersey and cotton-print dress, black and yellow, brown and white, men of every nation—but they all go pouring into God's Kingdom. And there go you! And there go I! My hands are not clean, your heart is not pure, Paul persecuted the Church, and Peter denied his Lord, but we all go into the Kingdom—not because our hands are clean, but because his are wounded; not because our hearts are pure, but because his was broken. Jesus is Saviour of Men.

> *Who is this King of Glory? Who?*
> *The Lord of glorious power possest.*
> *The King of saints and angels too,*
> *God over all for ever blest! Hallelujah*—(M.H.B. 222).

Charles Wesley, Charles Wesley, did not your fingers itch to write: 'The King of saints and *sinners* too'? For are we not, as you yourself have said:

> *The Church of pardoned sinners*
> *Exulting in their Saviour?*—(M.H.B. 251).

We may add two last words. Now we see a little farther, though only a little, into that mystery: 'Was the Cross God's Will?' We can now add that it assuredly was, for it was the gateway to the spiritual experience of death, and it was necessary for Jesus to endure death, that we might be saved from its outer darkness and nameless horror. Because he endured, we receive *now* eternal life, that when we die to this world, we enter into life everlasting. The Cross was necessary, that this might be so.

> *'Tis mercy all! let earth adore,*
> *Let angel minds inquire no more*—(M.H.B. 371).

The other word is that herein lies *full* salvation. God's Eternal Purpose was that we might be like Him and have fellowship with Him. Through sin we were made unlike Him, and alienated from Him. Christ Jesus, His Son, assumed our nature, lived our life, died our death, rose to life eternal, in order that we, identified by faith in him, might live his life for evermore. *But his life is perfect and sinless.* Thus to us is given, through him, the Holy Spirit that sin might no longer reign over us, that the fruits of the Spirit might be seen in us, that we might come unto a perfect man, unto the measure of the stature of the fullness of Christ! To be pardoned is not enough: we must become holy.

Brethren, preach the *full* Gospel of Jesus Christ. Do not be content with the watered message of moral improvement, and Jesus as Teacher and Example. Go on to preach the Law of Holiness, the Atonement of Jesus, the Gift of the Spirit, the goal of Perfect Love. It is the message of the People called Methodists. It is the Gospel of God Himself.

Book List

Jesus and His Sacrifice. Vincent Taylor, D.D., Ph.D. (Macmillan).

The Atonement in New Testament Teaching. Vincent Taylor, D.D., Ph.D. (Epworth Press).

Forgiveness and Reconciliation. Vincent Taylor, D.D., Ph.D. (Macmillan).

Christ and His Cross. W. R. Maltby, D.D. (Epworth Press).

Jesus and His Passion. R. Glanville (Epworth Press).

The Cross as Seen from Five Standpoints. J. Scott Lidgett, C.H., M.A., D.D. (Epworth Press).

The Bible Doctrine of Salvation. C. Ryder Smith, B.A., D.D. (Epworth Press).

If They Had Known. Studies of Everyman at the Cross. Leslie F. Church, B.A., Ph.D. (Epworth Press).

4. The Holy Spirit and the Trinity

By REV. DR. ERIC W. BAKER, M.A.

STUDY ONE. THE HOLY SPIRIT (1)

Bible Readings:

Is. 11 [1-10]; Joel 2 [28-32]; Jn. 14-16; Acts 2; Rom. 8 [1-17]; 1 Cor. 12.

Let it be recognized at the outset of these studies that they in no sense offer a comprehensive exposition of the doctrine of the Holy Spirit, but rather seek to select and deal with certain aspects of the doctrine which it is hoped may prove of use to some who at Whitsuntide or on other occasions choose this theme as the subject of their sermons. The portions of Scripture listed above are those in which the doctrine of the Spirit is treated at some length. There are very many others where reference to the Spirit is incidental and some of these are of great importance. An article such as that by H. B. Swete on 'The Holy Spirit' in Hastings's *Dictionary of the Bible* dealing comprehensively with the Biblical doctrine will well repay careful study on the part of those able to give it.

I

Most people would agree that there is in the mind of many of those whom we shall address in our congregations a good deal of vagueness as to the meaning of the event we celebrate on Whit Sunday. In a sense it is natural, indeed almost inevitable that it should be so, especially when that event is compared with those commemorated at Christmas and Easter. A baby in a manger, a man on a cross, an empty tomb, these are historical events which happened once for all. The significance of them may indeed be only imperfectly understood, but the events themselves took place within the realm of things seen and heard and touched. What is invisible may be just as real and more significant, but men find it harder to grasp and understand. Indeed the coming of the Holy Spirit can only be understood in the light of the effect it produced. The New Testament itself affords an illuminating illustration of this. It is recorded in Acts 19 [1-2] that when Paul visited Ephesus on his way back to Jerusalem he found there certain disciples. He asked them: 'Did ye receive the Holy Ghost when ye believed?' And they replied: 'Nay, we did not so much as hear whether there is a Holy Ghost' (R.V. margin). These Ephesian Christians had not been at Pentecost when the Holy Spirit descended on the assembled disciples. They had never heard of the Holy Ghost by that name, but they did know what it was to be delivered from moral impotence. They had experienced the sense of power which the indwelling presence of God confers. What would the members of our congregations reply if the same question was put to them that Paul put to the Ephesians? 'Did ye receive the Holy Ghost when ye believed?' Their answer would not be identical in words with that given to Paul. Though they were not at Pentecost they are all familiar with the story of what happened there. For many people, however, that doesn't make it any easier. The thoughts of Christians about the Holy Spirit are often bound up in a confused way with the different metaphors of doves, winds, tongues of flame, and the rest, under which the manifestation of the Holy Spirit is described in the New Testament. These metaphors are indeed not without their meaning and can be employed to illuminate the truth about the Holy Spirit as in the different verses of Hymn 289 (Spirit Divine, attend our prayers). But it is of the greatest importance that people shall distinguish between the reality of the Holy Spirit and the outward manifestations which are recorded in Acts 2. It was natural that, when the earliest disciples first became conscious of the Holy Spirit's power in their lives, that event should be accompanied by intense emotional excitement and fervour. Nor is the story of Pentecost an isolated instance in that respect. Again and again Christians have had similar, though not identical experiences. But it is a great mistake to associate the work of the Holy Spirit mainly with such *abnormal* occurrences. Above all, Christians should not be led to think of the Holy Spirit in vague ways as a kind of diffused power in the universe. Otherwise the inevitable result is that belief in the Holy Spirit comes to be regarded as a peculiarly difficult and remote part of our Christian faith. It is to be feared that many Christians do so regard it. By contrast note how naturally Jesus spoke of it. Any decent father, whatever his faults, will give his son bread and fish, the basic provision for the material needs of every day. So, our Heavenly Father will supply the spiritual needs of His children when they ask Him. 'If ye then, being evil, know how to give good gifts unto your children, how much more shall your Heavenly Father give the Holy Spirit to them that ask Him' (Lk. 11 13). The truth is that, far from being a remote part of our Christian faith, belief in the Holy Spirit concerns the whole traffic of our souls with God, for in so far as men today have vital dealings with God, it is God the Holy Spirit with whom we are in contact. Let us, then, try and clear our minds by recognizing two or three fundamental truths about the Holy Spirit which, if kept constantly in mind, will prevent us from ever becoming vague or uncertain, when we need to be clear and definite.

II

First and foremost, *the Holy Spirit is God*. He is not an attribute of God, but God Himself, the third Person in the Trinity. This being so the Holy Spirit can never be appropriately referred to as 'it', though it is very easy for us to fall into this error. We need to watch ourselves in this respect, as to make this mistake is a sure sign that we are getting woolly in our thinking. It might not be out of place to suggest here that whenever possible we should eliminate the word 'Ghost' and use the alternative and preferable word 'Spirit'. Whatever significance the word 'Ghost' may have had in other days, it suggests something eerie and unreal and is most unsuitably used in connexion with what is not vague at all, but utterly real and definite.

The Holy Spirit, then, is God. God is a Spirit: men also are spirits. They have bodies, but they are spirits. One practical definition of the Holy Spirit is 'God in man', the living God in the soul of man. Being God, the Holy Spirit is personal. He has a will and purpose which are wholly good. Man has been made by God and for God. He is constantly addressed by God and able to respond and enter into personal relationship with the Holy Spirit. For the Christian the supreme revelation of God is in Jesus Christ. It is through Jesus Christ that we know God to be our Father and ourselves to be the objects of his redeeming love. The invisible eternal Being, who made all things, appeared on the stage of history and men received a knowledge of Him which could only be given in the fashion of a human life. Through him came a revelation of God's character and purpose we should never have known or guessed if Jesus had not shown us. In the light of this revelation we interpret all God's other dealings with us. Ever since, Jesus has been for Christians the starting point of all their thoughts about God. This is not only true of God when we think of Him as the Creator and Sustainer of the universe but also of God the Holy Spirit at work in men's minds and hearts. It is, therefore, primarily in relation to Jesus that we should think of the Holy Spirit.

Historically, the gift of the Holy Spirit was made to the disciples assembled at Pentecost after our Lord's Ascension into heaven. The Holy Spirit was sent in fulfilment of our Lord's own promise as recorded in John's Gospel (14 [16], 15 [26], 16 [7], etc.). 'It is expedient for you', he told his disciples, 'that I go away; for, if I go not away, the Comforter will not come unto you: but, if I go, I will send him unto you' (Jn. 16 [7]). They did not understand his words at the time. What could possibly compensate for the loss of their Lord's physical presence? But they understood afterwards. Of necessity, the Incarnation had limitations. Jesus himself when in the flesh was subjected to them. They on their side were dependent on his external presence. This, though wonderful, was not enough. When the crisis came, they all forsook him and fled. But a few weeks later these same men became the nucleus of the new-born Christian Church, which was to prove the most remarkable of all human associations The reason for the change was the presence and the power of the Holy Spirit in their hearts. They no longer depended on Christ's presence by their side. From the first this link between Jesus and the Holy Spirit is unmistakable in the New Testament accounts. Their Lord was risen and ascended, but the Holy Spirit dwelt within them. Striking evidence of this connexion in their minds is afforded by the complete lack of dismay at their Lord's departure. When he had been crucified, they were a dejected and dispirited rabble, remnants of a disappointed hope. But now, bereft a second time of his physical presence, they knew no sadness or sorrow. He was not a tender memory. On the contrary he was more real than ever. His promises were continually being fulfilled in them and they faced the world with dauntless courage which nothing could shake. All that had come to them through Jesus is theirs still. It is to Jesus that the Holy Spirit bears evidence as he himself had promised: 'He shall glorify me:

for he shall take of mine and shall declare it unto you' (Jn. 16 14).
The Gospel had ended. What God had done once for all through
His incarnation in Jesus Christ, was over. But the Acts of the
Apostles had begun, and what God, the Holy Spirit, does through
those He redeems and transforms, has never ended yet.

For, as these disciples and others, notably Paul, carried the
message of Jesus Christ crucified, risen and ascended, outside
the narrow confines of Judea, where these events had taken place,
into the wider regions of Eastern Europe and Asia Minor, they
had another experience even more remarkable in its way than
the receiving of the Holy Spirit. They themselves, possibly even
Paul, though that is uncertain, had seen Jesus; many of them had
been eye-witnesses of his passion. But they discovered that when
they proclaimed the message of God's redeeming love in Jesus
to men and women who had never seen him, that fact made no
difference at all. If these men of other races responded to the
preaching of the Gospel by repentance and faith, they too
received power whereby they were saved from their sins and
became new. This from the first was recognized as the work of
the Holy Spirit. Neither passage of time nor distance of space
made any difference. And so it has been to this day. Otherwise
Christianity as a renewing and transforming power in men's
hearts and lives would have disappeared. The whole story of
Jesus would have been but an episode in history, the influence
of which would have faded in a generation.

We may define then the Holy Spirit as the new power which God
exerts over the spirits of men, when they respond to His love
revealed in the human life of Jesus Christ. That special and
distinctive influence was first exercised over the disciples, beginning at Pentecost, but it has never ceased to operate wherever and
whenever the Gospel has been preached and men and women have
responded.

III

This is God the Holy Spirit at work in men's hearts and lives
in every age and place since the coming of Jesus, at work in a
way which is only possible when men, through the preaching of
the Gospel, are made aware of God's character and purpose as
revealed in Jesus Christ. The link between the Holy Spirit and
Jesus is always a close one and sometimes in the New Testament
and elsewhere there seems to be no distinction between the Second

and the Third Persons of the Trinity, e.g., Rom. 8 ^{9}, 2 Cor. 3 ^{17}. Generally speaking, however, the distinction between the Spirit and the other Persons in God is quite clear, as it is consistently in John's Gospel. When we consider that in New Testament times the Doctrine of the Trinity had not been finally formulated, and the difficulty men with finite minds must needs experience in attempting to define the infinite God, we need not feel surprise, let alone dismay, at any apparent inconsistencies. Nor is it profitable to enter into theoretical discussion about the connexion between the risen Christ and the Holy Spirit in the experience of Christians. What has already been said should suffice to show how at all times the character and purpose of the Holy Spirit is always to be interpreted and understood in the light of God's historic revelation of Himself in Jesus.

IV

So far we have confined ourselves to a consideration of the Holy Spirit, first given at Pentecost, and at work ever since in men's hearts and lives. In this strict sense the Holy Spirit was given to the Church and it is within the Church that His power has operated. Later on in the next study we shall return to this and examine the Holy Spirit's activity in various aspects. Before doing so, however, it seems necessary to recognize that, if we apply the description 'God in Man' to the Holy Spirit, He has also been at work in other places and at other times. In point of fact, Christianity has already recognized this. After the coming of Jesus, not only did his followers interpret God's influence and power in their lives in terms of what they had learned in Jesus of his nature and purpose; they also, as the late Archbishop Temple put it, 'read back what they had learned through that experience into all the other activities of God at work within nature and within mankind in fulfilment of His own eternal purpose and in response to the manifestation of His character'. After all, God is eternal. He does not change. It is only our understanding of Him that may vary. The Holy Spirit was given at Pentecost, but God has been at work in the world and in men's lives everywhere from the beginning. The Fourth Gospel speaks of 'the light which lighteth every man' (Jn. 1 ^{9}). So what we may call an anticipation of the New Testament doctrine of the Holy Spirit is to be found in the Old Testament from the very beginning, and at this point we should notice some of its main features.

In the first chapter of Genesis we read how the Spirit of God was active in the creation of the world: 'the earth was waste and void and darkness was on the face of the deep: and the Spirit of God was brooding on the face of the waters' (Gen. 1 ^{2}). This is the religious explanation of what the scientists describe in evolutionary terms. Both descriptions are correct. The scientists can shed much light on *how* God created the world. The Old Testament tells us *why* God created it and reminds us of the Divine purpose in creation. The word 'spirit', as we know, originally meant 'breath', and we are told how God 'breathed into man's nostrils the breath of life and man became a living soul' (Gen. 2 ^{7}). Some of our Christian hymns, notably 'Breathe on me, Breath of God' (M.H.B. 300) and 'O Breath of God, breathe on us now' (M.H.B. 285) retain this form of speech. The writers of the Old Testament often refer to the work of the Spirit in sustaining and renewing physical life. In the same way the endowment of man with his various intellectual and spiritual gifts is attributed to the work of the Spirit. This is manifested in the special and exceptional powers given to individual men: the wisdom of Joseph, the strength of Samson, the inspiration of Moses, are alike gifts of the Spirit. Pre-eminently the gift of prophecy was due to the presence in man of God's Spirit. We may note as well-known examples of this the passage in Is. 61: 'the spirit of the Lord God is upon me . . .', which our Lord quoted at Nazareth (Lk. 4 ^{18} *et seq.*), and the Messianic prophecy in Is. 11: 'And the spirit of the Lord shall rest upon him, the spirit of wisdom and understanding, the spirit of counsel and might, the spirit of knowledge and of the fear of the Lord . . .'

V

With this Old Testament precedent in mind, we may confidently proceed to broaden our conception of the Spirit's activity everywhere. As when the world began it was His work to bring order out of chaos, so it is in response to the Spirit that man has sought to bring order out of chaos within communities and among nations. Spiritual development within individuals is largely a matter of what is called 'integration,' which is another name for bringing order into that which is chaos. Man as an individual is very complex; he is several selves rolled into one. He is made up of different instincts and impulses seeking expression and ranging themselves around different ideals. He resembles an army where every soldier marches in a different direction. He needs to mould into a unity the discordant elements in his nature, if he is to become a significant and purposeful being. That is the work of the Spirit.

Similarly, responding to the urge of the Spirit, man has discovered and made use of the ordered laws governing the universe. Bending to the Spirit, men have wrought out their inspiration in abiding form, enriching the lives of their fellows through sculpture, music, and literature. The Spirit is the source of all knowledge, the inspirer alike of the scientist's disinterested search for truth, the artist's vision of beauty, and the aspiration after good present, in some degree, in every man. His is the love wherewith a man loves his fellows and his God. He is the one eternal Spirit at work in the hearts of all God's children.

These two conceptions of God's Spirit find expression in two hymns placed next to each other in the *Methodist Hymn Book*. First, Charles Wesley's hymn: 'Away with our fears' (No. 278), in which the specific work of the Holy Spirit is linked at every point with the historical acts of God in Jesus and the gift of the Holy Spirit at Pentecost; and Percy Dearmer's hymn: 'O Holy Spirit, God' (No. 279), which tells of the wider activity of God in men's hearts and lives.

STUDY TWO.   THE HOLY SPIRIT (2)

We may well begin this second study of the nature and work of the Holy Spirit by recalling the two-fold function of the Spirit in relation to Holy Scripture.

I

The *inspiration* of the Bible is a truth universally accepted among us. What exactly do we mean by this? Let the New Testament itself be our guide. Three passages in particular may be cited. The first is of a general character and contains no specific reference to the Holy Spirit. 'Whatsoever things were written aforetime were written for our learning that through patience and through comfort of the scriptures we might have hope' (Rom. 15 [4]). The next passage is much more definite. 'Every scripture is inspired of God and profitable for teaching, for reproof, for correction, for instruction which is in righteousness' (2 Tim. 3 [16], R.V. margin). There is a slight variation in meaning, but none which affects our purpose, if we read with the R.V. text: 'Every scripture inspired of God is also profitable . . . etc.' Whichever rendering we prefer the point is the same, that Scripture is definitely described as inspired. The third passage is perhaps the clearest of all. 'No prophecy of scripture is of private interpretation. For no prophecy ever came by the will of man: but men spake from God, being moved by the Holy Ghost' (2 Pet. 1 20-21).

The Scripture referred to was presumably the Old Testament, as the canon of the New Testament was not yet completed, nor had it as such received official recognition by the Church, but all would agree today that what applies to the Old Testament which is the record of God's progressive revelation to the Hebrew people, applies even more to the New Testament, which contains the record of His supreme revelation in Jesus Christ.

It is important to note, as is made explicitly clear in the third passage, that Scripture is inspired because the Holy Spirit possessed the minds of the *writers*. The Holy Spirit, being personal, does this work through persons. These passages contain no warrant for the heresy, which arose much later, of the verbal inspiration and consequent inerrancy of every word of Scripture. Such a belief would have shocked the writers themselves.

What also needs constant emphasis is that, just as the writers of the sacred books were inspired to write, so the inspiration of the Holy Spirit is essential if the Scriptures are to be *read* with understanding. This is a favourite theme of Charles Wesley in his hymns, e.g.:

> *Come, divine Interpreter,*
> *Bring us eyes Thy Book to read,*
> *Ears the mystic words to hear,*
> *Words which did from Thee proceed*—(M.H.B. 306).

Or again:

> *Now the revealing Spirit send,*
> *And give us ears to hear*—(M.H.B. 304).

The clearest statement of this truth is perhaps in the well-known hymn 'Come, Holy Ghost, our hearts inspire' (M.H.B. 305) which has been described as the ideal hymn to precede the proclamation of God's Word. In this hymn the Spirit's part in inspiring writer and reader alike is made clear in the verse:

> *Come, Holy Ghost, for moved by Thee*
> *The prophets wrote and spoke;*
> *Unlock the truth, Thyself the key,*
> *Unseal the sacred Book.*

II

We turn next to the large number of passages, mostly in St. Paul's Epistles, which deal with the work of the Holy Spirit within the mind and heart of the believer. In Paul's teaching it is the Holy Spirit who, by His operation on the spirit of man, brings about regeneration (the new birth) and the restoration of the personal life of the individual disciple. Paul sees no limit to the Holy Spirit's work until its completion, the attaining of 'the measure of the stature of the fullness of Christ' (Eph. 4 [13]). This transformation is to include man's body, which is 'a temple of the Holy Ghost' (1 Cor. 6 [19]). The new life in the Spirit is a life of sonship of God: 'As many as are led by the Spirit of God, these are sons of God' (Rom. 8 [14]). Through the Spirit the redeemed are assured of this sonship: 'The Spirit Himself beareth witness with our spirit, that we are children of God' (Rom. 8 [16]). Here we are on ground which in later days Methodism has made peculiarly its own, and the reader is referred, among others, to Sermons IX, X, XI, XIII, XXXIX in the *Forty-Four Sermons* of John Wesley. It is this part of the New Testament which was Wesley's warrant in scripture, and is still ours, for the Methodist emphasis on Justification and Sanctification as together leading to the full salvation we proclaim. Equally impressive in this respect is the testimony of the hymns of Charles Wesley. In the section of the *Hymn Book* entitled 'Christian Holiness' we may note as typical Hymn 568, verses 3 and 4:

> *Heavenly Adam, Life divine,*
> *Change my nature into Thine;*
> *Move and spread throughout my soul,*
> *Actuate and fill the whole; . . .*

> *Holy Ghost, no more delay;*
> *Come, and in Thy temple stay;*
> *Now Thine inward witness bear,*
> *Strong, and permanent, and clear . . .*

It is significant that the risen Christ and the Holy Spirit seem interchangeable in this respect in this group of Charles Wesley's Hymns (cf. Nos. 550, 554, 558, etc.). In this connexion we should also note Charles Wesley's frequent use of the metaphor of 'fire' as a description of the Spirit's work in sanctification. The three magnificent verses at the end of Hymn 387, in which the Holy Spirit is described as 'Spirit of burning', are a good example. I quote the last:

> *Refining Fire, go through my heart,*
> *Illuminate my soul;*
> *Scatter Thy life through every part,*
> *And sanctify the whole.*

And the familiar 'O Thou who camest from above' (M.H.B. 386) will occur at once to everybody as another example.

Throughout the Epistles, while Paul deals so constantly with the work of the Holy Spirit in the individual believer, the conception of the fellowship is always in the background. The idea of a believer not closely linked with the fellowship would have been completely meaningless. The Holy Spirit was given to the Church and it is within the Church that His influence is exercised. In the earlier Epistles it is the local church he has chiefly in view, e.g. 1 Cor. 12, where he discourses at length on the diversities of gifts which are manifestations of the same Spirit. In the later group of Epistles, notably those to the Ephesians and the Colossians, his thought has developed and he is more concerned with the wider view of the Universal Church. It is in the classic passage about the Church in Eph. 4, where again he discusses the differences of function within the fellowship, that he speaks of the Spirit as the bond of unity (Eph. 4 [3–4]) and the source of the common life which animates the whole 'body of Christ'.

III

Two passages from St. Paul's Epistles are of special importance in relation to the gifts of the Spirit. The first is Chapters 12 and 13 of his first letter to the Corinthians. Chapter 12 makes it clear that these gifts are exercised within the Church and contains the celebrated passage about the relation of the members to the body and consequently to one another. While not despising any of the gifts, Paul does not hesitate to discriminate between them, urging his readers to 'desire earnestly the greater gifts' (1 Cor. 12 [31]) which are the spiritual gifts. Then follows the superb 'Hymn of Love' in Chapter 13, wherein faith, hope, and love are cited as the permanent results of the Spirit's coming. 'Now abideth faith, hope, and love, these three; and the greatest of these is love' (1 Cor. 13 ^{13}). This is the theme of John Wesley's sermon on 'The Marks of the New Birth' (No. 14 in *The Forty-Four Sermons*).

Emphasis on the essentially spiritual effects of the indwelling Spirit is laid with equal stress in the second passage which should be specially noted, namely, Gal. 5 $^{16-26}$. Here the comparison is between walking by the Spirit and fulfilling 'the lust of the flesh'. In contrast to the unclean and degrading works of the flesh, 'the fruit of the Spirit is love, joy, peace, long-suffering, kindness, goodness, faithfulness, meekness, temperance' (Gal. 5 $^{22-23}$).

> *And every virtue we possess,*
> *And every conquest won,*
> *And every thought of holiness,*
> *Are His alone*—(M.H.B. 283, verse 6).

IV

We now come to an aspect of the work of the Holy Spirit which we have not yet discussed but which is of the utmost importance, requiring to be treated at some length. Let our consideration have as its starting point the promise of our Lord, twice recorded in those chapters of the Fourth Gospel which contain his prediction of the Spirit's coming. 'The Comforter, even the Holy Spirit, whom the Father will send in My name, He shall teach you all things, and bring to your remembrance all that I said unto you' (Jn. 14 ^{26}); and again: 'I have yet many things to say unto you, but ye cannot bear them now. Howbeit, when He, the Spirit of Truth, is come, He shall guide you into all the truth: for He shall not speak from Himself; but what things soever He shall hear, these shall He speak: and He shall declare unto you the things that are to come' (Jn. 16 $^{12-13}$).

Here is a promise definite and clear. Our Lord is about to leave his disciples. It will be their responsibility to carry on his work. To guide them in this task he leaves them no list of codified regulations, but promises them the guidance of the Spirit of Truth. Far from stressing at this moment his own example and such teaching as he had been able to give them while on earth, He definitely reminds them of the limitations of this teaching.

'I have yet many things to say unto you, but ye cannot bear them now.'

Let us next recall how soon this principle was put to the test. It is recorded in the Acts of the Apostles, and was the consequence of Paul's successful missionary journey to the Galatian cities, in the course of which he had become conscious that Jesus Christ was the way for all men to God. Preaching first to the Jews in each city, he afterwards turned to the Gentiles and won from them a response to the proclamation of the Gospel which bore all the marks of genuineness. The question then arose whether, to become disciples of Jesus and members of the Church, these converts must first submit to the Jewish rite of circumcision. Must they accept the Jewish faith before Christ would accept them? This question was settled at the historic 'Council of Jerusalem' recorded in Acts 15, and it is the climax to which all the preceding narrative of the Book of Acts leads up. It was one of the great moments of history. Paul saw quite clearly that, if circumcision was to be insisted on, either the mission to the Gentiles would have to be abandoned or, alternatively, a united Church would become impossible. The viewpoint of the Jew is also easily understood. If the doors of the Church were to be opened to Gentiles as such, the Jews in the Church would soon be outnumbered by a majority of uncircumcized converts and it was unlikely that Jews themselves on any large scale would be won over to a predominantly Gentile institution. Such was in fact what came to pass. In Jerusalem the whole Church met, presided over by James, the brother of the Lord. Paul stated his case and Jewish advocates put the other side. When the leaders met by themselves, Peter, in the light of his experience, supported Paul's contention. James summed up, quoting Symeon and the prophets. Finally, the issue was decided in favour of the Gentiles. There were certain minor conditions laid down and accepted, but the great point was gained. Never to this day has the decision since been questioned. In principle, the world Church had come into being. The interesting fact in relation to our present concern is that, as far as we are aware—and surely had it been otherwise it would have been included in the account—neither side in the dispute appealed to any word or action of Jesus himself. This is more surprising when we remember that many of those present must have seen and heard him. Instead, the terms in which the decision of the Council is recorded are these: 'It seemed good to *the Holy Ghost and to us* to lay upon you no greater burden than these necessary things' (Acts 15 [27]). Thus early the Church of Jesus Christ was consciously under the guidance of the Holy Spirit.

This characteristic of the Church has operated throughout its history, not only in acts of the Church itself, but in the influence it has exerted in the world. Slavery was not, as far as we are aware, specifically attacked by Jesus, and it was a long time before it was realized how entirely irreconcilable it is with his teaching on the infinite value of the individual in God's sight, but its eventual abolition was due to the fact that it was an offence to the Christian conscience working through a Church which was under the guidance of a living Spirit. In our own day, the Temperance movement cannot claim any literal injunction of the New Testament as its charter, but its advocates have no doubt that in the circumstances which prevail today they are being led by the Spirit in their crusade.

It would not be true to say that the supreme authority of the Spirit has never since been questioned. Various attempts have been made to set up some other infallible authority for the guidance of the Church and the individual believer, notably the Bible as an infallible book, and the Church itself as an infallible guide. All such attempts, however, are doomed to failure. The plain fact is that no such infallible guide has been provided by God, and the Christian religion is essentially a religion of the Spirit, and it is by the Spirit that the believer must walk. This is made clear in the well-known Anglican collect for Whit Sunday: 'God, who as at this time didst teach the hearts of Thy faithful people, by the sending to them the light of Thy Holy Spirit: grant us by the same Spirit to have a right judgement in all things . . .'

Once again it should be emphasized that this promise of guidance is made to the Church and normally to be exercised in fellowship. In the instance we have already considered the whole Church was apparently assembled at Jerusalem and it has always been recognized that when a company of believers meets together to wait on God, animated by a sincere desire to know the truth, they can with confidence expect the guidance of the Holy Spirit. While it is true that the Spirit reveals the truth to the minds and hearts of individual men and women, it is in fellowship rather than in isolation that they are likely to receive the truth. Hence a man needs to test his conscience first by the tradition of the

Church and then by the counsel of his fellow Church members. It is a mark of spiritual arrogance for a man lightly to set aside this judgement. It is a departure from that attitude of humility whereby alone we may expect or claim the guidance of the Holy Spirit. No man by himself can receive or grasp all the truth. We need the help each can afford the other. This is, or should be, one of the main functions of the class meeting, to afford such fellowship in thought and prayer as will enable a group to perceive truth and arrive at a degree of insight beyond the range of any of the individuals who compose it.

With this safeguard ever in mind, we may, indeed must, go on to insist on the work of the Holy Spirit through the consciences of individual men and women. Faced with difficult decisions, in circumstances very different from those of 1,900 years ago, it is rarely, if ever, profitable for a man to ask 'What would Jesus do?' The real question is: 'What does God want me to do?', and to answer that question he must seek the guidance of the Holy Spirit.

A little reflection will serve to show the vital importance of this on the world today. It is in this sphere that Humanism is making one of its most deadly assaults today on our Christian faith. Believing that everything in the world can be explained without recourse to the existence or the activity of God, these foes of religion are invading the realm of morals. They tell us that ideas of right and wrong have arisen as society has developed and they deny alike the need and the fact of any divine sanction for human behaviour in individuals and in communities. Social pressure alone, they say, has both caused and sustained morality. The characteristic question of the age is 'Why should I be good?' To this question society by itself can give no ultimate answer, and it is not surprising that moral standards are in chaos. Against this viewpoint which can only lead to disaster, Christians are called upon to declare that the only ultimate sanction for human conduct is in the will of a righteous God. Conscience is the voice of God; we may agree that that voice is never perfectly mediated, being mixed up with human elements of various kinds, but it is the voice of God all the same.

> *And His that gentle voice we hear,*
> *Soft as the breath of even,*
> *That checks each fault, that calms each fear,*
> *And speaks of heaven*—(M.H.B. 283, verse 5).

Conscience has two main functions: first with regard to the past to pronounce judgement on actions already performed, and then with regard to the future to act as a guide and tell us what we ought to do. It is significant that while the first judicial function of man is primeval and world-wide, it has only been in the Christian era and under the influence of Christianity that the function of conscience as a guide to individual conscience has, save under totalitarian regimes, received universal recognition. There were, of course, anticipations of this, notably the Hebrew prophets, but it is one effect of the spread of Christian ethics, and it is one outstanding characteristic of the work of the Holy Spirit. We all need to pray in Longfellow's words:

> Holy Spirit, right Divine,
> King within my conscience reign—(M.H.B. 288, v. 4).

While conscience may often disturb us, it is one of God's greatest gifts to man. Nothing so marks him out from the animal creation and enables him to use to the full glory of his status as a child of God as this moral responsibility. His awareness of this and his ability to respond to it are alike the work of the Holy Spirit.

Book List

The Holy Spirit. G. B. Robson (Epworth Press).
The Holy Spirit in the New Testament. H. B. Swete (Macmillan).
The Christian Experience of the Holy Spirit. H. Wheeler Robinson (Nisbet).
The Spirit: a Symposium. Ed. B. H. Streeter (Macmillan).
Christian Faith and Life. Chapter VI. W. Temple (S.C.M. Press).
What we Believe. Chapter III. J. G. Riddell (Presbyt. C. of E.).
The Doctrine of the Holy Spirit. Headingley Lectures (Epworth Press).

STUDY THREE. THE HOLY TRINITY

Bible Readings:

Mt. 28 [16–20]; Jn. 1 [1–18]; Jn. 12 [44–50]; Phil. 2 [1–11]; Col. 1 [12–17]; Heb. 1 [1–4].

Trinity is not a Biblical word, nor was the doctrine of the Trinity formulated in New Testament times. That was a later development, as Christians felt the need of setting forth in logical terms the foundation of the faith. It was, however, out of the New Testament experience that the doctrine of the Trinity was eventually built up.

I

There are two passages in the New Testament where the three Persons of the Trinity are mentioned. The first is at the end of St. Matthew's Gospel where the risen Lord delivers to His disciples the commission: 'Go ye therefore and make disciples of all the nations, baptizing them into the name of the Father and of the Son and of the Holy Ghost' (Mt. 28 [19]). This passage is, as we know, incorporated in the baptismal service. It should be noticed that, though there are three Persons mentioned, there is only one name. The other passage is the concluding verse of Paul's Second Epistle to the Corinthians: 'The grace of the Lord Jesus Christ, and the love of God, and the communion of the Holy Ghost, be with you all' (2 Cor. 13 [14]). This passage, too, is in constant use among us as a benediction.

The other suggested passages at the head of this study deal for the most part with the Divinity of Christ. It was inevitable that the recognition by the Church of the Son as a Person with the Godhead should precede that of the Holy Spirit. As W. N. Clarke writes: 'The effect of the life of Christ was to enlarge the conception of God by the admission to it of what that life had exhibited, and by the admission of Jesus himself to a place beside the Father.' This had clearly taken place by the time the Fourth Gospel, one of the latest books of the New Testament, was written. Later came the recognition that as God Himself had come in the Son, so beyond all doubt He had come in the Spirit. This truth, one of transforming experience, was built up into the doctrine of the Trinity, which was regarded as something which had been *implicit* in Christianity from the beginning. There is no evidence that the early Church was in any way puzzled by speculative problems that from time to time have surrounded this doctrine in later centuries. It will help us to keep clear from confusion if, when we are thinking about the Trinity, we bear constantly in mind that it arose out of the *experience* of the early Christians, and contains their affirmation about the eternal unchanging God, which in the light of His revelation of Himself in Jesus and the subsequent sending of the Holy Spirit they felt constrained to make. We must remember all the time that, though God is personal, His nature is richer by far than any human personality could ever be, and that the truth we are trying to state is of necessity beyond our grasp. Above all, we need to avoid what is called 'tritheism', which has sometimes led their opponents to assert that Christians believe in three gods. In this connexion we may mark Brunner's words: 'The meaning is that one can know and love the Father only through the Son and the Holy Spirit; that one can love the Son, too, only through the Holy Spirit and, *vice versa*, the Holy Spirit only through the Son.' Creation, redemption, and inspiration are alike the work of the one God, Father, Son, and Holy Spirit.

We live in a world where the live controversies which exercise men's minds are not for the most part centred around such themes as the Trinity. It is an age of unbelief and the kind of error we encounter concerns whether there is a God at all, rather than, if there be a God, whether the doctrine of the Trinity truly and usefully describes Him. We are also faced with the demand on every hand that our preaching should be *practical* and deal with men's ordinary lives, not with abstract theories. But this is a very dangerous attitude. After all, nothing is more important than what a man *believes*. It determines how he behaves and what sort of person he becomes. What men in general believe determines the kind of world they create or to which they have to submit. What matters most in belief is what we believe about God. It makes all the difference, for example, whether we believe in a Creator who made the world and everything in it, with whom we have to deal, or whether we think that the world came into existence accidentally. If there be a God, no inquiry can be more important and exciting than that which seeks to understand His character and purpose. Our knowledge of God has been gained bit by bit in different ways, and in the doctrine of the Trinity we try to piece together what Christians believe about God and see it as a whole. That being so, it is of the utmost importance that when we preach on Trinity Sunday, and indeed on other occasions too, we should do our best to expound this unique part of our faith, which has no parallel in other systems of thought. Our people have a right to expect this of us. Accordingly, the rest of this study is devoted to an exposition of the doctrine which proceeds along the line of experience, which is historically the way in which the doctrine first came to be held and affords the soundest approach. By this means it is sought to show the value the doctrine has for an understanding of the Christian religion as not merely an episode but a faith for all time, after which the concluding section suggests that the doctrine throws light on those social problems with which men are endeavouring to grapple and on the solving of which depends the future of mankind. To the solution of these problems we believe Christianity holds the key, and the doctrine of the Trinity is at any rate one foundation for this conviction.

The trouble, as we have seen, about the doctrine of the Trinity, is that a great number of people, including many sincere Christians, regard it merely as an incomprehensible belief which they are required to profess, but which has little connexion with their worship and their prayers and none whatever with their life in the world.

There are two reasons for this. First of all, when men like us with finite minds and limited understanding try to set forth in human speech the nature of the Eternal God, we are clearly attempting something beyond our powers. It would be terrible if it were otherwise. If we could explain and understand God, the Source of all that is, as we can analyse a chemical substance, He would not be God at all but someone less than ourselves.

When we have done our best, there remains much that is mysterious, and we may rejoice that it is so.

The other reason why people stumble at the doctrine of the Trinity is because it was formulated centuries ago as the best explanation Christians of that time could give of certain facts of experience. However difficult to explain in speech, the experience was the most definite and genuine thing in all their lives. The doctrine was expressed in another language than our own, and moreover, since that day the terms used have changed their meaning, so that what originally was an explanation has, with the passing years, itself become a thing to be explained.

For all that, the doctrine of the Trinity contains those affirmations about God which Christians have felt compelled to make. They could not say all that the word 'God' meant for them unless they said Father, Son, and Holy Spirit, God in three Persons, Blessed Trinity. Behind this belief lies the living experience of our Christian forefathers, and if we are to enter into our Christian heritage we must make our own, not necessarily the exact words they used, but the experience that lay behind the words and caused them to formulate the doctrine.

II

We begin, then, with *Jesus Christ, God the Son, the Second Person in the Trinity.* Why do we begin there? Would it not be more natural to begin with God the Father? No, we are seeking to get at the *experience* behind the doctrine, and this is the order of experience. The whole Christian faith rests upon Jesus Christ. Christianity is an historical religion. It originated in certain things that happened in history, and everything follows from that. Nineteen hundred years ago there was born in Bethlehem one who, when he grew to be a man, lived a life of perfect purity and love. He not only taught men how to live, he was himself the perfect embodiment of his teaching. He called on men to repent and follow him. At first some responded, but his popularity was short-lived. He aroused the antagonism of the religious leaders, who plotted against him and finally brought about his death. He was crucified on the first Good Friday and his few disciples scattered. On the first Easter Sunday he rose again and they knew that what had seemed defeat was in fact a resounding victory. The scattered rabble became the glorious company of the Apostles, and they fell upon the world with a message of life and hope. That was how the Christian Church began, and from the first it has rested on the response of men and women to Jesus Christ as Lord. When those early Apostles came to reflect on their own experience and when they remembered claims he had made that they had not understood at the time, they came to the irresistible conclusion that Jesus Christ was none other than God Himself and that in him God became man for our salvation. Successive generations of Christians have endorsed that conviction. So it is that historically and in every other way our Christian faith rests on that central doctrine which we call the Incarnation.

III

Very soon, however, Christians began to realize that this belief in Jesus as God had to be related to all their other experience. As Jews or Greeks maybe, thay had believed in God before as Creator, a righteous lawgiver and ruler of the universe. They continued to do so; but now what they had had revealed to them in Jesus Christ enriched their knowledge of the eternal God and their faith in Him. The life of Jesus was not just a glorious episode; this was what God is like—always had been, and always would be. Especially, since Jesus had taught them, did they worship and draw near to the Eternal God as *Father*. Nature might reveal God's majesty and power; it could tell them nothing of His character and purpose. Jesus had revealed God's love and mercy in a way which they could never have guessed had not God Himself revealed it to them. So their experience of Jesus revolutionized and enriched the experience of God which they had had before.

IV

But that experience did not come to an end when the historical revelation in Jesus Christ ended. When Jesus spoke of his imminent departure they were appalled at the prospect. What could make up for that irreparable loss? But very soon afterwards they made, as we saw in the studies on the Holy Spirit, two great discoveries. First, that though Jesus was no longer by their side in the flesh, the Divine presence had returned to them in an even more marvellous way with the coming of *the Holy Spirit*. I say 'an even more marvellous way' because even the Incarnation had limitations. While Jesus was with them in the flesh they depended on his external presence. Under the stress of events this was not enough to hold them. As we know, they forsook him and fled. But now they knew God the Holy Spirit, present in their hearts. This experience of God within their own hearts was not, of course, entirely new. God had ever been present in the lives of men, seeking them for Himself, inspiring every right desire and every effort after truth and beauty. But now, through Jesus Christ, they understood as they never could have done otherwise the character and purpose of the God who spoke in their hearts. So the experience of God the Holy Spirit, first given to the disciples assembled on Whit Sunday is that special and distinctive influence God exerts within men, when they respond to His love and mercy in Jesus Christ. Even more marvellous and thrilling was the discovery that through their preaching and witness God could come in this way to those who had never known Jesus in the flesh.

This is what makes the Christian Gospel a message for you and me and for every age. Otherwise the Gospel would be a closed book to us for ever and the Christian story an ever receding glory at which we should gaze back wistfully across the centuries. That this is not so we specially celebrate on Trinity Sunday, which comes appropriately at the end of the Christian Year. From Christmas to Whit Sunday we trace in the calendar of our remembrance that pageant of events from our Lord's birth at Bethlehem, through his ministry, his passion, and redemptive death, to his resurrection and ascension, and then the giving of the Holy Spirit. Then on Trinity Sunday we assert that this story is no mere episode, however glorious, but a story about the Eternal God. The doctrine of the Trinity sums up the Gospel by telling us that the God of grace, revealed in Jesus Christ, is the same from all eternity and for ever more. He is the Father who reigns always on high. He is the Spirit who dwells in our hearts.

V

So far we have spoken entirely about the threefold relationship of God with men and women and we have said nothing about the *mutual relationship of the Persons within the Godhead*. This is, of course, something we find difficult to understand and which perhaps we need not be concerned with too deeply. There is, however, one practical consideration of vital importance for the life of the world. We live in a world where men are almost in despair, because of their failure to solve the problems of personal relationships. They have not learned how to live together. Men are grouped in opposing camps, nation against nation, class against class. At every point we are faced with conflicts of interest and motive. To resolve such conflicts seems completely beyond the power and ingenuity of statesmen. How can we hope for the peace and unity of mankind? The doctrine of the Trinity tells us that these problems do not arise within the Godhead, because the relationship of the Persons within the Godhead is one of mutual love. It is with that love that God has loved us in Jesus Christ. Jesus himself spoke of the relationship between himself and his Father as a pattern of the relationship between the believer and himself: he spoke of his love for men as a pattern of the love men should show to one another. This love is no weak, ineffective sentiment. It is the very nature of God, and therefore it is the strongest and most decisive factor in the universe, offering us the one practical method of solving our human problems.

So the doctrine of the Trinity, far from being of only academic interest, sums up the truth of the Gospel for us all by declaring perfect love to be the nature of God Himself, governing from all eternity the relationship within the Godhead, shown forth redemptively to men in Jesus Christ and affording the only sound basis for men and women in their lives together.

What makes life worth while? What fills it with warmth and richness? We can only answer that question by bringing in other people. We have seen that God's nature, being perfect love, can only exist and be expressed within some such relationship as the doctrine of the Trinity suggests. Similarly, in isolation our own lives have no meaning whatever. Most of us would begin with our homes where we live with those who are nearest and dearest to us. Our love for one another there is not something that we have achieved, it is God's gift to us and it is a reflection of His eternal love. We should then go on and include a host of people we meet at work and in our spare time, with whom our lives are bound up. Some of these it is easy to love, some more difficult, but all are, like ourselves, children of God and the objects of God's love. In that men are not different, but one: there is a unity deeper than our diversity. That is something common to us all, on which by God's help we can base right relations with everybody. So, in ever-widening circles which embrace all mankind, the doctrine of the Trinity has the one vital message for this distracted world. The future of mankind depends not on the ingenuity of politicians and economists, nor on systems established or maintained by force, but on whether man, himself loved with the everlasting love of God, can call out and give play to that all-embracing love, which is the very nature of the Triune God Himself.

It is He whom we worship and adore. In Him is life and hope for men and the world. Glory be to the Father, and to the Son, and to the Holy Spirit: As it was in the beginning, is now, and ever shall be, world without end. Amen.

A note might be added concerning the *hymns on the Trinity*. These are not numerous, but they are very valuable. Reginald Heber's majestic hymn: 'Holy, holy, holy, Lord God Almighty' (No. 36), is one which might well be used as the opening hymn of any service, not only on Trinity Sunday. Charles Wesley, as we should expect, has contributed a fine hymn for this, as for the other great festivals of the Church: 'Hail! holy, holy, holy Lord' (No. 37). Edward Cooper's 'Father of heaven, whose love profound' (No. 38) is a fine example of a penitential hymn, while Isaac Watts's 'We give immortal praise' (No. 40) is one of several examples of great hymns by that author which owe their preservation mainly to the Methodist tradition. Its two concluding lines are among the most illuminating in English hymnody:

> *Where reason fails, with all her powers,*
> *There faith prevails and love adores.*

All these are in the section on *The Holy Trinity*.

More likely to escape the preacher's notice is 'God the Father, be Thou near' (No. 952), which, for some unexplained reason, is included among 'Hymns for Week-day Services', but is an ideal closing Hymn for Trinity Sunday evening.

Book List

God was in Christ. D. M. Baillie (Faber & Faber).
An Outline of Christian Theology, *pp*. 161–81. W. Newton Clarke (T. & T. Clark).
What is the Faith? N. Micklem (Hodder & Stoughton).
What we Believe, Chapter IV. J. G. Riddell (Presbyt. C. of E.).
I Believe. Norman H. Snaith, M.A., D.D. (Epworth Press).
The Doctrine of the Trinity. L. Hodgson (Nisbet).

5. Christ's Challenge to Youth

By G. H. VALLINS

Our Title

'YOUTH' and 'challenge' are both dangerous words. The first is apt to imply a false division of life, as if youth were somehow a thing apart, unconnected with what goes before and what follows afterwards. The second suggests the crisis, the trumpet, the outwardly heroic, the gallant decision. It is a sentimental term, much bandied about, for propaganda purposes, at times of national peril and emotional stress. We should remember in our preaching:

(a) to stress the fact that youth is a part (and only a part) of the complete 'one-ness' of life; that it is not, as it were, a separate episode, with its own definite beginning and ending; and, therefore,

(b) that the challenge we speak of is something more than the urges and promptings peculiar to the psychological and physiological period we call adolescence. It is a demand that concerns the whole of our nature—body, soul, and spirit—and the whole of our life. Moreover, it is Christ's demand, which brooks no compromise.

Let us paraphrase our title: 'What Christ requires of the young man and the young woman.' That, stated simply, is the theme. It is no easy one to present without sentimentality and with sincerity. The appeal must be to the mind as well as the emotion. And it must be sustained. Too often Young People's Day, like some other festivals, comes and passes and is forgotten.

Challenge

(a) The general theme ('challenge') as distinct from the particular ('Christ's Challenge') is obvious in certain stories of the Old Testament: Moses (Exod. 3-4), Gideon (Judges 6 [11-24]), Saul (1 Sam. 16 [11-13] and 17), Solomon (1 Kings 2 [1-10] and 3). In the stories of Samson (Judges 13) and Samuel (1 Sam. 1 and 3), which have certain interesting points in common, there is an emphasis on boyhood; as there is also in the story of David (1 Sam. 16 11–12), the three children, with its searching 'but if not . . .' (Dan. 3) and, by implication, Daniel himself (Dan. 6). These stories demand careful treatment. They enshrine eternal truths; but they also reflect a primitive conception of God, life and even morality. It is important to face this frankly. To ignore it is as foolish as it is harmful.

(b) It is interesting, and not unreasonable, to speculate that Elisha was a young man when, as he was ploughing, Elijah 'passed over to him, and cast his mantle upon him' (1 Kings 19 19–21 and 2 Kings 2 1–14). But more significant is the fact, established by most scholars on general historical evidence, that Isaiah (that is, the Isaiah of the first part of the Book called after him) was twenty-one and Jeremiah about twenty-four when the call of the Lord came to them. That gives new meaning to the famous account of Isaiah's vision 'in the year that King Uzziah died' (Is. 6), and to the less vivid, but no less moving, account of the experience of Jeremiah (Jer. 1 4–10). It is not stretching things too far to imagine that Amos and Micah heard the call, and responded to it, when they were young.

(c) The 'challenge' is less obvious in one or two of the patri-archal stories—Abram (Gen. 12 1–4; but unfortunately this great and simple account of Abram's call is spoilt for our purpose by the statement—whatever it may actually mean—that Abram 'was seventy and five years old when he left Haran'), Jacob (Gen. 28 10–22, related to Gen. 32 22–31) and Joseph (Gen. 37 et seq.). The aftermath of the Joseph story, Jacob's blessing on his death-bed (Gen. 49 22–26) has its own point and interest. Other signifi-cant passages in the Old Testament are:

Deut. 6, 7, 8. As in other similar passages (cf. Micah 6 6–8), the challenge of self-discipline and holiness is accentuated in its application to the young.

2 Sam. 23 8–23. The roll of honour of David's young men. This passage is spoilt for us a little by its association with military glory and adventure; but the little character sketches and the beautiful story told in vv. 14–17 have a direct and searching appeal.

Certain Psalms, especially 1, 19, 23 (as representing, possibly, a song of David's youth), 119, especially vv. 9–16.

Certain passages from the Proverbs, part of which purports to be the advice of a father to his son (e.g. chapter 3). Ecclesiastes is, on the whole, better left alone, though 3 1–15, torn somewhat from its context, may be used with effect, especially if verse 15, last clause, is given its A.V. rendering: 'And God requireth that which is past.' The famous chapter 12 ('Remember now thy Creator') is not really apt; it is a poem on the sorrows of old age.

There is no better way of introducing any one, or all, of these Old Testament stories than relating them to the Hebrew writer's roll of honour of his own nation—the names of those who dared much and made their great adventure 'in faith' (Heb. 11). This chapter is, in fact, a fine starting place for any challenge to the young, always provided that 'faith' is clearly and properly defined. There is a further reference to it later in the article.

Christ's Challenge

(a) We begin with the *call* of the twelve disciples (or apostles), for we may assume that, though their ages varied, they were all young men when Christ—himself a young man—first met them. (Dorothy Sayers's characterization of the twelve in *The Man Born to be King* is worth special study.) The story is told in various ways by the four writers of the Gospels (Mk. 1 16-20; Mt. 4 18-22; Lk. 5 2-11; Jn. 1 35-51). All these passages are chiefly concerned with Andrew, Peter, James and John, though John himself includes Philip and Nathanael. Luke gives added detail, and John (1 41) emphasizes Andrew's part in winning his own brother— an important and significant point. The names of the twelve, without details of their call, are given in Mk. 3 14-19, Mt. 10 1-5, and Lk. 6 13-16. Matthew recounts his own call in 9 9; Mark tells the story in 2 13-17, and Luke in 5 27-32, both with the interesting detail of the feast made by Matthew in his own house. The surrender of Matthew, the man of business (cf. Zacchaeus, Lk. 19), has a special significance for the young man, even if we suppose that Matthew himself was not young; so has that of Judas, if we suppose him to be a young 'intellectual' agitator. It is profitable (and interesting) to make a study of each of the twelve, with, of course, special emphasis on Peter, John, and perhaps Judas. This study should be comprehensive: that is, it should follow each disciple, as far as we have knowledge of him, from the time of his call, to Pentecost and after. The application is obvious. To the familiar stories of, for example, Peter—his confession (Lk. 9 18-20), denial (Lk. 22 54-62), forgiveness and charge (Jn. 21 15-22), and Pentecostal courage (Acts 2 14-42)—add the brief glimpses we have of one or two of the other

disciples, e.g. of Philip (Jn. 14 [8-9]) and Thomas (Jn. 20 [24-29])
The challenge was not only to loyalty, endurance, and physical
courage, but also to the mind and the intelligence. Philip's
bewilderment and Thomas's doubt are as significant as Peter's
denial and Judas's betrayal.

(b) There is special significance in the '*charges*' given, either to
the twelve, or to the whole company of followers and 'disciples'.
The most sustained example of this is the series of exhortations
which Matthew collected together, and which we call the Sermon
on the Mount (Mt. 5-7). But there are many other examples in
the Synoptic Gospels—e.g. Mt. 10, especially vv. 24-42;
Lk. 12 [1-12]. John gives us the most intimate picture in chapters
13-16. It is through these passages, with their insistence on
absolute surrender, that we may present to the young the direct
teaching of Christ—again remembering that the twelve were,
for the most part, themselves young. One or two of the parables
should be stressed, especially the Sower (Lk. 8 [4-15]), with its
special application to the young in v. 13, and the Talents
(Mt. 24 [14-30]).

(c) Most instructive are the stories of certain *young men who
came to Jesus:*

Lk. 9 [57-62]. An interesting and symbolical passage. Three
young men (surely) come to Jesus 'in the way'. They are
emotionally excited—ready, they think, for a supreme surrender
and discipleship. 'Lord, I will follow thee, but . . .' In those
three young men, most of us are apt to recognize ourselves.
But the demands of the Master are stern and inexorable.

The rich young man (Mt. 18 [16-22]; Mk. 10 [17-22]; Lk.
18 [18-23]). An unforgettable story. Here, in a dramatic picture,
is the uncompromising demand of Christ. 'What lack I yet?'—
the answer to that is the supreme and hard challenge to every
individual man and woman.

'Who is my neighbour?'—the young man with a vital and
significant question (Lk. 10 [25-37]); and the answer to it, one
of the most striking of Christ's parables, is his call to the
service of mankind. 'I was a stranger, and ye took me in,
naked, and ye clothed me, sick and in prison, and ye visited
me.' It is Jesus himself who lies beside the road we take—the
road 'from Jerusalem to Jericho', from our own town or
village to the next, from our home to the place of our business,
or of our worship.

The Young Men of The Acts and Epistles

(*a*) *Mark*. The story of John Mark, the writer of the Gospel, is easily pieced together, from his own writing, from the Acts of the Apostles, and from the Epistles of Paul. It is the story of a young man in a 'Christian' home (probably the home where Jesus and the Twelve met and ate the Passover together, in the 'upper room, furnished') who followed after Jesus, faltered in his service, and afterwards recovered himself mainly (we may surmise) through the encouragement and help of his uncle, Barnabas, whose name—by an inspired mistranslation of the Authorized Version—means 'the son of consolation'. Here is the story. Its meaning for the young is likely to be intensified because it is apt to touch so nearly their own experience, and because it affords them both warning and encouragement.

Mk. 14 $^{51-52}$: Tradition has it that Mark is writing of himself. The 'certain young man', in that tragic hour, tries to reveal his eager love.

Acts 12 ^{25}: It is some years afterwards. Barnabas, having come to Jerusalem with Saul (Paul) from Antioch, visits Mark's mother; and persuades young Mark to go back with him and Paul to Antioch.

Acts 13 ^{13}: Paul and Barnabas come to 'Perga in Pamphylia', but Mark goes back home. Perhaps he was homesick; perhaps he was ill. We don't know.

Acts 15 ^{36ff}: Paul was so disappointed in him that he refused to take him on a second journey; but Barnabas went so far as to part from Paul, and took Mark with him alone to Cyprus. We hear nothing more of Mark except through a casual reference by Paul in his letter to Timothy:

2 Tim. 4 ^{11}: Paul the aged desires Mark to visit him in prison. 'Take Mark,' he writes to Timothy, 'and bring him with thee, for he is profitable to me for the ministry.' It is the happy ending of a story which, more than most, illustrates the relationship of youth with experience (Mark with Barnabas and Paul).

(*b*) *Paul*. It is almost unnecessary to stress the significance of Paul as an example of Christ's challenge to the young—yet Paul is so great and overwhelming a character that we are apt to forget he was himself a young man when that challenge came. The story, that of a man who 'endured to the end', has a special dramatic appeal at his beginning:

Acts 7 ^{58}–8 ^{3}. The young Pharisee, persecuting the Christians. Notice Paul's own account of those early days in Gal. I $^{11-14}$.

Acts 9 $^{1-9}$. The vision and the conversion. The story is told again, by Paul himself, before the people of Jerusalem (Acts 22 $^{3-11}$) and before King Agrippa (Acts 26 $^{2-23}$). It is a good thing to read all three accounts, if only because it gives added weight to the narrative of one of the most decisive and dramatic episodes in human history. The third account is, of course, the most vivid. Note especially v. 19: 'Wherefore, O King Agrippa, I was not disobedient unto the heavenly vision.' In strong and beautiful words Paul declares his acceptance of the challenge.

For the rest, the letters of Paul, with their light on his journeys, adventures and perils, are a fine inspiration. They record the fulfilment, as life went on to the final sacrifice, of the magnificent dedication of youth. Certain passages, with many others, will suggest themselves, e.g. his brief reference to his time of quiet contemplation and (probably) fasting in Arabia (Gal. I ^{17}); his account of his sufferings and adventures (2 Cor. II $^{23-27}$); his emphasis on the tremendous responsibility of life, and our relationship one to the other (Rom. 12–14); and his characteristic metaphors of the runner (I Cor. 9 $^{14-17}$; Phil. 3 $^{12-16}$) and the soldier (Eph. 6 $^{10-18}$). A telling contrast may be made between Saul the King and Saul (Paul) the Apostle. Notice the two confessions: 'I have played the fool' (I Sam. 26 ^{21}) and 'I have fought the good fight' (2 Tim. 4 ^{7}).

(c) *Timothy and others.* The two letters to Timothy consist of the advice of an old man to a young man. They have, therefore, a special bearing on our subject. It is interesting, with the help of a good reference Bible, to piece together from Luke's narrative (*see* e.g. Acts 16 ^{1} and 17 ^{14}), and various salutations and references in the other epistles, a sketchy narrative of Timothy's connexion with Paul. The letters to Timothy stress the likely weaknesses and failings and temptations of a young man (*see* e.g. I Tim. 6 $^{3-14, 20}$; 2 Tim. 2 $^{16-26}$). Though much of these letters is no more than routine instruction to a young 'minister', both, but especially the second, are charged with the deep and wise spiritual counsel of a man experienced in the Christian way.

It is tempting, and interesting, to speculate that many of the men (and women) whom Paul salutes in his letters were young. If that speculation is allowed us, the endings of the letters become important. To take one example. In Col. 4 [17], he sends a message to a man named Archippus that he should take heed to the ministry which he had received in the Lord. Possibly, even probably, Archippus was the son of that Philemon to whom he wrote a short letter about another young man, Onesimus (Ep. *Philemon*). Archippus, perhaps, had been failing a little in his ministry. He is mentioned in Philemon, v. 2, as our 'fellow-soldier'. Perhaps Paul's gentle reproach and wise encouragement had rekindled his enthusiasm and his faith. There are, for the finding, other examples in the letters. They are often, in their homely way, full of meaning for us still.

(*d*) *All Saints*. We do not normally in Methodism observe the festivals of the saints. But 'All Saints' (November 1) has a special and legitimate appeal to the young. It is the festival of those who have gone before; those who, in the race, have passed on the torch to the new runners. That great passage in *Hebrews* (Heb. 11) already mentioned above, is, as it were, our text. Here the writer makes the roll of honour of his people, the mighty heroes of old as well as those whose names were forgotten but 'of whom the world was not worthy' (cf. the famous passage in the *Apocrypha*, Eccles. 44). They are the watchers, the 'cloud of witnesses' (12 [1-2]), and we are in the arena. It is again Paul's familiar metaphor of the athletic contest (perhaps, indeed, the writer was here influenced by Paul?); and it is a metaphor that has a peculiar appeal to the young, since the modern parallels are so obvious. Moreover, it is a passage that leads our thought onwards in time; the saints belong also to the later ages—those known, like our own Wesley, or unknown except to those among those whom they lived and moved. And here is the opportunity to develop that idea of 'oneness' and fellowship, too often forgotten or neglected in our modern Church, where a sharp division is apt to be made between youth and age. This same chapter of *Hebrews* (11) will suggest also the figure of the pilgrimage, the onward march; and this is a reminder of *The Pilgrim's Progress*, a book which cannot be neglected in any dealings with youth. The Bible is not the only revelation of the Word of God. I remember a great sermon by F. L. Wiseman, who took as his text the passage where Bunyan says that if the pilgrims bore any brunt it was when they were on the Enchanted Ground. What about this, when courage is failing?—'The lions were chained, but he saw not their chains'; or this, for a salutary warning against religious complacency?— 'Then I saw that there was a way to Hell even from the gates of Heaven.' There are dozens of other suggestive phrases, whose application is strengthened by the personification and allegory of the narrative.

A Reminder

It is important to remember that the whole service, not merely the sermon, should present Christ's challenge. If the prayers are extempore, let them be simple and strong without vain digression or undignified colloquialism. If a collect or any other written prayer is used, let it be (usually) from the Methodist *Book of Offices* (itself based on the Anglican *Prayer Book*) rather than from modern collections favoured, for example, by the B.B.C., most of which play down to the common sentimentality of youth. Beware of phrases like 'gallant and high-hearted happiness'. They are sentimental and false. The same principles hold in the choice of hymns. Choose 590 rather than 588, 182 rather than 354. Not that Wesley and Watts are the only good hymn-writers! There are in our collection a number of fine modern hymns, like, for example, 632 and 979. The appeal of Christ himself to men and women was uncompromising. We have tended to forget that today: to invite the young not to the stern responsibilities and high privileges of the fellowship of His Church 'militant here on earth', but to a table-tennis club and a discussion circle. Yet the tremendous challenge remains.

> *When I survey the wondrous Cross*
> *Where the young Prince of Glory died . . .*

That is how Watts originally wrote the hymn. Christ is still the *young* Prince of Glory. It is well to remember that, when we think or speak of His challenge to the young.

Book List

Youth and the Gospel. Godfrey S. Pain (Epworth Press).

Youth on Fire. J. W. Skinner, M.A. (Epworth Press).

Youth at the Helm. J. W. Skinner, M.A. (Epworth Press).

Six Clues to the Mystery (Broadcast Talks to Youth). Douglas A. Griffiths (Epworth Press).

The Manhood of the Master. H. E. Fosdick (S.C.M. Press).

Tom, Dick, and Padre (In Talks on the Christian Faith and Life). P. E. Morton-George, M.A. (Epworth Press).

1. The Christian Doctrine of Man

By *the* Rev. EDWARD ROGERS, M.A., B.D.

STUDY ONE
INTRODUCTION TO AN URGENT THEME

Aim: To show that this doctrine is not merely 'useful for preachers', but is, in fact, a specially relevant and vitally necessary doctrine for today.

Bible Readings: This is an introductory study, and the readings chosen illustrate aspects of the theme.

Exodus 21. Early examples of 'fair dealing' between men.

Amos. Righteousness as the basis of national life.

1 Kings 21. The story of a conflict of doctrine.

Ephesians 4. The perfect man.

Hebrews 2. A commentary on Psalm 8. What is Man?

If the wily Local Preacher, looking at the title of this study, 'Introduction to an Urgent Theme', decides to knock off fifty per cent for writer's enthusiasm, and re-titles it in his own mind: 'Introduction to a Theme which a Local Preacher with Plenty of Spare Time and a Taste for Speculative Argument might possibly find interesting,' he will be wrong! Putting it soberly and without exaggeration, the 'doctrine of man' is probably the most important fundamental issue of our generation; critically important because opposing views are fighting for the soul of man and the battle has entered on a phase which will be decisive for long years to come.

For example, do you think that a man who is accused of theft should be given a fair trial and an opportunity to defend himself against the charge in court? That, you reply, is elementary justice. Every man should have the right to a fair trial. But why? After all, if the State condescends to give us what we call certain 'rights', there is no reasonable ground for complaint if the State takes them away. But, you reply again, the State does not give us our rights. It looks after them, or it ought to, but it doesn't give them. Every man has his rights, and justice is one of them.

Are you sure? Isn't man a product of his economic class? Are not all so-called 'rights' merely relative to the economic organization of society? Is it not the duty of man to subordinate himself in all things to his class? Isn't it old-fashioned reactionary nonsense to talk in these days about individual rights? Very many people think so; and in some countries the people who don't think so keep quiet or they get put safely away without any fooling about with 'fair trials'.

At this point I expect you, as a good Local Preacher, to protest. 'I don't care how many people say they don't believe in justice, and I don't take much notice of their clever arguments. To shove a man in jail, or worse, and keep him there without trial is a crime against humanity.' Of course it is! But why? There isn't any answer to that awkward question unless we have the right answer to an even more ancient question: What is man? And that is what we are going to think about in this study.

Naboth's Vineyard

Look at 1 Kings 21. Naboth had a vineyard. Ahab, King of Israel, wanted it, so he offered a fair price or a good exchange. Naboth the peasant, with a peasant's reluctance to give up his land, wouldn't consider it. So Ahab, deeply disappointed, took to his bed. If the man wouldn't sell, that was the end of it; for Ahab had been brought up in the Israelite tradition that another man's rights had to be respected. But his wife Jezebel, brought up in a different tradition, could not make out what was worrying her husband. He was the king, and a king took what he wanted. So Naboth was framed, and died. This vivid story of centuries ago is fundamentally a story of conflict between two doctrines of the rights of man. More than that, it is the story of a man who gave way to temptation when the insidious appeal of self-interest revealed that he did not really believe in the tradition in which he had been reared.

Was Ella Wheeler Wilcox Right?

The point we are working up to is that the prevalent conception of the nature of man in any society is a major factor in determining the life of individuals and nations within that society. It was the official doctrine in Nazi Germany that a man existed to give complete obedience and service to the State. So rebels were sent to concentration camps, and incurable invalids were put to death. It is the unofficial doctrine in most countries that man exists to 'enjoy himself' . . . you only have one life, so make the most of it! . . . and as a result Pubs and Pools and all the other substitutes for life flourish. It is like an axiom in geometry. Get your doctrine of man wrong, and your civilization goes wrong.

We are all familiar with the lines of Ella Wheeler Wilcox:

So many gods, so many creeds,
So many paths that wind and wind,
While just the art of being kind
Is all the sad world needs.

How pleasant it would be if that were true! How pleasant if it didn't matter what we believed so long as our intentions were good! But the plain truth is that the things we do, and even our interpretation of 'kindness', depend on what we believe. We cannot live without a creed. It may be a good one or a bad one; well thought out or a woolly jumble; but there is no getting away from the fact that our life reflects our creed. Christianity was first called 'The Way', because it was a new way of life based on a new way of thinking about God and man (*see* Acts 19 [1-9].). 'Eat, drink, and be merry, for tomorrow we die' is a different way of life based on a different set of ideas. The important, the essential thing is to get the right faith to live by.

The Popular Contemporary Doctrine of Man

Now, we are not merely interested students of the social situation. We are preachers of the Gospel, seeking to win men and women into the saving way of truth. (Look up Rom. 10 and 1 Cor. 1.) And that means that we have to go where they are to bring them where we know they ought to be. Paul quoted from the Old Testament when he preached in the synagogue; but he quoted Aratus and Epimenides when he preached in Athens (cf. Acts 13 [14-41] and 17 [16-31]). So we shall beat the air in vain with our preaching unless we have both a sympathetic understanding of contemporary ideas and a clear conception of our own faith.

What, then, is the popular contemporary doctrine of man which is acting as the motive force of contemporary life? It is a mixture of remnants of Christian theology, half-understood old-fashioned popular science, simplified and falsified psychology, and the optimistic belief than man can perfect himself and his society by his own efforts. It reminds me very strongly of an old sea-faring cook's comment on hash. 'You don't have to make it,' he said. 'It just accumulates.'

Out of the 'accumulation' has come a vague and illogical doctrine of man which is altogether one-sided. It is thought, quite mistakenly, that science has proved that man is a creature of this world only, and that nobody with any claim to intelligence could possibly believe in immortal souls. Which is why so many people nowadays think that the worst thing that can happen to anybody is to die! (In debate with an ardent young Communist recently I was attacking Marxist 'materialism'. He was most indignant, and replied that Communists were as fond of music and literature as anybody else. When I explained that music and literature could be as materialistic as engineering, and that I was referring to the absence of faith in the eternal and spiritual, he looked at me as though I were a refugee from a Museum.) It is also thought that psychology has explained all the nature of man in terms of animal instincts and emotions, and that religion has been finally accounted for as an infantile 'running away from reality'. (In fact, Jung, the greatest living psychologist, and very many others, have come to realize and have said very plainly that religious faith is both reasonable and real.) But although man is now generally regarded as a creature of this world only, it is believed that one day he will at last succeed in building a perfect and happy civilization, that he is destined to be the Lord of Creation. Actually this is a hangover of Christian teaching, retained because it gives a sense of purpose to life, but with the Christianity that made it sensible left out.

The result is that we are living in a civilization which is pre-carious and unbalanced because it is founded on a one-sided idea of man. All the stress is on the half-truth (half-truth, please note, and not error!) that he is a 'citizen of this world'; and the other half of the truth, that he is a citizen of the world of the spirit, is forgotten. Furthermore, because men have got on the wrong lines they are always unreasonably expecting brighter days to come, and always being disappointed. Now that the lesson of the first half of the twentieth century is beginning to sink in, it looks as though, following two generations of optimists, we shall have to do our work in a generation of thorough-going pessimists. And one way in which we can 'serve the present age' is to preach the full, true doctrine of man.

The Social Gospel

We are not altogether blameless! There was a manner of preaching that was growing in popularity at the beginning of the century; preaching that owed a good deal more to the Collected Works of Emerson than to the New Testament. Influenced by contemporary ideas, it turned its back on Heaven and Hell and preached the Kingdom of God on earth—and sometimes it sounded more like the Kingdom of Man on earth! The miraculous, the supernatural, the other-worldly, was soft-pedalled, and pride of place was given to the Sermon on the Mount, with a strange forgetfulness that the Sermon taught the way of life for men who believed in the Son of God. The battle-cry was Hymn 910. Study it carefully! Admirable sentiments. But never a word about the grace that alone can make these things be.

I am not for one moment suggesting that it is foolish to preach the Social Gospel. I shall be preaching that gospel, and urging you to do so, in these studies. But what I *am* suggesting is that you can't preach the Social Gospel without the Gospel! We don't get very far with sinful men with no more than a moral appeal to their better nature. Much earnest, sincere, and often passionate, preaching has been labour in vain because it had too easy a doctrine of man. 'Christianity is good news about God. It is also news, good and bad, about man' (*The Message and Mission of Methodism*, p. 7. The whole section, pp. 7–11, will well repay study). We didn't think enough about the bad news, and so we didn't say enough about the Saviour. Those who long for a better order of society find a more searching song in Hymn 906; and a profounder message in 'Seek ye first the Kingdom of God, and all these things shall be added unto you'.

Education

And now let us move over into another field to consider the equally popular notion that education (magic word!) will solve all our problems. Mark Twain neatly summed up the philosophy of a generation when he said: 'Soap and education are not as sudden as a massacre, but they are more deadly in the long run.' But as soon as we probe beneath the surface we find ourselves landed in the same conflict of ideas about man.

I must not forget that these are Study Notes—so here are a few pertinent questions to be going on with. What sort of education do we want? Is the purpose of education to adjust the individual to the community in which he lives? If the community is not as good as it ought to be, is the purpose of education to prepare the child to work for the improvement of the community? Then who is to decide what is an 'improvement'? What is the standard for a good community? Is it material comfort and security? Or more than that? Is it good enough to concentrate on relating the individual to the community? Ought not education to aim at the full and free development of the individual personality? But then, is it not true that there are potentialities in the human mind and soul that ought not to be developed? Can an education be sound which is primarily self-centred? And if we agree that education ought to balance both individual development and social responsibility, can we safely assume that the Christian virtues can be taught and practised as ends in themselves and not as the fruits of the Spirit?

These questions are still being debated—but the children are not being kept at home till the argument is settled! What we find in the schools today is a 'working compromise' that muddles up all the answers so that no-one can really tell what is the purpose of the school curriculum. The fundamental problems of education are just about evenly divided between those which are concerned with the nature of man and those which are concerned with his destiny. If you have a child at school, remember that his training and the direction given to his impressionable years depend upon a 'doctrinal argument'. It wasn't just enthusiasm that made me call this an urgent theme!

A Mixed Bag

It would be easy to pile up illustrations of the pressing, even desperate, importance of our theme. I will go so far as to say that whatever practical piece of Christian service interests you—and you can interpret that as broadly as you like—this business of the doctrine of man is bound up in it. I have taken the following examples at random. It would be a useful exercise if you were to add two or three of your own.

1. One of the most momentous tasks of political planning now being undertaken is the work of the United Nations Commission on Human Rights. It deals with such things as freedom of speech, religious liberty, and the security of family life. It has inevitably become the battleground of conflicting ideas. The struggle within the United Nations Commission over the right of free speech, for example, is an ideological struggle. It all turns on what doctrine of man you accept.

2. We are trying to build up an order of society which will give security to the worker and his family. It is a very good thing that starvation is no longer to be the incentive to work, and that illness will not be a crippling blow. But we find that we have raised a whole crop of new problems. What is the incentive to work in a society of full employment? What is 'work,' anyway—social service, or earning a living? What is the best use to make of the new leisure gained? And so back we go again, as we must do when we are talking about men and women and not about 'hands' or 'personnel', to the old question: What is man? And at the risk of becoming wearisome, I repeat once more that until we answer that question correctly we shall not make much headway with the others.

3. One remarkable feature of our age is the apparent insignificance of the individual. Our lives seem to be dominated by vast, impersonal forces that we can do very little to influence. The sad thing is that so many people seem ready to accept their own presumed insignificance. It means that they don't have to think. But the Christian is not over-awed. He is not proud, but he knows that he matters. From whence does that conviction come? From the knowledge that God loves him, and so there is an innate dignity in man that cannot be denied.

Conclusion

A steady survey of the world in which we live reveals that the popular doctrines of man are unbalanced. They are either too cynical or too sentimental. We should do well to look upon men with the eyes of Jesus. He knew that they were sinners, and he knew that they were worth dying for. In the Christian doctrine of man there is a refreshing, salty realism. The problems are not simplified, and there are no easy answers. We have had too many of them! The problems are seen as they are, and the answers are often hard but true.

And that lays upon us the responsibility of knowing, and of faithfully proclaiming, that doctrine. We can all do our full share of pointing out where the politicians and the Communists go wrong; and a fat lot of good it does! Most people know well enough that the world is in a mess, without our having to rub it in. In its desperate state, the world needs a positive word. It is not sufficient to say: 'That way is wrong.' We must be able to proclaim: 'This way is right.' Quite simply, in the Gospel we have a doctrine of man that can both diagnose his ills and offer him healing.

STUDY TWO.   THE DOCTRINE EXPOUNDED

Aim: Convinced that it is a vital necessity to reach a true estimate of man, we shall consider the Christian doctrine.

Bible Readings:

Genesis 1, 2: The origin of man.
Jeremiah 17 $^{1-10}$: the nature of man.
Romans 1, 2: the rule of sin.
Psalm 103: the mercy of God.
Ephesians 2: the destiny of man.
1 John 2: the destiny of man.

'Man is Heaven's masterpiece,' said Francis Quarles three centuries ago. 'Man is Nature's sole mistake,' said W. S. Gilbert two generations ago. 'Man is an embodied paradox, a bundle of contradictions,' said Charles Colton, about half-way between the two of them in time. And a great many other writers have said a great many witty things about this curious creature; but these three will be enough to indicate that we face no easy task when we set out to expound the Christian doctrine of man. After our first study, that should not surprise us. We discovered that the trouble with most contemporary teaching about man is that it over-simplifies, though the basic and unjustifiable simplicity is often hidden by a cloud of long words. There is no great merit in making an easy subject look difficult; but there is real danger in making a difficult subject appear to be child's play, especially when, as we have seen, the subject is the doctrine which directly affects the whole of life. I give fair warning that in this study we shall have to use our intelligence!

Man and Nature

We start with the undeniable fact that man is a creature of this world. Like the gnat or the camel, he is born into this world, lives in it, and dies. The scientist can trace the progress of our diseases, and is learning to overcome them, by experiments carried out on rats or guinea-pigs—because our bodily organism obeys general natural laws. Unless we eat, we die. Those who have known real hunger, or the grinding pressure of poverty, know what are the 'necessities of life', and have no doubt that we are creatures of this world.

But that is not the *whole* truth. Man is an intelligent creature, a remembering creature, a creature with gifts and abilities unequalled by any other form of life on this planet. Admittedly, there are those who argue that, all the same, he is entirely of this world, and that mind, for instance, is the result of pure chance in the million-fold possibilities of the universe. But it doesn't make sense when you consider it seriously. Reason is something that could never develop out of unreasoning nature. It might evolve from lower grades of intelligence; but by no accident could it begin where there was no glimmer of reason. So, too, the sense of moral obligation, though it can obviously be channelled by custom and directed by training, could never come into existence out of purely natural processes though they went on from everlasting to everlasting.

We must not let that very useful servant, science, become our master. The scientist can *describe* man as an organization of intricate molecules, themselves composed of very involved atoms (which is true!), but he cannot explain how that organization can reason about the structure of atoms. The psychologist can *describe* the working of the human mind in terms of emotions and reflexes and responses; but he cannot explain the origin or fix the limits of mind. Indeed, those scientists and psychologists who are studying the relationship between mind and matter, and who are experimenting with the strange powers of mind (telepathy, pre-cognition, etc.), are not only making a sorry mess of old-fashioned materialism but are being driven by the weight of the evidence to the conclusion that, in a way that science cannot explain, man is a being both inside and outside Nature.

The Child of God

You will observe that there has been so far no quotation from the Bible, and not a single phrase of theology. It is not the usual approach, but I have chosen it deliberately. I want to press home my conviction that when we refer to the Bible we do not enter a special 'Sunday' world which has to be fitted on very gingerly and tactfully to the normal world of experience. On the contrary, we meet Reality. Our generation thinks loosely in terms of science, and will listen to the scientist when it turns a deaf ear to the prophet. It may come as a salutary shock to some to learn that, without leaving the ground of the scientist, we have found evidence that man is a dual creature—of this world, but not altogether.

Several explanations of the fact are offered to us. Some say that man is a 'freak of Nature'; which is just giving up trying to explain. Others say that he has not yet fully evolved, and that we now see him in the half-finished stage; which is very impressive until you realize that this does not explain why he should have a dual nature at the 'half-way house'. Others say there must be a realm of existence and a quality of life which is not of this world; and that man, as it were, has a foot in both camps. This is the Christian interpretation, and it fits most closely all the facts of experience. The first chapters of Genesis, which speak of the dust of the earth animated by the breath of God, form a fitting prelude to a Bible which is supremely concerned with the relationship between God and His creature, man (see, for instance, Ps. 104; Is. 43 [1]; Mal. 2 [10]; Rev. 4 [11]).

The orthodox statement is that man has been created by God, and depends upon God for his very existence. He may rebel against God; he may say in his heart that there is no God; but he cannot escape the insistent reality of his nature. If he accepts the rule of God, he lives in the grace of God. If he rejects that rule, he lives under the judgement of God. However he behaves, and whatever he believes, it is in God that he lives, and moves, and has his being. (See Acts 17 [24–28]; and Hymns 42 and 55.) We have no truck with the teaching that man is an accident of evolution. He is God's creature; and if that is so, his only hope of true happiness lies in fulfilling the purpose, whatever it is, for which God created him. 'Our hearts are restless till they find rest in Thee.'

Man, the Sinner

Having got so far, we shall turn away again from theology to look at the men and women we know. There is obviously something wrong with all of them, including ourselves! (The only people who would claim to be completely satisfied with themselves are those with least reason to be satisfied: the stupid and conceited.) If we are honest, we have to admit that we are not what we ought to be. (Ponder very carefully verse 5 of Hymn 689.) We must keep our sense of proportion. There is a good deal that is right with people—affection, courage, love of truth, willingness to sacrifice for others. I don't think that I have ever met a completely bad man in all my life. Have you? So we shall have to remember the 'problem of the goodness of man' when we estimate the truth of the Christian doctrine. But only a fool would say that this world is now inhabited by perfectly good people. 'Man's inhumanity to man' is a byword. The catalogue of such typical human characteristics as greed, lust, envy, pride, jealousy, cruelty, is far too long and all too true.

How can we account for it? The animals and the plants appear to fulfil their destiny without this mingling of contradictions (*see* any good Commentary on Mt. 6 [28]). There is a measure of reason in the modern argument that the course of evolution gives us a clue. As the human mind has developed it has overlaid, but not conquered, the old animal nature; so that ancient sub-human instincts survive to wreck our complacency and disorganize our plans. But it just won't do if it is offered as the whole story. Blinding murderous rage may be a sub-human survival, but cold intellectual spite, which is as bad, is obviously not. Cleverness and goodness do not invariably go together—and if 'goodness' is begging the question, it is just as true that cleverness and happiness do not invariably go together.

The Christian is neither comforted nor convinced by the specious argument that these faults and failures are things we shall 'grow out of' in a couple of million years or so. He says that man is a sinner! If the word is blunt and unfashionable, so much the worse for fashion. The fact is that man, the dependent creature of God, has tried to assert a fictitious independence; has put his own 'self' in the place where God should be—and the precise, technical word for that is 'Sin'. It is a very great pity that the word has come to be associated only with its more lurid and spectacular manifestations, such as drunkenness and adultery. The modern Pharisee, condemning with complacent self-righteousness the failings of others, has just as great a need to pray: 'Lord, be merciful to me, a sinner.' (Have a good look at 1 Kings 8 46; Prov. 14 9; Ezek. 18 4; Dan. 9 1–15; Lk. 18 13; Jn. 8 7; 1 Jn. 1 8; and the twenty-five references to sin in Rom. 6 and 7.) Man is the creature of God. Man is a sinner.

More Bad News

We are all caught in the web of sin. It enters into all our relationships—personal, social, industrial, international—and spoils them. And as we all have to live in relationships with others, none of us can escape the effects of sin. We are born into the tainted body of this world and when one member suffers or sins all the rest are affected, even as the ripple of a stone dropped into the ocean touches every far-distant coast. It is plain fact that man is so completely involved in present sin and the consequences of past sin that he cannot extricate himself. As Paul said, using the customary language of his own day, we are all 'in Adam'; all in the grip of sin.

I know quite well that this is a message offensive to the pride of man. We still cling doggedly to the hope, after centuries of experience to the contrary, that we can save ourselves by our own efforts; by better planning, better education, better discipline. But it won't work! Snugly concealed at the heart of all such plans is the master-sin of pride. Here is the place where Christian doctrine is unpalatable medicine; but here is the place where it is healing truth. We do no good by substituting soothing syrup! Until man learns his helplessness (see Jn. 6 68) and allows his need to conquer his pride (Micah 6 8) there is no real hope for him; and it is our job as preachers to proclaim this truth.

But if all this is so, would it not be better to leave man even in the false warmth of illusion if the only alternative is a bleak hopelessness? If ignorance is bliss, 'tis folly to be wise! The answer is that it is not Christian doctrine that man is utterly and irredeemably corrupt. We have already noted that there is real good in man. There is a world of difference between 'man cannot save himself' and 'man cannot be saved'. The fact is that man is not 'corrupt'; he is 'perverted'. And that is not merely playing about with words. Man can recognize that which is good and can long for it because the 'image of God' in his own nature, though sadly tarnished, is not finally destroyed. If it were destroyed he would be out of the reach of salvation. The deep-rooted conflicts in the inner life of man, so vividly portrayed by Paul (Rom. 7 $^{22-24}$) and equally vividly portrayed in our own day by Freud and Jung, witness to the ineffectual longing of perverted man for the bliss he cannot attain. On a greater scale, the long story of social and economic frustration mirrors the same spiritual frustration. But—if help came from outside man—there is that within him that could respond!

The Good News!

At this stage, when the bad news about man is clearly grasped, the good news of the Gospel speaks the word of release. In barest outline that good news is: 'God was in Christ, reconciling the world unto himself' (2 Cor. 5 ^{19}). Into a world dominated by the infection of evil there was born a person, thoroughly human (for we know that he hungered, wept, and bled), who was yet free from the contagion of sin ('in all points tempted like as we are, yet without sin,' Heb. 4 ^{15}). There was no tragic inner conflict in his nature, no spiritual frustration; because he lived in the right relationship to God (Jn. 15 ^{10}). In Jesus, the Son of Man, we see man as God intended him to be, the unspoiled image of the 'true self' of man.

But this does not mean that God has shown us again the 'pattern of humanity' in Jesus Christ, and now commands us to live like that as though we could manage quite comfortably with a pattern to work from. The idea that the Christian Gospel is no more than knowledge of the right way of life is an ancient heresy, which keeps cropping up because it feeds our pride. The Gospel is an offer of power; of strength to do what we now know we ought to do. Through Jesus, real 'life' (see Jn. 10 ^{10}) has now come into the world, freely available to all who are in fellowship with Him (Rom. 5 $^{5-6}$). The Son of God laid his glory by in order that he might seek out and save the lost.

Observe how all the great lines of theological teaching converge on this point. Repentance, Justification, Sanctification . . . these are not 'theological problems'. They tell how the lost sheep of God comes home. The doctrine of the Atonement, centred on Calvary and the Resurrection, witnesses to our faith that when Jesus voluntarily accepted the Cross (for you realize, I hope, that he was not trapped by cunning enemies, but deliberately took that way) he fought and defeated, for our sakes, Sin and Sin's lieutenant, Death. Because Jesus was both true Man and true God He is the bridge for us between the two realms of existence. All of it is in John 3 [16].

Summary

It is time that we brought all the threads together in a statement of the Christian doctrine, for we may see its strength and truth more clearly in the light of our introductory argument. (1) Man has been created in the image of God; therefore he is both 'natural' and 'spiritual'. (2) Historic man is so perverted by sin that his 'human nature' is now in opposition to his 'original nature'; so that his life is made up of conflict and frustration. (3) By the grace of God, who has revealed to man in Jesus Christ his true nature and the reality of its perversion, man is redeemed and the 'image of God' is restored. (4) The way of restoration is faith in Jesus Christ.

And I ought to add that this is not just one more of the thousand human speculations about man. There is Divine authority behind the doctrine. The historic person Jesus, the foundation of our faith, manifested his nature in his life, death, and resurrection . . . and no one should dare to deny its truth who has not faced up to the fact of the resurrection and the experience of countless believers.

Outworkings of the Doctrine of Man

In closing, I want to suggest some ways in which the doctrine is relevant to our lives. First of all, it will be noticed that it is no airy-fairy teaching which denies the reality of evil or the importance of this world. Because we believe that man matters in the sight of God, it is laid upon us as a duty to fight against all social evil, all that degrades and despises man. We have no right to acquiesce in evil by assuring ourselves that such things are beneath the notice of 'spiritual beings', or that it will all be straightened out in the next world. It would be a useful exercise to work out the implications of the prayer 'Give us this day our daily bread' in the light of the faith that *all men* matter to God.

When we have got that worked out, we should restore the balance by thinking out 'Man shall not live by bread alone'. It is essential, if man is to live according to his true nature, that his spiritual needs should be met. That means, among other things, worship . . . and freedom to worship.

Again, it is not true that our doctrine takes away all freedom from man and makes him a puppet in the hands of God. Our modern dictators make men into puppets; but that is not the way of God. He offers salvation, shows us the way of life, offers us power to live; but we have the responsibility of accepting or rejecting the offer. In the Kingdom of God we are children, not conscripts.

Again, and this is particularly relevant today, the Christian doctrine shows the way of release from the conflict between individual needs and social claims. (Look again at the questions on Education in the previous Study.) If all other human beings are the children of God, they are my brothers and sisters, not my rivals. I can only attain the fullness of my individual nature in a proper relationship to God and to my neighbour. There is no doubt that those who stop short at 'individual salvation' have halted at the beginning of the Way. Is it not true that when, through faith in Christ, I willingly accept the discipline of his Body, both my individual and social needs are fulfilled? (Eph. 4 16; 1 Cor. 12 25–6).

Again, the doctrine speaks of man as a citizen of eternity and gives him dignity as an immortal soul. It is a sobering thought! How many people would live as they do if they really believed in immortality? It is the lack of this faith that drives many to such strange and useless expedients to find happiness in terms of this life only. The Christian experiences, here and now in all the limitations of this mortal life, the quality of life eternal. He fights a good fight with cheerful courage, because he is full of the hope of immortality (see 2 Tim. 1 10). He also has a clearer view of history . . . but this must wait till the next Study.

Finally, as this is the truth about man, all social planning and all personal conduct must be tested by it. This doctrine lays upon the preacher the task of the prophet; for man ignores it at his peril.

STUDY THREE. COMMUNISM

Aim: To test the Christian doctrine of man by contrasting it with its great modern rival.

Bible Readings:
    Deuteronomy 30: The choice between life and death.
    James 4: The cause of strife.
    1 John 4: Judging the teachers of man.
    Acts 4 31–37: Apostolic communism.

Several times in the course of our two previous Studies we

have reached a stage in the argument that could best have been
illustrated by a reference to Communism, but I have kept away
from it because it is so important a subject, and so much in the
minds of men today, that we ought to consider it in detail.
The Christian faith is being challenged by a rival faith which is
deliberately out for world dominion; a faith which is founded
upon quite definite ideas about man, society, and history. This
rival faith must be taken seriously, and studied thoughtfully.
Unhappily, a great deal of nonsense has been poured out about
Communism, both for it and against it; and Christian preachers,
picking up odd pieces here and there in the newspapers, have
not been wholly guiltless!

I would draw your attention to some very wise words in the
Report of the 1948 Lambeth Conference: 'The most highly
organized, consistent, powerful, and destructive form of secular-
ism is beyond doubt Dialectical Materialism, and the type of
Communism in which it is embodied. This is perhaps the one
live alternative to the Christian interpretation of man. Between
the two there can be no compromise; and it seems to be increasingly probable that it is between these two that the world must
choose. Neutral positions may not long be tenable. No presentation of the Christian world-view can command the assent of the
rising generation unless it has squarely come to grips with the
dogmas of Dialectical Materialism. For Marxism, by an ironic
paradox, is at some points nearer to the Christian doctrine than
any other philosophy in the field, and this makes its rivalry all
the more formidable.' (In passing, the whole of the Lambeth
Report on the Christian Doctrine of Man will repay study.)

I must make it perfectly clear at the beginning that we are
going to look at Marxian Communism. The old word 'communism' simply means 'common ownership', and has nothing to do
with atheism or commissars; but it has now been grabbed by the
Marxians and identified with the official and orthodox doctrine
of the U.S.S.R. There is, indeed, a steady stream of 'pure
communist' teaching in the Christian tradition. The main stream
of Christian commentary on Acts 4 is that, in a sinful world and
taking men as they are, private property under legal obligations
is a necessity of ordered life. So long as men are selfish and
unloving, everybody's property is nobody's property. (Your chapel
caretaker could give evidence on that theme!) But there is at the
same time a strong tradition that, if all men were Christian and

able to bear the demands of the best, the ideal form of society would be 'communist' in type. That is an arguable proposition, but I will just state it and leave it there. My point is that Christian opposition to Marxism is not based on love of dividends or satisfaction with things as they are.

Nor do we necessarily disagree with the long-distance goal of the Marxian Communist. He says (quite sincerely) that he wants to see all men free and equal, and living in a state of society where each gives according to his ability and receives according to his need, and where life is not organized and controlled by money power. We must remember what Jesus said about God and Mammon; Lk. 16 [13] ('Mammon' is the impersonal power of wealth; as great an evil in Roman civilization as in our own). When Marx and Engels get down to details, and paint their childish picture of a society where everybody does as he likes and nobody ever disagrees with anybody else, we begin to suspect that there is something wrong; but so long as it is kept vague it is very close to the Christian ideal. Our quarrel comes when we begin to consider how we shall get there.

What is Marxian Communism?

You see, one source of the strength of Marxian Communism is its confident assertion that communism is 'inevitable', that the whole historic process has been scientifically demonstrated by Marx—with a few additional touches by Lenin, and that there is not the slightest need to call in the aid of a God who does not exist. Man can do the job. Indeed, he will have to, whether he likes it or not. If he fits in with the flow of history it will come more quickly; if he resists it will come more slowly; but he cannot prevent it.

The basis of Marxism is the Materialist Interpretation of History. This we must get hold of if we want to understand our adversary. I will summarize it as briefly, simply, and fairly, as I can; but it will not be easy going. (Marx was a dreadful writer, incurably lazy, who could not be bothered to think out clearly what he wanted to say. Though this is the heart of his teaching, of which he was most proud, he never wrote the promised exposition of it and we have to gather scraps and suggestions from all over his works.) We begin with the argument that the life, organization, and social structure of any society depend upon the form of industrial production. There is one sort when man is a hunter, another when the basis is slave labour, another when workers are employed by an owner but work at home, another when they work in factories with power-driven machinery. Thus, the governors of one type of society are feudal nobles; of another, industrial capitalists. It is not too much to say that the form of industrial production really determines customs, habits, opinions, and ideas.

The next step in the argument is that the forms of production are always changing, as a result of 'economic laws' over which individuals have no control. The form of production of which the typical example is the hand-loom, created such problems of sale, distribution, wages, etc., that the only solution was to change over to power-loom working . . . but though this would have solved the problems of 'hand-loom' society its final effect was to create a new 'power-loom' society with new problems. So the world changes, under the steady pressure of economic laws.

The historic method of the change is that the social class which is next to the top fights and overcomes the class which holds power, because the class which holds power has lost its economic strength when the form of production changed. We have now arrived at the final phase of history. Only two classes are left: the *bourgeoisie* and the proletariat. The last struggle has now begun. The result is inevitable. Soon will come the victory of the proletariat, the society which has only one class, and a happy world for everybody.

Underlying all this is very definite teaching about the nature of man. He is 'concrete, actual, and material'; which means that he belongs to this world only. Religion is wrong in theory as a useless superstition; wrong in practice as a drug which prevents men from putting an imperfect world right by their own efforts. Man is not perfect. He cannot be in an imperfect society, because he gets all his personal consciousness from the society in which he lives. But he is perfectible, and will be perfect when the Communist Utopia comes. He is naturally selfish and egotistical; but that only means that in practice you can rely on the working out of economic laws, as men will always strive for that which they think will give them the greatest security.

The Christian Answer

The first reaction of the intelligent Christian is to wonder how anybody could be taken in by these assertions. There is so much talk about 'scientific proof' (Marx first called his system Scientific Socialism) that it comes hard to find so much flat, dogmatic assurance, and not a word of proof. But when we remember how many, especially of the industrial workers and particularly on the Continent of Europe, have lost all touch with the Christian Church and its teaching, we should not be surprised that they accept this sort of stuff.

The Marxist doctrine of man is out-dated eighteenth-century philosophy, and we need not trouble to point out all its fallacies. We have already considered the weakness and partiality of materialist doctrines. But we may note that when Communism is put into practice one side of the doctrine is dropped. Logically, if our ideas depend upon our economic circumstances, nobody is personally responsible for his ideas; but you would be ill-advised to rely on that as a defence if you were accused by the N.K.V.D. (Russian security police) of being a Fascist reactionary. We may also wonder how, if Marxism is correct, the *bourgeois* Marx managed to get hold of the right ideas! The real trouble, of course, is that such a doctrine permits and condones the most ruthless and inhuman cruelty by lowering and degrading the status of man; making of him a mere cog in a gigantic machine.

The fundamental fallacy is that Marxism only thinks of 'man in the mass'. It has no use for those individual variations in which the Christian sees evidence of the infinite creativity of God. It is not true that a man is merely a unit in a social class, and that he can only find fulfilment in 'class solidarity'. The Marxist doctrine of the 'class war' is thoroughly bad psychology and a distortion of history. There *are* conflicts in history, which are real and important, but this idea of two classes at war on every issue is ridiculous. It is significant that when Karl Marx was developing the Labour Theory of Value, on which much of the economic theory hinges, he turned away from questions of individual skill and energy and based his theory on 'an undifferentiated jelly of socially necessary labour'. The Christian does not believe that man, whether he be a poor Bolivian peasant or a high Soviet official, is no more than a statistical addition to an undifferentiated human jelly. (Think over Mt. 10 [29–31].)

It is this underlying weakness in the attitude to man that spoils the Economic Interpretation of History. There is so much in it that is true and valuable, such a refreshing emphasis on those social and economic motives which earlier historians had either forgotten or ignored, that one cannot help regretting the simple credulity that tries to give an economic motive to the whole of history. Patriotism, loyalty, love of adventure, religion, the effects of great personalities . . . all these have played their part in history. If Marx himself had never lived and written, this world would have been a different place.

The Christian, who freely accepts the place of economic motive in history, has a wider vision. He does not have to put all his hope in the happiness of some distant future generation. The idea that all the struggles and sorrows of the centuries are justified if in the years to come a better way of life is achieved, is not, by itself, a very cheering thought or a very sound idea. We who believe in God, and trust the promises of Jesus, look forward both to a purer world for future human generations and also to a fullness of joy for ourselves and those who have gone before us in the life that lies the other side of the grave (*see* Heb. 11 [39]–12 [2]).

And finally (not because there is not more to say, but because I must watch my space) we do not believe in those automatic 'economic laws'. Marx 'proved' that hours of work would grow longer and wages smaller as the years went by; and he was wrong! He was wrong because he argued from the notion that man is altogether selfish and merely an economic unit. Improvement in working conditions and care for children was at one time regarded as foreshadowing the collapse of England; but Christian men who trusted in God and defied 'economic laws' in His name were abundantly justified.

Marxism in Practice

The Christian does not oppose Marxism, let me repeat, because he disapproves of the Communist idea of society, but because the Marxian theory is so far from the truth that the practice based on it cannot possibly succeed. And as a very determined effort has been made for over thirty years to make Marxism work, we can test the effect of the doctrine in experience.

We believe that man is a spiritual being, and that he can only fully live by the power of the Spirit of God (*see* 2 Cor. 4, especially verses 13–16). So we expect a flagging of energy where the spiritual life is weakened or denied. There may be a spurt of energy when there is a change (new Government, new manager, new minister?), but unless there is a spring of renewal it flickers away. The abiding faith of Christian believers in Soviet Russia, which has surprised and discomfited the League of the Godless, must not be forgotten. The heroism of the defence of Stalingrad has made 'official' Russia begin to wonder again about the human 'soul', and may lead to a healthy transformation of crude Marxist materialism. But the orthodox teaching of Marx is still proclaimed, and the obvious result is a flagging energy which can only be driven to effort by fear—fear of the slave labour camp or fear of 'capitalist aggression', so assiduously proclaimed by radio and Press. When the vision of baseless enthusiasm fades, as it must, the whip returns. There are more exiles, more prisoners, and more police in Soviet Russia than in the worst days of the Czars.

And how the rosy dreams have faded! Marx, the theorist, believed that the Communist Utopia was at hand. Stalin, who has to tackle the practical problems, now says that there will be a thousand years of painful struggle before it comes. The easy talk of liberty and the withering of the power of the State has given place to the iron dictatorship of the proletariat; which is, in practice, the Kremlin and the elite of the Communist party. The confident assumption that equality could be established by passing a law has come slap up against the reality of sin (for it was soon discovered that if all men got equal wages many of them were willing to let others do the work!), and a marked and growing inequality has returned. Liberty and equality are good things . . . but they are qualities of spiritual beings, not of economic robots (2 Cor. 3 [17]; 8; 14).

The Challenge to the Christian

On the field of doctrine the Christian has everywhere the advantage of the Marxist, and it is right and proper that the emptiness of Marxist promises should be exposed. But I cannot, with a good conscience, end on a note of complacent superiority. It is both a challenge to us, and a criticism of us, that so much courageous devotion has been enlisted in so poor a cause. The plain fact is that our doctrine is true, but we do not always practise what we preach. For many years, and often with good reason, the Christian Church has been associated with 'God bless the squire and his relations, And keep us in our proper stations'. Too often the sound doctrine that we should be content with that station *to* which God should call us has been interpreted to mean that we should be content with that station in which man has put us.

The report of the first Assembly of the World Council of Churches is a sign of the deepening realization that the Christian cannot be content passively to accept injustice and exploitation. We have a Gospel for society, which is not merely politics with a flavour of preaching but a word from God of warning and hope. But we cannot expect the world to take much notice of us unless, like the Church of the apostolic days or the early Methodist societies or the Primitive Methodist revival, we live the faith we proclaim (*see* 1 Tim. 4 [12], noting that 'conversation=manner of life').

There is a fight now on for the soul of man and the future of the world. Sustained by the infinite resources of God and the power of His Spirit, there is no reason for us to be despondent or fearful; but there is every reason for us to be alert and disciplined; ready to instruct those that oppose themselves, if God peradventure will give them repentance to the acknowledging of the truth (2 Tim. 2 [25]). Without malice, without prejudice, we must out-think and out-live the Marxian to recapture the enthusiasm of youth for the service of the Prince of Peace and for their own good.

But though we are called on to oppose Marxian doctrines, our preaching *must* be without malice and without prejudice. There are those who would be most willing to take the Christian Church as an ally—for their own purposes. For them the appropriate message would be Lk. 12 [14-21]. The spring of our witness is not an opposition to change, but a call to man to inherit the Kingdom that God intended him to have.

Book List

The Scrutiny of Marxism. J. M. Cameron (S.C.M. Press).
A Christian Looks at Communism. Edward Rogers, M.A., B.D. (Epworth Press).

STUDY FOUR. DOCTRINE AND CONDUCT

Aim: To consider the Christian doctrine of man as it affects personal conduct, with particular reference to two great social problems.

Bible Readings:

James 2: Faith and conduct.

Isaiah 28: A solemn warning.

Romans 14: The guide to Christian conduct.

1 Corinthians 8–10: Not all things are expedient.

2 Peter 1: Faith . . . virtue . . . knowledge . . . temperance.

In this Study we shall be principally concerned with the two questions of Temperance and Gambling, looking at them with the great doctrine that has been our main concern well in our minds. After the call to service in a mighty cause which was our theme in the last Study, this may seem to be a considerable come-down—if one may judge by the way in which the Conference direction that the third Sunday in November shall be observed as Temperance Sunday is quietly side-stepped by ministers and local preachers alike!

But is it really a come-down? We are in very good company, and in a great tradition, when we bring home our doctrine to details of personal conduct. The letter to the Ephesians begins with the great cosmic conflict between good and evil, and the purpose of God that all creation shall be harmonized and redeemed by the work of Christ. But the wise apostle does not end there. The redemption of this world is to be accomplished through the work of Christ in his Body, and we are members of his Body (*see* Eph. 4). So *all our actions* will either forward or retard God's purpose. Covetousness, drunkenness, the relationship between parent and child or master and servant—these have all to be regarded by the Christian as things related to this great and universal purpose.

I suspect that the real source of our diffidence is that, as preachers, we have a healthy dislike of negative preaching. We have heard it said so often that the Christian Church is like the mother who ordered: 'Go and see what Bobby is doing, and tell him not to!' that we tend to steer clear of 'Thou shalt not'. We have a positive Gospel to preach. We remember that Jesus took the negative Rule of the Pharisee (Don't do to others what you don't want them to do to you) and changed it to a positive and effective command (Lk. 6 31). It is possible to have a reputation for being 'nice and quiet and good', when the truth is that you would like to assert yourself and follow the black sheep but haven't the courage or the energy!

But when all the excuses are weeded out, and the valid reasons accepted, it remains true that there can be no positive preaching which has not its negative side. The positive command to take the narrow way which leads to life necessarily involves turning away from the broad way that leads to destruction. Paul commended honest work—and at the same time laid it down that those who stole should steal no more (Eph. 4 28). In fact, unless both notes can be heard in our preaching, our positiveness may end in vague high-sounding generalities, and it may justly be charged against us that we give too little clear guidance about the problems of daily life. Jesus taught and lived to offer men the love of God; but the wonder of the offer is enhanced and made distinct by the background of solemn warning to those who rejected that life-giving love (N.B.—It is sometimes said that Jesus laid down no rules, but gave general principles. Do you agree? Read Mt. 7).

Moreover, as we saw in our quick glance at Ephesians, the New Testament leaves us in no doubt that conduct matters (Rom. 6 1-2; Col. 3 for example). I select two thoughts for our guidance. (1) Our conduct is a real reflection of the vigour of our spiritual life. This is the personal side. I know something of the quality of the life that is lived in the power of the Holy Spirit. As I look at Jesus I see what a 'true man' is like. We can always justify ourselves by comparison with others (2 Cor. 10 12), but not when we measure ourselves by his standard. If we are boastful, impatient, quick tempered, easily discouraged (1 Cor. 13), it is a sign of spiritual weakness. We are known by our fruits; and we know whether they are the fruits of the Spirit or not. (2) Our conduct, giving the weight of example to our preaching is the way in which we can best witness to the outside world. This is the social side (see Col. 4 5). It is the Christian 'way' that will win the world; a way of living and a sound doctrine. It is true that we preach not ourselves but Christ crucified; but our listeners have a habit of assessing the truth of our doctrine from the evidence of its effect on us—which is a sound enough method! A bald-headed barber is not the best salesman of hair-restorer. A bad-tempered preacher is not the best exponent of

Christian love (cf. Gal. 1 [24-25]). James 1 [26] is a word to be taken very seriously.

So, remembering both our duty to ourselves and to our neighbours, remembering that we are all the creatures of God and that 'no man liveth to himself', let us examine the two matters which our Church has declared to be social evils with the conviction that they are as important as, for instance, Marxian ideology.

Gambling

If the size of the financial turnover is anything to go by, gambling today provides one of our major national industries. Annual expenditure has steadily risen, and is now close to the astronomical sum of £1,000,000,000 per annum; spent on horse and greyhound racing, football betting, and 'amusement' machines. We can estimate this total because we have reliable statistics on these forms of gambling; but if we could add the expenditure on personal bets, local raffles, and factory pontoons the figure would swell to even more bloated proportions. This is a very big thing; which means that it is either a very big social good or a very big social evil. The Christian ought not to have much doubt as to which it is.

It would be well for us to define what we mean by gambling, lest we become entangled in the sophistries of those who say 'All life is a gamble' and go on to argue that there cannot, therefore, be anything seriously wrong with the practice. By gambling we mean 'a stake upon chance for gain without labour'.

(a) There must be something 'on' the gamble—money or goods. Tossing up for choice of ends in a football match is not gambling. Playing 'Happy Families' with the youngsters is not gambling. But if I bet you ten shillings that I win the toss, or if the winner at 'Happy Families' gets the Christmas pudding, that *is* gambling.

(b) The transaction must depend upon luck. The cardsharper, who can 'place' his deal, is not a gambler—he is a criminal. If I could read the future, and *knew* that Bubbly Boy the Second would win the 2.30, I should not be gambling if I put my money on him; I should be fraudulently gaining money by false pretences. But I am gambling when I fill up my Pool form, though I do it with mathematical devotion to permutations and combinations round my 'bankers', for I am staking my money on the unknown.

(c) Life is full of risk, and made up of probabilities. (A great door and effectual is opened unto me, and there are many adversaries; i.e. I don't know how this will turn out, but I must take the chance in the service of my Lord. 1 Cor. 16 9.) The founder of a new company, the man who leaves one job for another, the explorer—all these take risks. But they do not expect reward without effort. The appeal of gambling is 'Twenty thousand pounds for a penny', or 'This lovely tea-cosy for threepence'.

And now to face the issue! It's my money, I get a kick out of waiting to see if I've won or not, I don't hurt anybody else, so why shouldn't I have a flutter?

Because, in fact, I do hurt other people, and so offend against the law of Christian charity. There is a fundamental difference between gambling and every other economic transaction. If you study carefully industrial statistics or estimates of family expenditure drawn up for fixing such things as pension rates, you will find no mention of gambling. The reason is that in gambling there is no mutual satisfaction, but simply the transfer of money from one set of pockets to another. If I buy a pair of kippers, my money pays for the labour and services of the fishermen, curers, transporters, wholesalers, and retailers; and the kippers satisfy me. In a sound economic transaction everybody gains, for that is the basis of exchange. But if I win £1,000 by guessing four draws, others *must* have lost that amount. If I win the raffled tea-cosy, all the others lose their threepences. A system whereby one can gain only at the expense of others runs directly contrary to the Christian basis of society.

We could go on farther to show that, through the haphazard and chancy redistribution of money through the community by gambling, there is a serious net economic loss and a lowering of the general standard of living; but we have already said enough to make good the point that the practice is socially bad. It can just as vigorously be condemned as individually harmful. Its great appeal is that it offers an artificial thrill to people wearied with the dreary monotony of life. In other words, it offers a poor substitute to those whose supreme need is the real zest of life. It perverts and leads astray that longing for fullness of life which can only be satisfied when a man enters into the inheritance prepared for him by God. It feeds the soul-destroying tendency to greed, and breeds all manner of superstitious folly. Its dearly cherished dream is the lucky windfall. It tries to build the house of life on the uncertain sands of chance. How can the Christian, knowing that he is the beloved child of God and that Christ has called him so to labour that he may build his house upon the rock, reconcile his Gospel with gambling?

For these reasons, our Conference expressly condemns all gambling on Church premises, and all gambling methods to raise funds for Church causes. Admittedly, it seems a trifle priggish to refuse to fork out threepence for a ticket, when the proceeds are to help a family in distress. 'I don't want the tea-cosy! But it's a good cause.' So what? The obligation of Christian discipleship is clear. If the cause is really good, I can help without mingling my generosity with gambling, and I ought to.

Temperance

We made up our mind about gambling by trying to fit it into the whole body of Christian doctrine; and we face this second question in the same way. Gross over-indulgence in alcohol is immediately and obviously condemned. Drunkenness is among the works of darkness that the Christian has cast off (Rom. 13 [13]) because it impairs the judgement, enfeebles the reason, and makes man lower than the animals. The individual personality created by God, redeemed by His Son, whose body is intended to be the temple of the Holy Spirit, is corrupted and spoiled.

Nowadays we don't preach much about drunkenness. Perhaps, to my mind mistakenly, we assume that it is not a serious problem today. Surely the revelations of the war-time evacuation measures, which spot-lighted a half-forgotten section of our nation and appalled 'decent folk' by unmistakable evidence of the way in which many of our fellow-citizens have grown accustomed to live, should shake our too comfortable complacency. Perhaps, too, we take it for granted that all our people know where we stand; forgetting that it is one part of our duty as preachers to repeat the obvious—for there is always a new generation rising which needs to be taught.

But what about moderate drinking? Even if over-indulgence is wrong, it does not logically follow that moderate indulgence is. An inordinate fondness for ice-cream is a bad thing, it might be argued, but an occasional sixpenny tub is not thereby forbidden. We can agree with that logic. The clear arguments against drunkenness are not automatically valid against moderation, and we should not speak as though they were. But there are other arguments to consider. Let us remember again that our approach is to be doctrinal, along the lines of personal self-discipline, personal example, and social responsibility.

Concerning social responsibility, I begin with the fact that the Liquor Trade is a very efficiently organized industrial colossus. If we had not grown up with it, we should be amazed at the quiet acceptance of an industry so highly organized to profit from human weakness. The total expenditure for 1947 was £678,000,000. The brewers' profits, after allowance for wear and tear of plant and machinery and deduction of National Defence Contribution, Excess Profits Tax, and Profits Tax payable, were no less than £49,000,000. (Up-to-date figures and useful information are regularly given in *The Christian Citizen* the magazine of the Order of Christian Citizenship—to which every Local Preacher who takes his commission seriously ought to belong!) There is no comparison between conditions in the pastoral community of Palestine, with an irregular and often dangerous water-supply—think how pleased the woman of Samaria was when she thought that Jesus was talking about a spring of fresh water—and our community, in the grip of this commercial mammoth. My 'moderation' strengthens and supports a system that may lead to the undoing of my brother.

As for personal example, we cannot do better than work out the argument of Paul in 1 *Corinthians*. He is talking about 'meat offered to idols', and is emphatic that he has a perfect right to eat it if he wants to. Even though his eating shakes the faith of a 'weaker brother', there is no legal obligation on him to refrain. But, as a Christian who loves his brother man, he is under the obligation of love. 'All things are lawful for me, but all things edify not.' For the other man's sake, I will not eat. (It would be a good idea to trace the course of the profound argument of 1 Cor. 8-10, preferably with the help of the Moffatt N.T. Commentary).

Paul is dealing with a practice which he considers to be quite harmless, but he is ready to abstain for the sake of others. (Note particularly 8 [12]). We are dealing with a practice which we know to have led to the downfall of others. We follow Paul, and have never declared total abstinence to be a legal obligation, but we commend it as an obligation of grace.

As for the individual and personal angle, we have to seek understandingly and charitably for the reason why men drink alcohol. The basic reason is that they are not satisfied with themselves as they are, or with their life as it is. They feel they need to kindle the 'fire of soul' with the 'taper of conwiviality' —which is not a printer's error, but a quotation from *The Old Curiosity Shop*. They have to 'sink one or two' before they warm up at the Club dance. They feel better with a little drop of something inside. They can forget their troubles for an hour or so. And all of this is substantially true. Alcohol depresses the higher brain, which controls memory and judgement—and that is just what the drinker wants!

And here we are back at the point we reached when we analysed gambling. This is the substitute way, the deceptively easy way of escape from life; to be condemned because it drugs the 'divine discontent' that is there to lead a man to God. If this thing is a hindrance to the spirit's search for God we cannot take it light-heartedly into our own lives.

The statement issued by our Conference in 1948 admirably and pointedly summarizes the issue. 'Alcoholic indulgence inflicts heavy loss and damage on the community in deterioration of character, impairment of health and efficiency, discord in domestic life, neglect and suffering of children, public disorder, the creation and intensification of poverty, economic waste, and in the undue influence of the liquor trade on public affairs. Since the social, economic, and spiritual consequences are so formidable, moderate drinking is a refusal to lay aside a disabling weight, a condonation of the traffic, and a compliance with evil. In the light of New Testament teaching, a habit so hurtful to ourselves, our fellows and the cause of God must be included in the things that are renounced for the sake of the Kingdom. The Methodist Church, therefore, calls upon its members not as a burdensome duty, but with a high sense of privilege, to abstinence from alcoholic beverages as an essential part of their witness to that abundant life in which no harmful thing can find a place.'

One Last Word!

The two social problems we have been considering are not ends in themselves, The man who has never touched a drop in his life but is a tyrant and a bully at home has missed the way of the Gospel. There is no cause for self-satisfaction if you never gamble, but are too mean to spare a copper for a worthy object. The Christian life is a unity. 'Thou shalt love the Lord thy God with all thy heart and with all thy soul and with all thy strength and with all thy mind; and thy neighbour as thyself' in every sphere of life.

Book List

The Message and Mission of Methodism (Epworth Press).
Lambeth Report, 1948.
Doctrines of the Creeds. O. C. Quick (Nisbet).
The Red Prussian. Leopold Schwarzchild (Hamish Hamilton).
The Way of a Christian Citizen. E. C. Urwin (T. & S. W. Dept.).
Christian Character in the Early Church. F. B. Clogg, M.A., B.D. (Epworth Press).
God and Man. J. Scott Lidgett, C.H., M.A., D.D. (Epworth Press).
The Christian Doctrine of Man. Wheeler Robinson (Nisbet).
The Christian Estimate of Man. Sydney Cave (Duckworth).

2. The Life of Jesus

By the Rev. F. WARBURTON LEWIS, M.A.

I

THE Gospel of Mark opens with a dramatic scene. Away from the haunts of men, crowds are gathering day by day at the call of a mighty prophet who has aroused in Israel expectations of a Day of the Lord that had lain dormant for long. But he has bid them know that the Day will not dawn until they have renounced their sins and themselves made response to their Saviour God. Their answer is to all outward seeming nation-wide and complete, and their expectation is of an opening heaven and a Divine Deliverer clothed with power, who will bring them 'deliverance from our enemies and from the hand of all that hate us . . . that we may serve our God without fear in holiness and righteousness all our days' (Lk. I $^{71-5}$). The mighty prophet is welding them into a company committed to this hope, thronging about him in tumultuous excitement stimulated by the long pent-up desires of a captive and fanatical people longing to regain its freedom among the nations of men.

As we watch this great multitude crowding the brink of Jordan, our eye is caught by a young man in workman's garb slipping quietly through the crowd until he reaches John. So Jesus comes from Nazareth—to John's surprise, for this young carpenter is surely already ranged on God's side—and, with heart and mind burning with flame of devotion, commits himself to the cause of God and Israel. If we ask whence he came, we find no answer in the stories with which Matthew and Luke preface his appearance at the Jordan; neither shepherds watching their flocks nor 'wise men from the east' make any contribution to our knowledge of him. But Luke, before telling his own great story of that life and death, has gathered precious records of a group of godly folk who were 'looking for the consolation of Israel' (2 ^{25}). Zacharias and Elizabeth, Mary, Joseph, Simeon and Anna belonged to the quiet folk of the land who cherished the things of God in their hearts; folk from whom in days past not a few of the Psalms had come. Out of this environment came Jesus to offer himself with full heart and burning will to his God, and, all unexpectedly, to make discovery of himself as he was in God's eyes.

There had never been an hour on earth like this. For Jesus, the heavens were rent and the earth fell away. He was alone with his God who claimed him as 'My Son'. He was caught up into the chariot of the Most High and held eternally in His power. Amazedly he knew himself to be the Son of God. The experience at the Jordan was not play-acting, but the actual Word of Revelation calling Jesus to his true stature and destiny. We can do no more than dwell here, and let the 'sense' of it—the amazing, staggering revelation of the eternal truth—fill our minds and hearts. 'Son of God' is what he had been before the gates of birth closed behind him, and now the hand of God has drawn back those gates, and he is once more at home with the Father. His call henceforth is to live in this hour and make his sonship real upon earth. Then at last would the kingdom, that is the Sovereignty, of God be here. The Revelation, 'Thou art My Son,' had a twofold meaning for Jesus. Supremely it meant the knowledge and possession of the Eternal Sonship which had been his 'before the world was' (Jn. 17 [5]). And it also had its Jewish meaning, 'Messiah,' being thus a call to fulfil that name and show himself to be Israel's Deliverer.

Seized and possessed by this overwhelming Act of God, Jesus finds himself in the wilderness alone with the wild beasts. We cannot measure the loneliness. To him alone of men has God so spoken, and with no one can he yet, if ever, share his incredible secret. As the days pass the Word of God wholly possesses his mind: he is Son of God on earth, and his call is to make that Sonship the salvation of men. Again, we cannot fathom the depth of heavenly joy, wonder and peace that filled his soul in its communion with the Father. But who would believe him, and how indeed make that life of communion a daily and an eternal fact in the streets and then in the hearts of men? Days of thought on this level at length left him weary and hungry, to find himself in the grey wilderness under grey skies, with the wild beasts. 'God's beloved Son?! Tell it not in Jerusalem, lest the daughters of the circumcized scoff and deride. Do you feel like Son of God? Do you still really believe that hallucination of the Jordan? Then why not act on that conviction

—nay, prove its truth by making these stones bread? It is proof you want—take it' (Mt. 4³).

This was one of the moments when the angels held their breath; the fate of God is in the balance, and that of the Devil. The battle is set and the fight is on. The Prince of Evil cannot but endeavour with all his might to pluck this faith of Jesus from his heart. Salvation is by faith always, and Satan is the Prince of unbelief: he would not believe in Job (1¹¹), nor in Israel (Zech. 3¹), and he will not now believe that the carpenter's son can bear the stupendous weight of this revelation: he will tear this faith from his heart. 'Son of God, alone, untended by angelic hosts, clad in homespun with a carpenter's bench awaiting your return to sanity, with grey skies unbroken by any word from on high? Messiah, called of God, but left alone to tell that to an Israel which slays her prophets? What have you to rely on, to stand on?' Then Jesus arose and threw Satan down: 'I have the Word of my God, and by that Word of His to me ("Thou art My Son"), and by that alone, I will live.' The battle is won.

But it is not finished. We already see that, so far from Jesus being exempt from temptation, the depth of his temptation was greater than anything we can experience. But so also was the range greater. His immediate task was to win Israel for God. How? But surely that is easy: 'If you *are* Son of God, act on that as a fact; assume your rights and fearlessly fling yourself on the battlements of Israel—they cannot resist you and the hosts of God.' And so here Jesus puts all that aside once for all. He has been called amid the ways of men, and amid those ways where God has placed him he will work out his salvation and the salvation of men. Not presumption, but obedience is the way of Sonship (Mt. 4 ⁵⁻⁷).

But the range of the temptation is wider still (Mt. 4 ⁸⁻¹⁰), matched only by the range of his mind. He is facing life—nay, life is wrestling with him. The exhilaration of the conflict is flooding his spirit with energy and power. Life calls him, all the kingdoms of life are calling him, all of them may be his. He has but to go the way of men, and what realm is beyond his grasp? What realm of art or of thought? What realm of conquest? The world of men is one under Caesar? If that were his, easy were it to bring a world to God. He had magnitude of mind for greatest things: all may be his. But he is God's, and God's only shall be the service of his days and the undivided worship of his mind. His armour is adjusted, his mind attuned to the Father's; he bids Satan be gone, and sets forth for Galilee clad only in faith, to make good that faith wherever the days lead him.

What that faith was is revealed in the Fourth Gospel, where the story of Jesus begins just here as he returns from the dread field of temptation (Jn. 1 ^{36}). He makes a tremendous impression on the Baptist (1 ^{29}): he has come out of a great experience and is being carried forward by an overwhelming consciousness of fellowship with the Father which is almost visible to onlookers 'as he walked'. He is conscious now (1 $^{1-18}$) of a communion with the Father reaching back to the beginning when 'the Word was with God', as it is now on the earth. The light that had lit the hearts of men in a world that knew him not was now burning in his heart. This light he would now take to the people of Israel —would they receive him? And he knows amazedly that, if they accept him, he can give them 'the right (authority) to become children of God'. He is going to pitch his tent in the streets of men that they may see the glory of God, and that so grace and truth may at last dwell among them. Thus it was that 'Jesus returned in the power of the Spirit into Galilee to preach good tidings to the poor . . . and to proclaim the acceptable year of the Lord' (Lk. 4 $^{14-19}$). 'See the Christ stand!'

II

So irresistible was Jesus as he returned from his consummate mastery of life in the dread conflict in the wilderness, girt now with the Spirit's power and triumphant joy, that men left the Baptist, and on his way back to Galilee some half-dozen young men gathered at his side. With them he lit the marriage day of a friend in Cana, and then went on with his mother—What a change she would find in him!—to Capernaum (Jn. 1 ^{37}-2 ^{12}). And here, in Capernaum, he made his headquarters during his Galilean ministry, ever returning home to this city from his journeys. Here (Mt. 4 $^{13-16}$) in the heart of 'Galilee of the nations' the great light sprang up. That light came from the heart of Jesus as we see it shining in his wonted place of worship at Nazareth, when he riveted the attention of his audience who only sit in wonder at the words, not of thunder but of grace, that fell from his lips (Lk. 4 $^{16-22a}$: the rest of this paragraph must

be dated two years later, as in Mk. 6 $^{1-6}$). Here in Capernaum
he summoned to his side some of the young men who had
walked with him from the Jordan to Cana and who left their
fishing nets and boats to serve him (Mt. 4 $^{18-22}$). In a few days
(Jn. 2 ^{12}) he was ready and set out to tour all Galilee (Mt. 4 $^{23-5}$),
and in this paragraph, one of the most neglected in the Gospels,
the first Evangelist gives us a very remarkable account of his
earlier ministry, teaching in the usual places of worship which
for some time were quite open to this new and amazing prophet;
preaching broadcast the good news of God and His approach to
men in His kingdom now being established in their midst; and
withal scattering the demons of sickness and disease that
oppressed the people. The climax comes after months of labour,
when it was seen that the whole land (v. 25) was thrilled by his
work and presence.

Mark (1 ^{21f}) gives us a flash-light glimpse of this work as it
fell out on one Sabbath day. In the synagogue men realized that
here was a new kind of teaching, utterly removed from the formal
professional disquisitions of their customary teachers. Though
unable to explain it, they recognized an authentic note of
authority. Long years afterwards this was put into memorable
words of ultimate truth: 'The Law was given through Moses;
Grace and Truth came through Jesus Christ' (Jn. 1 ^{17}). The
Scribes' teaching was nought but commentary on their Law;
Jesus was free of the mind of God. And in the presence of this
burning mind of the preacher, the demons of evil were disturbed
and then thrust out of their ill-gotten and illegitimate citadels
in the minds and bodies of men. As the congregation streamed
out of church that morning, his fame went out on every tongue
and by every highway into all Galilee. So was it only natural
that, as he entered Simon's house, radiant in mind and glowing
in health, sickness should vanish as darkness before light, and
the family, with his friends, should be gathered in quietness and
peace as their hostess attended to their needs. But no sooner had
the Sabbath ended with set of sun than the city broke into action
and thronged the street with their helpless and hopeless sick
folk. Had Jesus ever so filled a day with labour? Had he ever
slipped into his mother's home so wearied—and so satisfied?

Nevertheless he was up and away before dawn, praying in
some lonely spot (Mk. 1 ^{35}). Here we meet what became a habit
with him—to seek counsel with the Father whenever confronted

with a problem in his work. It is idle to talk of Jesus habitually spending nights in prayer; that was not a habit of his, but our historians record for us occasions when, as here, decisive decisions had to be taken, and they were always taken in the solitude of the Father's counsel-room. For the very success of that Sabbath day was in itself a temptation—the temptation to build on it, to make his headquarters his throne. Victory seemed nearer than he had thought. He had found what the people wanted, and along that line he could run and be glorified. But would this be the glory of God? Would it be building on rock or on sand? The answer came clearly, and he is away on another long tour of the towns of Galilee, that there too men may see the light, if, peradventure, they will turn from their chosen gods to him, and find life that is life indeed. But the curious embarrassment of Capernaum kept on meeting him, and his popularity became a furore (Mk. 1 [45]). His very solitude became a hospice for wounded men—from every quarter they came, and after some weeks of work he went back to Capernaum. We must recognize here a critical fact that Jesus, in communion with the Father, knows once for all time that the supreme salvation which is his work does not lie primarily on the plane of physical well-being, but in the sovereignty of his own spiritual life which must become for men the bread of heaven come down from above.

During his evangelistic tours Jesus has been confronted by a stubborn fact—the fact that, by the unassailed and inviolable custom and tradition of his nation, two sets of men and women were shut out from his ministrations, for it was the unquestioned dictum of the day that for these religion had no message—they were beyond the pale. These were the tax-collectors, the outcasts of society, with whom it was more than your position in society was worth for you to be seen dining; and the religious outcasts, the folk who 'kept not the law' and had no lot or part in the true Israel. These folk Jesus would see on the outskirts of the crowds listening, wistfully it may be, but themselves convinced that they had no part in all this. (Seventeen centuries later, Wesley found the same thing in a nominally Christian land and church.) Here then is the next call to Jesus of the flaming heart. But how bridge the impassable gulf? He cannot preach to men who regard themselves as beyond the pale. They cannot cross to him; he must cross to them. So he summons a tax-collector to his side, and bids Matthew (Mk. 2 [14-17]) know that he is needed, for his own sake indeed, but chiefly for the sake of the folk dwelling in the land of hopeless night. To break bread with others was the final proof of fellowship, and he can now pour out his heart to them. Wherever now the Galilean preacher goes there are no longer any outsiders. But concurrently with this conquest of the unclean land there goes out the horror-stricken cry: 'He is eating with publicans and sinners.' In the judgement of men, his first strategic mistake. In the mind of Jesus, his clear declaration that there are two classes of men: those who are satisfied with their religious standing, and those who know themselves lost in the maelstrom of this life but for the mercy of God now come down from heaven to earth. He takes his Gospel to those beyond the pale, let the 'righteous' think and say what they may. Jesus is standing before us, *Saviour of men*.

III

The ministry outlined in Mt. 4 [23-4] has by now lasted anything up to nine or ten months and has covered all Galilee, echoing through Syria. There is yet Judea to be evangelized (v. 25), and it is here that the Fourth Gospel, when rearranged in its original order, helps us. We have seen that John records the beginning of the Galilean work in 2 [12], but he does not encroach on Mark's narrative. Now we have to take Jn. 3 [22-30], which falls properly between 2 [12] and 2 [13], as our guide. Having for the time completed his Galilean ministry, Jesus leaves Capernaum and carries his Gospel into 'the land of Judea', taking with him a band of disciples for his work, encountering the Baptist by the way. And in Judea, Jesus will meet official opposition, inspired from Jerusalem, from which he has so far been mercifully free in Galilee, and soon the skies will darken.

It is the season of the Passover and of the ripening corn (Mk. 2 [23-8])—the first spring of the ministry at the end of what we may think of as the first year, though we cannot exactly date the opening of it. He and some of his men, one Sabbath day, are walking radiantly through the ripening fields, glad to be alive and glad to pluck and eat the corn around them, as was the custom of the land. A pleasant enough picture! But then the storm broke. They are breaking the Sabbath! Anathema! Their exuberant life in God's open air and in the vivid fellowship of their Master is clamped down by the ordinances of a statutory religion of Law shutting out liberty and light. And here we see Jesus arise in that might which met the challenge of Life in the wilderness. No barren victory in argument will suffice: there must be deliverance once and for all. The ears of corn are for men; the Sabbath is for Man. No longer shall men be victims of a statute, prisoners of a 'sacred' day. He stands forth Master of the Sabbath, and war is declared in Israel.

But it is when he enters the synagogue that this becomes clear beyond gainsaying (Mk. 3 $^{1-6}$). Apparently it is a quiet enough scene: a congregation gathered for the customary Sabbath worship. But the air is charged with electricity, for sitting there are a crippled man and Jesus. If they meet, the discharge will come. Jesus has only to sit still and the threatened storm will pass. But to remain unmoved by that man's mute appeal were to rivet more tightly the Sabbatic chains. Jesus accepts the challenge, and bids the man stand up. How tense the scene! But how surprising the question Jesus asks: 'Is it lawful on the Sabbath day to do good? to do harm? Is it the day that matters, or the deed? To save a life—of how much more value is a man than a day? to kill?' Kill? Yes, the rapier of the Deliverer is right through; these men who would forbid him to heal this man on this day are at the very moment planning in their hearts to kill Jesus. And out they went to perfect their plans. The work of Jesus may yet cost him his life.

And now Jesus completes the first year of his ministry by going to Jerusalem at the time of the Passover (A.D. 27) that from the very Temple of God he may make his great appeal to men (Jn. 2 ^{13f}). For some twenty years the thrill of his boyhood's visit had dwelt in his heart. 'If only from that place he could win a sway over the hearts of the children of earth, then verily that Temple would become the centre of his Father's Kingdom.' And on his entry, in the only place assigned to the children of earth, he is met by the reek of a cattle-market and the chaffering of merchants. He has come to gather Jerusalem with the love of God and enters the place that should have been sacred with the prayers of the spirits of men, sensibly the focus of God's presence and man's awareness of Him, only to find it a house of fraud and the haunt and refuge of the crooks of the Empire, a den of brigands (Mk. 11 ^{17}). Then, with the anger of God sweeping through his heart, this son of the hills and winds of Galilee clears that court, and knows now that he must clear much else.

All that might have been glowed, a lovely picture, in his heart; what Israel had made of it lay before him—and he drove it out with the sword of God's wrath, eaten up with zeal for God's House.

To understand the crisis that followed, we have absolutely to ignore Jn. 2 21–22, which, like some dozen other verses, is an interpolation interrupting and misinterpreting the narrative. The break with Judaism has come, suddenly, but finally. Confronted by the authorities in charge of this Temple, of this travesty of God's hope, he bids them go on with their ghastly work till Titus makes an end; there is no hope here for man's salvation. He will build another religion and he will begin now Then he leaves them to their doom; he will never keep another Passover in Jerusalem. There must be a new Israel, a new Act of God. Two years later they will quote his words, words never forgotten, against him at his trial when he is being hounded to death for this very thing, his attempt to build a Temple not made with hands (Mk. 14 58). But by then he will have instituted a New Covenant and his foes are too late.

He leaves Judea and turns northward (Jn. 4) by the shortest and usual route to Galilee, suddenly liberated from all that had cramped his days; he can now find his own way without reference to Israel and his early hopes that in Israel he might find the vehicle for the will of God. 'Find his own way?' How do you build the Church of God? What are her foundations and where the pinnacles of her hope? His mind now is wholly here, and his men find him strangely silent and absorbed. They leave him to his reverie, sitting by a well, relaxed for an hour, wearied, not so much by the journey, as by stress of thought and labour of heart, thirsting to drink wine new in a new kingdom of God with those that shall be his.

And one of them is drawing water in the mid-day heat—it is like the opening of a window on to long vistas of hope and light. His thoughts are of a religion free from all that has cramped the spirit of man—free from Jerusalem and from Gerizim—and here is one thirsting for that truth. It is a new situation, and not only the parched lips but the parched heart of the Father's Son is refreshed as he draws to himself a mind free from inhibitions and vainly hoping for that Christ who should come and 'declare unto us all things'. Jesus is not answering her questions so much as thinking aloud of the Gospel newly born in his heart. 'I that speak unto you am he'—he now knows himself as never before, the Founder of a new City of God, into which many like unto this woman will enter to find the peace of God at last. It is an hour of exhilaration—the weariness has gone, his fingers are on the organ of God's hope; he lifts his eyes to see the fields white unto harvest (v. 35). And above all that, he lifts his eyes to the Father who 'seeketh such to be his worshippers' (v. 23). Above the thirst of Jacob's well is the thirst of God; he tells her so; and then sets out on his life-long task of slaking that thirst, that his Father may at last also have rest. He stayed two days with her people, and they, first of all men, declared him to be 'the Saviour of the world' (v. 42).

IV

In that consciousness Jesus returned to Galilee, soon to be followed by crowds from every part of the land which he had visited, this being the culmination of that early ministry which we have seen summarized by Matthew (4 25), now recorded by Mark (3 7–8) as he leads us from the first year of the ministry to the opening of the second. And here we have not the mere passage from one year to the next, but a definitive change in the work. In his work at Nazareth, Jesus had seen good builders dig down through the sand and rubble to the rock which alone would hold the weight of a house. A similar need faces him now, and a temptation. The temptation is to take the easy way and let the enthusiasm of the crowd carry him to a swift and spectacular triumph, thus confounding his enemies. But the Church of which he dreamed by Sychar's well cannot be built on sand; crowds afford no sufficient foundation for the Eternal; it is clear that work more thorough and permanent is needed now. He will not yet use the word, but Jesus now sets himself to build his Church. He turns from the crowd (Mt. 5 1) and gathers a company of disciples into what we may call a Summer School on some fair spot among the hills, and this school we must think of as continuing, not merely for a few weeks now, but from time to time through the ensuing months. Fortunately we have record of this teaching in Mt. 5–7, and these pages become properly luminous for us as we come to them thus and find them to be, not a system of Christian ethics issued for mankind, but an unfolding in fellowship by Christ of the manner of life in the new City of

God. Our record (Mt. 5 ³ᶠ) begins with the colours of the Christian character as the light of the everyday plays upon it. Founded in a fathomless humility, a complete willingness not to gain but to be blest with the fullness of God's grace, and a faith for ever unshakable that it is the Father's determined good pleasure to give us the kingdom of His own life (Lk. 12 ³²)—here is the foundation of our salvation, even salvation, not by merit or by achievement, but by grace (cf. Eph. 2 ¹⁻¹⁰). It will be found that 'the kingdom of heaven' is, as Paul discovered, 'righteousness and peace and joy in the Holy Ghost' (Rom. 14 ¹⁷). It was here that Jesus lived, and into this life he would gather his beloved. They will find all life redeemed by being raised into a light from heaven. Sorrow will no longer overcome the disciple, but be transformed into, not exchanged for, joy. Earth, and its daily beauty, will become a daily gift of the great Father's will. But, above all that, the insatiable longing of the heart for righteousness, that is, for life that is life indeed and is our very own—even this hunger shall be met and satisfied. Gratefully, as the gentle dew from heaven, will pity and mercy light upon our needy souls as we ourselves look upon men as God looks in His great compassion. And as this life of single-hearted devotion dominates our minds, we shall see Him who is invisible and be caught up into the Divine Fellowship. This Fellowship will then be worked out in the labour of life, in the building of peace, that is, the true wealth of life upon earth according to His will. Thus will our sonship be completed in Him.

How long did Jesus take to show his friends all this, and to fill their hearts with the assurance that this, in God's will, was their lot and inheritance? He then goes on to unfold their fortune, as, heirs of heaven, they make their way among men; it will be derision and persecution, through which they are to pass with gay hearts, greeting the unseen with a cheer (5 ¹²). From this world they are not to turn away or seek to escape; their calling is to live there as the redeeming salt and conquering light. So Christ links his company of disciples with the crowds down below. Those crowds need redemption, and first of all redemption from false gods, and, specifically, from the false ideals standardized among them by the Pharisees and their interpretation of religion in terms of law. Here Jesus finally puts all that aside, bidding his men know that God desires a righteousness of an altogether other and higher kind (5 ²⁰), surpassing incommensurably any life found in legalism. This life must express itself, not in abstention from forbidden deeds, but in a heart clear of intent and purpose of evil (5 $^{21f, 27f}$). Reverence, constant awareness of the presence of the God of Truth, must be the clothing of the mind (5 ^{33f}). Supremely, it is a life of grace; the day's duty duly performed (Lk. 17 ^{10}), we go on to the second mile of uncounted beneficence (5 ^{41}), the liberty of the sons of the God of all grace (5 ^{45}), in tolerance, self-forgetfulness, mercy and love, sons of the Most High (cf. Lk. 6 ^{35}).

With such light from above were the days on the uplands filled, and with such light were the groups of disciples raised into the veritable Kingdom of Heaven, now established on earth, not to be overthrown by storm or flood (7 ^{25}). And we must always bear in mind that this ministry of discipleship went on intensively through this year and the next, and that this heart to heart association with Christ remains for us the only sufficient house of Salvation. One definite act of Jesus, carried out only, as was his habit, after fellowship in prayer and counsel with the Father, was the selection from among the disciples of a small group of Twelve who might be more continuously with him and whom, on occasion, he might be able to use as his colleagues and representatives among the people, better equipped than some for publishing the Gospel through the land (Mk. 3 ^{13f}). And, before leaving the sunlit hills for the vales below, Jesus would look round with a full heart; the Shepherd has gathered and formed his flock; for them he must live; no man shall snatch them out of his hand (cf. Jn. 10 $^{27-8}$); they will follow him, and unto them he will give eternal life—his own life, now and ever. God has given them to him, and they with their successors shall be God's holding among men, a Church where God finds a home —to this end must the Christ work directly, amid all of duty and labour that may meet him on his way.

V

On his return to Capernaum (Lk. 7 ^{1f}), Jesus is strangely and opportunely encouraged by meeting a very unusual man who has thought out a philosophy of life for himself. This Roman captain is awake to the fact that he in himself has no authority, but that being under the authority of Rome, all the power of Rome backs him as he issues his orders. Astonishingly enough, he recognizes that Jesus is in like case, under authority from above and thus empowered for his work. Jesus marvels to meet such understanding, the very insight of faith itself, surpassing any yet found in Israel, and on the next day, upborne by this quickened sense of fellowship with the Most High, meeting hopeless sorrow in the face of a widow bereft of her only son, he speaks the word of God and restores her to her rightful home of joy and love (Lk. 7 [11-17]). Once again in that hour the people knew that 'God has visited his people'. If only they had been faithful to the vision of their highest moments! This veritable Gospel ran like fire through the province and penetrated the prison of the Baptist. If only he could have buried his expectations and with a transformed mind (=repentance) recognized the Christ of God! But the same purblind prejudice prevailed everywhere, and prevented the friendly Pharisee who opened his home to Jesus from recognizing the sheer divine beauty of his guest, as Jesus lifted the sin-haunted woman into pardon and peace (Lk. 7 [36-50])—the act and mien and power of a Saviour in clearest reality and beauty.

Perhaps these months of A.D. 27–28 were the happiest ever lived by a company of men and women on what must have seemed to them God's earth; summer months in the open country, and winter months in and around Capernaum, their days enriched beyond all telling by the presence of their beloved Master. We see them, the winter past, setting out again on their work of evangelizing, and it is here that Luke delivers us from a notion prevalent in many minds, that the only companions of Jesus were the Twelve. Our Evangelist (Lk. 8 [1-3]) shows us a goodly company of women, ladies of Galilee, who had formed themselves into a noble band of helpers who saw to it that Jesus should be free from material cares and anxieties. It was the offering of their love: 'To them 'tis little that they bring; to him 'tis very much.' And what a home of refuge into which to bring such as the woman whom we have seen rescued in the Pharisee's house. How Magdalene and Joanna and Susanna, infused by the spirit of Jesus, would welcome, guard and guide such as she. We must not miss the greatness of Christ's effort; the winter is past and he rallies all his resources for yet another appeal to Galilee, city by city, village after village; his greatest effort in the labour of evangelization, and that of him who spake as never man spake. And the result, nigh unto heartbreak, is given us in what we carelessly label 'The Parable of the Sower' (Lk. 8 ^{4f}). It is only Luke who gives us this *connexion*, and we have generally taken the parable at its surface value and never found in it a nerve of Christ's experience and a tragedy of his life. As the tour went on, the crowds increased day by day, and Jesus became more and more conscious of the contrast between these people who just came, heard, and went their way—between them and the company that had left their tackle and were his very own. The climax was a measureless anti-climax; he faced the crowd and told them a story about a farmer. Then he left them. Not a word about religion. 'It is of no use'; he said, 'they have eyes, but they see not; minds have they, but they think not. The seed of God is good and living, but the soil of their minds, thin, lazy, preoccupied, stuffed with notions, kills it'. So Isaiah had found, so Paul found, and here our Master enters into the very travail of God (which he has bound us to share ever since —'Woe is me, if I preach not the gospel!') So he left the people with a question: 'What does he mean?' If only he can break up the soil of their one-track minds, that the light and seed of God may save them! And, leaving all that desert of unfruitfulness to the Father, Jesus bends himself, from now on, more and more fully, to the company around him, dedicating himself to them and their successors even unto this day. Such is the story of the kingdom, and here we find the great Master dedicating himself to the narrowness of his calling, bringing the choicest seed of his mind to those who will take heed. 'Narrow may be the way, but deep and soft and clean is the soil I shall find, and at the end of the day I shall see of the travail of my soul and be satisfied. The rest is afterwards. Meanwhile my work is just this, my comrades.' To hearts and minds, simple, sincere, and true, he would ever give his uttermost (cf. Jn. 17 $^{6-10, 19}$). But Jesus knows now that his personal effort to win disciples from the towns and villages will fail to cover the ground, and so makes a great venture (Lk. 9 $^{1-6}$), with bated breath it may be; he summons the Twelve and sends them out to extend his ministry far and wide, with results other than he desired. When the Twelve return, exulting and elated (Lk. 9 ^{10f}), they are followed by crowds streaming toward Capernaum to find the new Messiah.

The early instinctive first impression of two years before (Jn. 1 $^{41, 45, 49}$) had by now filled the hearts of his Apostles and overflowed in eloquent and vehement proclamation of the Christ throughout the land. 'We have found the Messiah' echoed through the countryside, and the folk, with unleashed desire and intent, converged together 'from all the cities'. It was in vain that Jesus sought to escape with his men, who were themselves the captives of their own ecstatic preaching. As the next day dawned, he found the landscape covered with a congregation of five thousand men, often enough with their families (Mt. 14 21), in his eyes a great shepherdless flock of sheep knowing not and inherently unable to find their way to green pastures and waters of life. Then was Jesus caught up in the compassion of God (Mk. 6 34), and, flinging aside all hesitation and reserve, with glowing heart he welcomed them, throwing wide the gates of his kingdom (Lk. 9 11). That day—all day long—Jesus spoke as even he had never spoken before. Israel stood before him, and he makes his supreme effort to win her. Neither he nor they notice the passage of the hours eaten up in the eloquence of the burning heart of God pleading for acceptance that He might gather the sheep in peace for evermore. So he kept the Passover, not of Jerusalem, but of God (Jn. 6 4).

Then through the mighty heart of Jesus there strikes the chill of failure. There is no response, and he will never again speak as he has spoken this day. We cannot measure the effort or fathom the grief of the Christ. Even the Apostles know that it only remains to send the people home. This Jesus will not hear of until they have been royally fed, for they have listened all day. A lovely gesture, and a daring, for great is the risk. Jesus chances the risk and loses; for now, at this sign of power, power that may suffice to drive the Roman into the sea, the gathered sons of men who have longed for this hour through the centuries rise as one man and surge upon him to carry him to Jerusalem and the throne of David (Jn. 6 15), and thence to 'all the kingdoms of the world and the glory of them' (Mt. 4 8f). No Caesar could resist such a nation led by such a king. 'Get thee hence, Satan; the kingdom of God is not of this world, and is founded only on his worship.' Alone—he had sent his men away—he sent that surging multitude away; feeding a crowd was child's play compared with that act of mastery and will.

Chilled to the heart, the lone man seeks the solitude of the mountains and the fellowship of the Father. There the night was spent, for there had been no crisis like this. Two years' labour has ended in failure. Israel will not understand and accept. A year before, Jesus had broken with the official religion of priest and Pharisee; now he has broken with the nation. Which way tomorrow? Never before on this earth had there been prayer like unto the prayer of this night. As the day breaks he descends to do his Father's revealed will; to build a New Israel out of his own flesh and blood, in faith divine, at whatever cost. I am not surprised to find him, with heart aflame and mind braced to this mighty task—I am not surprised to find him walking on the water of Gennesaret and calling Peter to follow without doubt or fear, nor that his men bowed in awe in his presence (Mt. 14 [33]). The Christ of God has come.

Jesus then has parted with the people as a nation. They had tried to make him king in their own world and for their own purposes, and he had sent them away; that is over. In the morning he comes down from the mount of divine communion to tell them (Jn. 6 [26-40]) that he, and he alone, is God's Gospel for this world. For two years he had striven to speak to them in their own language; that is now discarded, and from now on *he himself* is for men the Word of Life. So he walks forth among men, God's Word to them. He offers himself as the bread of life, the only life that is life indeed. 'Your fathers ate the manna in the wilderness—and they died' (v. 49). And here we must note a very marvellous thing, a revelation of the innermost being of God; humility, a splendour, not of this earth—the Greeks and Romans had no word and no use for it. God giving Himself to be our bread, our daily bread, come down out of heaven that we may eat thereof and live for ever; 'my flesh, for the life of the world' (vv. 50-1). Upon this, many of his disciples left him, and there now comes before us the picture of a company of men and women who know finally that with their Master alone can they find eternal life (vv. 66-8). But, mark you, the Devil is there; the day will come when this incredible humility will be betrayed into the hands of men (v. 70).

As Jesus sets out on this life and death adventure, he is met by the final challenge of Judaism in the form of an official deputation from Jerusalem (Mk. 7 [1]). Four hundred odd years before, there had come from Babylon a man whose lasting significance has not been properly or fully acknowledged. Ezra, armed with the now fully-developed Jewish Law, made the life of Israel into an inviolable ecclesiastical organization, for ever fenced off from the wider life of man. The voice of the living

Spirit was smothered, and within this hedge of law Israel became narrow and bitter, until she came to pray that her enemies might rot on their feet as they stood and their eyes drop out of their sockets as they fought (Zech. 14 ¹²,¹⁵). Within that wall of Judaism, men like the author of *Jonah* died in despair, and Jesus was born. There he too will die. But not yet. Not before in words of consuming flame he has burned up the prison-bars of their legalism and set men free. Man is defiled—*defiled*—only by what comes out of the heart (Mk. 7 ¹⁵), and there is damnation found (vv. 21–23). So he flings back their Law, impotent before these vices of the heart, and in so doing seals his own fate; the Pharisees are scandalized (Mt. 15 ¹²) and will never forgive; the day will come when a certain Saul of Tarsus will watch Jesus on Golgotha pay for this sacrilege. But that will not be the end; a day will also come when this same Saul will write to the Galatians to carry on this revolution for the salvation of men, that they like him might die unto the law and live unto God (Gal. 2 ¹⁹). And even at the cost of Calvary men must be delivered from every prison into the liberty of sons of God. But this means for Jesus the end of his Galilean ministry; he will return, secretly and hurriedly, now and again, but the glory has departed from Capernaum.

VI

Then Jesus leaves his native land (Mk. 7 ²⁴) where now he has not where to lay his head. He must escape for a while into solitude until he has recovered from the terrific strain of his fight with Judaism. The plaudits of Capernaum would stifle him, and for once the great physician prays that no sick be laid at his feet. He even tries to hide himself. He will do nought until he sees his way once more, and the Father's will. The revelation of this comes in the strangest way, through a woman distraught with anxiety for her child. A year before Jesus found himself opening his mind to a woman (Jn. 4) in a space of freedom from the jurisdiction of the Temple and priestcraft. Now again, it is with a woman that he adjusts the compass on an unknown sea. What is the relation between them? There is none. She knows that she has no claim on the Messiah of the Jews; he is known to her, 'Son of David' (Mt. 15 ²²). And he is thinking of other things, and giving no heed to her intrusion. Then there breaks through upon him that this woman is like the Roman captain (Lk. 7 ⁹) of unusual penetration—she penetrates his consciousness of being rejected by Israel, as men brush the crumbs from the table. Once more, here is more understanding than he has found in Israel. And for her, she makes no claim to sit at Israel's table—'All I ask is to share the crumbs discarded—to sit just inside—may I?—You are opening the door for me thus far? That is all I crave.' 'Thank you from my heart,' says Jesus, 'for that and all that it means. Sit down in my kingdom, open now to all who will; with me from henceforth there is neither Greek nor Jew, barbarian or freeman; the door is open to the flowing Will of God. He is now her Lord, and she one of his company, harbinger of many that shall come from north and south, east and west, home to God.

The break with Judaism is naturally emphasized by the wanderings of Jesus and his companions outside Galilee, from Phoenicia to the district of Caesarea Philippi (Mk. 8 ²⁷). The disciples, it may be, have been surprised and puzzled by the mood of their Master; a certain absorbed aloofness during these days; and at last they are equally startled by a sudden and unprecedented question: 'What are men saying about me now? Who am I supposed to be?' The answer is much as Jesus suspected; the tide has turned, the enthusiasm curbed, the spate of incandescent and revolutionary popularity canalized within safe channels; at the best he can only look for acknowledgement as one of the Lord's prophets. No longer can he look for the support of the people against the bitter hate and assault of the leaders of Judaism. Then what has he left? Anything? Anyone left who has heard and seen the Word of God? And in that fatal hour of crisis, when God's fortune has reached its nadir, steps one into the drift of men's verdicts, the drift of Satan's lies: 'Thou art the Christ of God.' Not we, but only Jesus can measure the significance of that, the permanent difference it will make. But the immediate effect is the release of Christ's heart, breaking out in benediction on Peter's head (Mt. 16 ¹⁷). Now Jesus stands on assured feet. He had not built on the early enthusiasms of these men, but, at every risk, has lived himself out in their midst; and he has won. Against the judgement of their national church, against the resultant vote of the people around them, they have chosen their Christ, and their Christ, and more, he will be.

Gathering these men around him, Jesus begins his final work.

Two years of labour and patience have cleared the sand, and he is down to bedrock. Then comes the creative word: 'Now I will build my Church.' With hewn stones such as Simon, he who learned a builder's trade in Nazareth will now begin to build for eternity. Since the Passover of last year (Jn. 2 ¹³, ¹⁹) he had known and chosen this to be his life work, and now he can begin. He can only leave Jerusalem to Titus, and build where neither moth nor rust, nor storm nor fire can come. But what of Caesar, the towers of whose Temple, indicative of a world-wide sway of unquestioned power, are flashing before him in Caesarea? 'I challenge thee, Caesar. Empires pass away, but behind my Church the gates of Hades, the gates of Death, shall never close.' This is tremendous, and it commands the future, even unto this day.

We can now understand why Jesus forbids them to proclaim him as the Christ—their blunder on their recent preaching tour. He has turned from all that Israel expects her Messiah to be, a conqueror borne from triumph to triumph, visibly omnipotent before all men. Jesus will have none of that, and these men dimly see that he is worth more than all the leaders of Israel. Then Jesus makes another of his critical ventures; he trusts these men to stand the revelation of what awaits him as he pursues this his chosen way, the way of God for His Christ amid recreant men. Crash go all their dreams of seats on a throne. Judas curses inwardly and Simon gasps in incredulous amazement, as Jesus tells them that in the end of the earthly story the leaders of Israel—of Israel, mark you—will get him into their hands and glut their ruthless hearts with his blood. Jesus is deliberately breaking the images of Israel's Messiah dwelling in their hearts. And it is desperately hard work, for Israel had never allowed suffering to have any place in her expected Deliverer's fate or fortune. The Suffering Servant of the prophet of the Exile had not been heeded or understood. Only in the mind of God is the true Christ understood, and the task of Jesus is the seemingly hopeless one of holding his disciples—how many?— to himself until the light of God fills their redeemed and liberated minds. Mark (8 ³¹⁻³) tells us simply that Jesus said all this quite freely and without reserve, and at once nails down the loving and burning protests as the very coin of Satan, the great Seducer of men from the mind of God. And, he bids them know, this in due measure is God's will for them too: if they would still follow him, there is no place for 'self'—that must be crucified now, and, thus liberated, they are to take their lives in their hands, shoulder each man his cross and so follow him to where men crucify. Jesus lifts them into an unearthly realm where earth's values cease to damn, and the truth of eternal life breaks in. It must never cease to amaze us that Jesus expected his people to stand for this, and to stand up to it? Can you imagine what it feels like to be crucified? You would not like your best friends to see you there. And that picture is pale to what it would all mean to men of that day and of Jewish blood. Yet here is Christ's great venture, and he won. Such was his power —may we for once call it his spell?—that in the end even the aristocrat, Saul of Tarsus, will glory in nothing but this (Gal. 2 [20], 6 [14]). So began (Mt. 16 [21]) for men the revelation of what God is like, still only half-believed among us, God in the hands of men who do unto Him what they will. This revelation Jesus will enshrine in his own life as far as Golgotha—and beyond. There are men present who, before they die, will see it and know that the Kingdom of God, not after man's imagining, has come with power (Mk. 9 [1]).

A week later followed the greatest hour (Lk. 9 [28f]) whose significance is so seldom realized by us. The founding of an Eternal Church amid the wrecks of time calls for a supreme session of prayer, and into the quiet of the uplands Jesus went with three of his most intimate disciples. The secret of the Transfiguration is that the hour of his ascension had come, the hour when that perfect life of holiness, of complete personal devotion to God, blossomed into flower and fruition, the natural climax of life on earth when lived unto God, for death is only the wages of sin. Once in man's story has the perfect end been accomplished, and Jesus now stands beneath the heavens opened to receive him, body and spirit blended in perfect triumph of life and beauty. This consummation had been inspiring his consciousness for some little time, and he had recently (Jn. 6 [62]) asked his disciples what they would do if they saw 'the Son of Man ascending where he was before', and our great historian plainly tells us that the time of his assumption had come (Lk. 9 [51]). Jesus has gained the right to enter heaven and sit down on his throne; Moses and Elijah are there to escort him, and all the celestial orchestras are waiting to raise the acclaim as he goes to the Father.

It was not only Peter who wist not what to say in that amazing hour, but far more astounded were Moses and Elijah when Jesus would speak of nothing but a departure, not from Hermon, but from Jerusalem where prophets were wont to be slain. The heavens are opened to him, and the Father's home; but Jesus closes the golden curtains, turns his back upon it all, and sets his face like a flint to go to Jerusalem (Lk. 9 [51]). It was on Hermon first of all that the supreme sacrifice was made. For love of us, Jesus gave up all his rights, all that he had won for himself; refused to go by a way we could not follow; and descended again into fellowship with us in the tragic war with sin and death, that he might blaze a way, at whatever cost, through whatever suffering, a way where we might follow, upborne by love and redeemed by his blood. And—mark you—it was then, when the clouds were once more upon them and all the pageant of glory gone, when Jesus has laid his all on the altar of high sacrifice and is going down to the dumb multitudes in the darkness—it was then, and not till then, that God spoke: '*This* is my beloved Son; hear ye him.' And then there was Jesus only. Today there is Jesus only.

VII

Strangely poignant is the cry wrung from the heart of Christ as he finds himself, after the exaltation of Hermon's open heaven, in the midst, once more, of the feverish life of men: 'O faithless and perverse generation, how long shall I be with you—how long must I bear with you?' Here we suddenly look into an unveiled heart for one sacred moment (Lk. 9 [41]), before he braces himself to face the ultimate issue (v. 44), shoulders the inevitable cross, and sets his face to go to Jerusalem (v. 51). In the supreme hour that will be his on Calvary, we may think of him as uplifted by the very challenge of the dire situation. But meanwhile, he finds himself, like the Suffering Servant in Isaiah 53, despised and rejected in a nameless Samaritan village (v. 52), so contemptuously that James and John are provoked to vengeance—'how long' indeed? But the soul's armour is braced, and to that vulgar reaction he will give no place, he is leaving Galilee, where no longer has he any sure place to lay his head (vv. 57–62); the dead past is buried for him, and he has to create the future; He has set his hand to the plough, with eye fixed on that fellowship with the Father which lies beyond Calvary. Only the Kingdom of God (v. 60) matters now, and, though Capernaum become a jungle mound, though the ploughman's fingers show white and eyes grow tired, surely the furrow will be straight.

It is well to note here that so far we have only covered five of the Chapters in John; that Chapter 5 must be placed after Chapter 6; that it gives us a date, the Feast of Trumpets in the year A.D. 28, and accordingly it becomes clear that for the last six months of his work Jesus has his face set and his heart fixed on Jerusalem. At this Festival the Jews will be recalling the giving of the Law, talking of creation and of judgement, settled in a world of their own where nothing ever happens. It is sixteen months since Jesus was here, and he is for the hour untrammelled by commitments and circumstance. It is a Sabbath made for God, and Christ walks the streets free from all the inhibitions of Judaism, set free to fling the power of the life of God into the task that lies ahead of him, and into any hour that confronts. He is alone, and it is good to be alive in the September sunshine—to be alive in the exuberance of God and the exhilaration of mind inspired from above. With his eyes on the day when the dead shall hear his voice and live, he turns a corner to be suddenly confronted with a picture of all that should not be; a life wrecked by sin, crippled by helplessness, and sunk in loneliness, friendless, and unheeded by men to whom the invalid has become part of the familiar landscape—that which has no right to exist accepted as normal in the city of David. I like to think of Jesus here forgetting where he was, moved by a veritable instinct of the heart of God, sweeping the evil off the street and lifting the victim of evil out of hopeless imprisonment into the health that was the divine will for him—and let all know by this sign, the will of God for all men everywhere. Jesus is telling the Truth, Reality as it is in God's mind, unbesmirched by the sin and folly of earth.

For the moment, God is at large in Jerusalem—and Jerusalem is utterly shocked! The God of Jerusalem is a God of statutes, many of them, that cripple life, hindering the outlets of health, love, grace, and beneficence. Jesus stands for the moment startled; and then sweeps them aside. 'Do not get in my way; my Father is working, and I am working; there is much to be done. The Sabbath—it was made for God: He is Lord thereof. I am only doing what I have seen my Father doing, and greater things than this will He do by me. I have given to this man to draw sweet breath of daily life: I am going on to raise men, men who will, to life that is life indeed.' Jesus is taking to himself his rightful power (authority), conscious fully now that the Father has given all things into his hands, conscious that the Father has dowered him with life which he can bestow on all who will hear his voice—and live.

And it was at this time that he lifted his heart to the Father (Lk. 10 ^{21f}) in utter thankfulness for his own people, given him by the Father. They are the simple-minded and the single-hearted (cf. Mt. 5 ^{3,8}), and Jesus takes them as his portion, just as today he takes us. He gathers them as a hen gathers her chickens, and lifts his heart in exultation to God whose gracious and determined will this is. Among such folk will Jesus ever live, and of his fullness shall we all receive. Here we have the exceeding greatness of Jesus; though he knows that in the mind of God all things are his, yet is he radiantly content to be the Master of the lowly, of those despised in the eyes of the learned who held in their hands the keys of knowledge and could not see God when He walked in Galilee. For the true knowledge of God lay only in the mind of Jesus; no one can know the Father save the Son, and—with leaping heart of exultation—'those to whom I will reveal Him. Oh, come to me, all of you who are striving to know God; lay your arduous burdens down—leave that method to the learned—and come to me; learn of me, and you will find that the learner's yoke is easy, the way of the child: I will give you power to become His children and will lift you into the knowledge of the Eternal (cf. Jn. 1 ^{12,18}).' Once more, see the Christ stand.

VIII

It is worth while to read chapters 5 and 7–11 of the Fourth Gospel and note the number of times—not a few—that the word 'kill' occurs, and always with reference to Jesus. The first reference is at the Feast of Trumpets in 7 ^{19} (7 $^{15-24}$ is part of Chapter 5) in September, and then in October we get 7 ^{25}. Now it was at this time that Jesus told a great story about a man known to us through the centuries as the Good Samaritan (Lk. 10 $^{25-37}$), an utterly incredible story to Jewish ears, because there were no good Samaritans! Jesus can only tell the story because it is a true story (not a parable), and his hearers know it to be true. They know that the priests had decided that he must die; it was an

open secret; and their first clumsy attempt was to hire brigands
—'robbers' (R.V.), not 'thieves'—to assassinate him on the
notorious road to Jericho. If we are sensitive, we can hear Jesus
telling the story, see the ambush, feel the brutal attack—but it
was difficult to kill Jesus: priests would have done; the brigands
leave their work only half done. We can sense the victim lying
helpless, listening to approaching footsteps once and again, only
to lie back disappointed of help, with the blood slowly ebbing
away. Then the startled exclamation of the merchant on his way
to market—the swift and tender tendance; the sweet comfort of
the oil and the wine; the strength of the arm that raised him
and eased the jolting of the journey to mine host's good hostel,
the indescribable luxury of a couch, a nurse's care, and the long
sleep of a quiet night. Jesus is safe; it is only in Jerusalem that
such murder can be carried through.

On the morrow, agitated disciples find him, and find also
the problem of what to do with him. Then they learn that in a
village, Bethany way, lived a woman not unknown for her beneficence, and so it came to pass that 'a certain woman named
Martha received him into her house' (Lk. 10 [38]). It was Martha's
house in an unnamed village—Lazarus was a rich man living
in Bethany—and here Jesus found what must have been heaven
on earth. The incident given us of that one meal indicates the
lavishness of Martha's care—soon to become loving care; he
who had not where to lay his head these last months has now a
home; and in that home the answer to all his seeking, the perfect
disciple whose mind is open to the living Word of God, harbinger
of victory—he *will* find faith in the true Israel of God. Lazarus
would join that sacred circle, and as the days of convalescence
pass 'Jesus came to love Martha, and her sister, and Lazarus'
(Jn. 11 [5]); record that of the richest experience in his life on
earth, foretaste of that joy in heaven where his beloved have
been ever gathering at his feet.

It were idle to miss the good wrought on Jesus in that resting-
place granted him of God. With the bodily convalescence went
such a reinforcement of fellowship with his Father during this
veritable Sabbath of peace, that we find him going on his way
from now on in consummate mastery of circumstance, difficulty,
and even death, and in serene confidence of mind stayed on the
eternal values of life as it lies hid in the divine purpose. We have
carefully to read the great story—all one story—of his next

sojourn in Jerusalem given us in Jn. 9, 10 $^{19-29}$, $^{1-18}$, $^{30-42}$, in that order, and dated in December, the time of the Dedication Festival (10 ^{22}).

Radiant in spirit renewed at the fountains of divine inspiration, Jesus finds himself confronted by a man locked in the prison of blindness, and in the darker dungeon of despair built for him by the cruel Jewish theory that all suffering was the immediate response of God to a man's sin. In this case they taught that he was born in suffering because of his parents' sin. The greatest book in their Scriptures, *Job*, had been written to banish this doctrine, and written in vain—in vain even unto this day. The man was a hopeless prisoner in body and mind, imprisoned through the evil of mis-shapen physical life and by a theology of untruth born of the Father of Lies, whose lusts corrupt the whole earthly scene (Jn. 8 ^{44}). Then did Jesus step forth out of Martha's home in his might of Saviourhood. The sightless eyes are anointed with light and the spirit of the man redeemed into invincible faith by the touch of the heart of the Christ. The Jews may excommunicate him (9 ^{22}, ^{34}), cast him to the dogs, but he has found his Saviour, and is free of Jerusalem and all her earth-born fogs. For him there is no more night. We need not wonder that on this undeniable fact of deliverance and power, there sprang up in every street dissension and controversy (10 ^{19}), but the truth is penetrating *some* minds; 'This is not the way a mad-man talks—this makes sense,' and peace.

When challenged, in answer Jesus raises his crook and club —'I am a shepherd, and I know my work. Moreover, my sheep know me; to them my voice is as the spell of life, compelling; they know my guiding crook, and the wolves know my guarding club (In Lk. 2 ^{8} we should translate 'keeping guard'). My sheep are my own, given to me of my Father, safe for ever in His keeping and in mine; eternal life is theirs.' We must not miss either the ever-present grief of the inexplicable fact, 'You are not of my sheep'—this will help to still that mighty heart in the surging sorrow of Calvary; nor the fierce determination of the great Shepherd who here bends and binds himself, for ever, to his sleepless task of selfless devotion. A shepherd lays down his life in ceaseless care and work, guiding the often witless sheep to living pastures of rest and of life, guarding his heedless folk when, all unknowing, they rush down the slopes of the valleys of deep darkness (Ps. 23 ^{4}: R.V. marg.) where lurk the wolves

of hell. A very noble Shepherd this ('good' is insufficient: 10 [11]),
beautiful to look upon in the divine vigour of his action and the
divine love of his own—was not his Father a Shepherd
(Ps. 23)? Nor will he ever lay aside his crook; he lifts his eyes
to distant moorlands of earth's travelling to greet such as we
are who shall yet be his (v. 16), a great flock, flock of one
Shepherd, gathered in many a fold beyond that day's horizon.
We do not well to turn to what have been recorded as formal
foretellings of Christ's resurrection, while failing to notice this
tremendous affirmation that a shepherd is immortal till his work
is done. 'Fear not, little flock; for this very thing, that I lay down
my life daily for my sheep, does my Father love me, and His
fathomless power is mine. It is my Father's bidding; I and the
Father are one' (Jn. 10 [16–18, 30]). Our hearts are moved, nerved
and won; but the Jews took up stones to smash him. Surely
their house will be left unto them desolate.

It is good to see him (10 [40]) leaving the fateful city for the
countryside, settling there with his sheep in green pastures by
waters of rest (Ps. 23, R.V. margin), and beginning the glorious
work of winning to himself many who shall be his for ever.
That quiet village, could we find it, means more than a desecrated
tomb in Jerusalem. There must be sacred spots up and down the
lands of men to which the heart of Jesus still goes out in the
dreams of memory, joy and peace.

To understand the tremendous story that follows (Jn. 11), it
is needful to keep in mind as background the determined policy
of the priests to kill Jesus (10 [31, 39]), and the necessity of instant
vigilance laid upon him. The home that had sheltered and blessed
Jesus was rent by the desperate illness of Lazarus at Bethany, and
Jesus is drawn from his retreat beyond Jordan by an urgent and
secret message in code: 'He whom thou lovest' is sick. But
Lazarus learned this and, alarmed at the risk to the Master, must
have sent a message as urgent, bidding his friend beware of the
priests and all their wiles. This explains why Jesus delayed for
two days, to evade the assassins, and why he declared that the
sickness would be to God's glory. In this part of the Fourth
Gospel 'the glory of God' always meant *sacrifice*—and here is his
friend risking his own life by urging delay. Such love is the end
of all God's seeking and labour. But it is clear that Jesus was
profoundly shocked when news came that 'Lazarus is dead!'
'Lazarus dead! That cannot be. He who so loves me is immortal.

Such a death violates the essential Truth of God's real world.'
And to wipe out that lie Jesus bids his men prepare to return to
Judea. But this foolhardy recklessness, as it seems to them, is
too much for them. To return to Judea is to walk on to the
daggers they have seen drawn, and his men shrank back in
sheer dismay, for this is the end of their dreams—to them it is
sheer madness. Then strikes the hour for which Thomas (who
had no dreams) was born. He agrees with his brethren, but what
then? Desertion? 'Desert our Master? That is beyond the bounds
of possibility. But there is nothing left you say? Nay, manhood
is left; honour is left—let us also go, that we may die with him
—*that* is left to us.'

And Jesus is walking on, aloof, lost in outraged love, and
wrapped in dream-like meditation. 'There are twelve hours of
daylight—my way of love, of love's vindication, is clear; it is best
to press right on in the light, whithersoever it leads.' So Jesus
comes to Bethany, and walks right into a company of his
enemies, many of whom—called 'the Jews' (11 [19])—had come
from Jerusalem to console the bereaved sisters. This makes
clear what we are prone to overlook, that Lazarus and his sisters
had come over from the company of the bitter enemies of Jesus
and risked everything for the love of him. Could such friendship
be the victim of lying death? Jesus stands, then, at that graveside,
with Mary and Martha weeping at his feet, and girt with foes
who would willingly lay him cold and dead at his friend's side.
Thus Jesus stands, torn by the tragedy of man's age-long sorrow,
outraged by man's pitiful fate at the hand of Death, and pierced
by pitying love. Then, as never before, he rises in the fullness
of Saviourhood. In himself is the answer to all this. He sweeps
aside all the best orthodoxy of the Jewish faith: 'At the Last Day?
Nay, I am the Resurrection and the Life—he who puts his trust
in me cannot die; such love as this is not meant for the dust.
Lazarus, come forth!'

It behoves us to look at Jesus here, standing with his hand on
the shoulder of Lazarus, as the two friends look into each other's
eyes. Here, and not in any philosophical arguments for the
immortality of the soul or doctrines of its resurrection, is the
basis of our faith in everlasting life. Jesus stands before us,
himself the Resurrection, Life Everlasting amid the shoals and
quicksands of time. And with him Lazarus, and that for ever.
Jesus (we may suggest) had fallen in love with him at first sight

(Mk. 10 21), had called him from his world of wealth and position in Bethany, had ultimately won him even to the jeopardizing of their lives, and had chosen him as part of his own eternity. Eternal Life for us is to be so chosen and rapt from earth's entanglements and death's tentacles into 'the vision of that loveliness which is the life of heaven'. Glowing in the heart of Jesus, as he looked upon Lazarus, were his own later words, 'Yet a little while, and the world beholds me no more; but . . . because I live, you shall live also' (Jn. 14 19). In after days, another member of that bitter Jewish party met this same Jesus in his journeying, and he too was rapt out of a veritable prison of bonds, and went on to declare: 'I have seen the Lord,' and 'To believe on the Lord Jesus Christ is to be saved' (Acts 16 31). Such was the consoling brought to Martha and Mary, not by their friends, the Jews with their newly-found doctrine of a future life (Jn. 11 19), but by him who could say: 'I am the Life' (14 6).

IX

Need we wonder, as we sense the tremendous power of that scene where Life stood visible in the flesh at their side, that not few of Martha's friends went over, risking all, to Jesus, flaming in victorious strength and love, liberated from the shackles of earthbound humanity? But not all. Some hied them to head-quarters to report the shattering event and the portent of a threatened triumph for the Nazarene (11 48). The Jewish Council was promptly summoned to tackle the startling situation and the only too obvious danger to their nation, the nation of God Himself. Discarding the interpolated editorial note in vv. 51-52, we see Caiaphas stand out as the arch-conspirator, a man trained and expert in priestcraft, assuming command of the final campaign against Jesus, priestcraft skilful enough to draw the Roman, hated conqueror, into league against the man more hated still. 'From that day' (v. 53) the state of war stands clear for all to see. As the pilgrims to the Passover met on the way to Jerusalem, the conversation turned most frequently on the chance of the Festival being marked by the appearance of the Galilean for whose head, they all knew, a warrant was out (vv. 55-57). He had not been seen for a little while, having made another withdrawal into the country to spend precious days with his disciples—how many?—days to which they would all their lives look back, days snatched from the devourer for God's eternal harvest, days wherein he harvested his strength and clarified his sense of fellowship with the Father that he might the more surely fulfil His will in the storm-lashed days to come. For the last time, he would know days of quiet light from the arousing of the sun to the setting thereof, amid quiet villages with their sweet life of family concerns and fruitful labour, with occasional hours when children were brought to his knees by mothers perceptive of his grace and beauty; days of encounter with inquiring minds, or, it may be, a leper laying at his feet the grateful wreath of a rare gratitude, all amid the refreshing intercourse of his nearer friends and future ambassadors.

From these green pastures and quiet waters Jesus steps forth into the concourse of events, nerved to meet the hour and the power of darkness. He returns (Jn. 12 ¹⁻¹¹) to the scene of the mighty deed which had signed his death-warrant, and, surprisingly enough, he is royally greeted by the chiefs of Bethany who, scornfully ignoring the warrant for his arrest issued by the authorities of Jerusalem, welcome him and Lazarus as guests at a city banquet in their honour. We cannot take our place within that lighted hall with understanding until we have eradicated v. 6, which is an interpolated note interrupting the narrative and completely misinterpreting the situation—incidentally also giving a quite erroneous view of Judas. Even the Judas of popular estimation could hardly have the impertinence to suggest (v. 5) that a lady had no right to do as she would with her own. His query: 'Why was not *this* ointment sold?' is only possible if we understand that *all* had been sold and given to the poor, Lazarus being no longer able to offer his house, nor Martha to be his hostess. All the more remarkable is this spontaneous gathering of the gentlemen of Bethany to honour Jesus and the friend wedded to him in sacrifice, danger, and love. They would share the danger with Lazarus (v. 9), for after this evening every one of them would be a marked man. Let Jerusalem know that her writ does not run in Bethany, and that when she has gone down, not one stone upon another, the name of Bethany will smell sweet in an everlasting spring. It is good for us to realize this hour, when he who was to become the despised and rejected sat crowned with honour among his fellow men. Caiaphas does not speak for all, nor Judas. Can we too lay our tribute of adoration at his feet?

But it was done for us, the very thing we would have done, had we thought of it. Out of the dispersal of the family wealth, Mary, who understood as none other except the beloved disciple, had kept back, in clear prevision of the need, a priceless cruse of precious ointment, and, as the company were longing to express the overflowing of their hearts in gratitude and something akin to adoration, a woman slips into the room and over the feet of their beloved guest she breaks all that vase in the reckless divine abandonment of grace (cf. Jn. 3 [16])—it was all she had—it was to her the least that she could do: to her, so little; to Jesus, so much. 'She hath wrought a good work on me' (Mk. 14 [6]). He would go to his dying anointed; the worship of that hour would outlast the Empire and the powers of Hell (Mk. 14 [9]). He would go to his dying knowing that the grace of God had triumphed for all time. And in that banquet-hall men sat back satisfied; the perfect thing had been done, and the name of Bethany would live for ever. But so real was the danger that the early evangelists told men the great story, but held back the name of the woman whose deed was to be carried on the wings of the Gospel throughout the world (Mk. 14 [9]). The next day the priests would enter the name of Lazarus on the roll of death, and Jesus would give his people a new command: 'Love as I have loved—Greater love is there none than this, that a man lay down his life for his friends' (Jn. 13 [34], 15 [12–13]).

X

The days of decision have arrived, and Jesus, leaving Bethany with its eternal repose of truth, love, and honour, flings himself into the maelstrom of conflict and controversy in Jerusalem. It seems one of the strangest acts of his life to enter the city in what was meant to be recognized as the garb of the Messiah. But the hour of decision has come, and Jerusalem must accept or finally reject the Christ who will not swerve from his true revelation of himself and the thought of God, refusing to have aught to do with popular desires and expectations. During days of controversy and plotting, Jesus walks safely, guarded as yet by the popular enthusiasm. But the day wanes, and Jesus finally withdraws to the room lovingly reserved for him by one of his unnamed disciples, the secret of it being so jealously guarded that the Apostles themselves, including Judas, are in the room before they know its location—until he dismissed Judas and for, say, two hours after that, Jesus is safe from interruption for the supreme completion of his work. He leaves the crowd, he leaves Israel, to devote himself to his Own. On the evening before the Passover day, as is made clear in Jn. 19 [14, 31, 42], he will keep a Passover meal, a sacramental meal of his own, to which he has been looking forward, and for which he has longed (Lk. 22 [15f]). No Jewish Passover of national pride for him, but a Session of light and love in the presence of his Father. And so we come to the hour (Jn. 13 [1]) of Christ's overwhelming consciousness of God, the consummated consciousness that he had come from God and was about to return to God. The room becomes for ever The Upper Room, portal of Eternity, where we, even we, may sit down in heavenly places with Christ Jesus.

Let us enter with the first entrants. May be, if we are hypersensitive, we shall 'feel' the presence of the Devil (v. 2), but that is suppressed by the overwhelming power of the mind of Jesus, lit by light of his Father's fellowship and will, the revelation of which is now the instant task and call of the hour, so that he may at long last be able to say: 'He that hath seen me hath seen the Father' (14 [9]). How then, in this supreme hour of the revelation of the divine, will he bear himself? On Hermon he had refused his rightful entrance into an expected heaven; now he draws heaven into that hidden room, that God may be known as He really is. Jesus lays aside his robe, girds himself with a homespun towel, pours water into a common basin, and washes his disciples' feet—the unguessed beauty of God, the hall-mark of real divinity in humility: in the climactic hour of revelation Jesus thus wrote out the name of God. 'If you have seen me, you have seen the Father. It is not enough to hold your inherited and traditional faith in God—to know Him as He really is, you must believe also in me (14 [1]). And this is the Life Divine which I now bequeath to you' (14 [15]).

But when Jesus had risen from his knees, he knew that he had failed with Judas. Electric with emotion, tense with fate, were the moments when, washing his feet, Jesus raised his eyes in a last appeal to those of Judas—and knew that he had failed. Such a Christ was only anathema to this nationalist Israelite. The Devil had won in the heart of Judas, whose resolve to betray his Master was now finally confirmed. He finally gave his adhesion to the old Israel and rejected the new, even with contumely. But there are two swords in that room, and Jesus has only to tell

Peter, 'That is the man,' instead of whispering a secret to the beloved disciple—and it will not be Jesus who will hang between the two brigands on the morrow. Jesus gives his life for Judas, and now knows that he can wear the robe of the divine glory, which is sacrifice, and die for all men. The glory of God is in the Upper Room (13 [31–32]). For a little space Jesus is free of all distraction to devote himself to his beloved, and through them to all 'that shall believe on him through their word' (17 [20]). Here is the life-blood of the New Covenant, which means the New Religion and in his own blood, not that of the Egyptians as of yore, will he seal his men his for ever. They drink that wine, and we drink it still, 'new in the Kingdom of God' (Mk. 14 [25]), pledged to the life that cannot be achieved by any effort or gained by any merit, but only received from above, from the riven heart of God. So Jesus accomplished on earth the work which the Father had given him to do (Jn. 17 [4]).

XI

From the sure peace of that Upper Room Jesus goes forth to work out in the flesh the revelation of God made there in the light of heavenly fellowship and love. He has given his life for Judas—is it clear that he can drain the cup of man's sin? So terrible is that sin, so terrible is the situation in which he finds himself caught up and manacled, that they tell us the grass was red with his blood. What, we must ask, what was the so bitter cup from which he shrank—'If it be possible, let this cup pass'? Threefold is the agony. To bear man's blackest sin in his own dying, in the very act of that death to become the incarnation of the crowning crime of man, is, surely, in his own person to put the seal on man's damnation. To bear in his own self the sin that would make man's forgiveness impossible—this is also impossible to the Lover of Man. And, beyond even that, there is the breaking of the Father's heart—is not his dying the sure seal of that? Here is a cup of threefold bitterness from which Jesus may surely shrink back. For to go forward means all that.

'Nevertheless, not as I will, but as thou wilt.' He drinks it. In that last intense agony of prayer the divine secret has been revealed. 'Drink my cup—it is mine—drink my cup. We can bear all things, we can endure all things—and we can forgive.' The Gospel of forgiveness comes right out of the dying of Jesus. He is bearing, not inflicted penalty, but sin itself. Sin is killing him. But sin cannot break him. He will do only as he has seen, in Gethsemane, the Father do; he will bear it. And, bearing it, forgive. Here we behold earth's final sin, God's deepest agony, and God's ever-present forbearance and forgiveness. The cost of forgiveness is the bearing of sin. Only God is equal to that. 'No man hath seen God at any time; the only begotten Son, who is in the bosom of the Father, he hath declared him' (Jn. 1 [18]). Supremely, on Calvary.

Out of the lighted fellowship of the Upper Room he had gone to the solitude of a garden at night to take to himself finally the fact and bitterness of sin; from the high joy of love's giving and the wine of heavenly response he had gone out to accept for himself the inescapable burden of Israel's suicide and the Father's shame. The mighty heart failed not here, but met the Father at the appointed place of tryst. Is it not finished? Nay: all that must be held fast and carried out of the solitude, out of the warm room of human love, into the open unshielded glare of publicity lit by the hate of enemies and pierced by the laughter of Hell. The odour of the ointment is exchanged for the gibes of a crowd—for the pitiless taunts of men—here is the barb in the arrow of his suffering—whom he would fain have gathered as a hen gathers her chickens under her wings. His enemies have him now where they want him. Victorious unbelief is now blatantly triumphing. He who posed as Son of the Highest ('What blasphemy!') now hangs between two brigands above the dung heaps outside the walls of the Holy City. At his feet—perhaps the most piercing of his sorrows—a group of women, with one man, whose hearts are being crushed, nay, crucified with him.

The helplessness of the Sufferer is not the least part of his pain. He cannot reply to the taunts. The Master Mind of Evil has so woven the tangled skein of earth's happenings and of Israel's thought that his suffering and dying, wherein he is entering into the nearer fellowship of the Father, are to the people the last and perfect proof that he has been a fraud and an impostor. He has only to come down from the Cross—and that were easy, if he were the Son of God—to *prove* that he is the Son of God. Such their shattering logic. To have turned stones into bread in the wilderness would only have proved that he was a magician; to have come down from the Cross would only have been to gratify the lust of a holiday crowd—and to have deserted his Father. For this is the final hour, on earth, of his fellowship with the Throne of God where God ever bears the sin of the world. To reach that Throne, Jesus must take all the sin that is killing him into his heart, and so penetrate more and yet more into the Divine Fellowship. The crowd see only a felon crucified for his effrontery; Pilate a revolutionary whose strange proceedings rendered him dangerous to Caesar; Caiaphas and Saul of Tarsus a victim of damnation, for 'damned is every one that hangs on a tree' (Gal. 3 [13]). The day will come when Saul of Tarsus, the brilliant devotee of the Law (Gal. 1 [14]), will have to decide between the Law and the Crucified. But that is not yet. The Damascus road for Jesus is on the other side of the dark in which sin and hell have now wrapped him.

And in that darkness the battle of faith is fought out. The Devil, who has now won the nation of God to his side, now wings his reburnished dart of poisoned unbelief: 'If—if you are Son of God.' Salvation is only by faith—and can Jesus still believe in himself, believe in himself as the Revelation of God, believe in the God who needs must hide Himself in the darkness and silence where He ever bears man's sin, and so leave him helpless that he may know the last bitterness of the Eternal Cross, its utter loneliness? The tides of pain surge on. Amid it all, Jesus finds strength to pray for the soldiers (Lk. 23 [34]) who knew not what they were doing—Caiaphas knew well enough—and to lift a thought of love to a quivering Heart in heaven, a Father's heart. He finds strength to send his mother into the stricken night with a son's arm around her. Then he clothed himself in the rulers' taunt: 'He saved others; himself he cannot save.' Then the veil of the Temple was rent, the heart of Jesus was rent, and into the hands of the Unseen and the Eternal, Jesus commended his spirit, his faith unbroken, his trust triumphant and complete. 'He that hath seen me, hath seen the Father.'

'I saw a Lamb, as though it had been slain, standing in the midst of the Throne' (Rev. 5 [6]).

XII

They that had loved him went home to derelict hearths, the silent stars came out, the Sabbath dawned with needless glow, a Sabbath haunted by the consciousness of a silent form lying wrapped in grave cloths on a raised ledge in a garden tomb. Endless seemed that day, and incredible seemed the day that followed. Jerusalem was a turmoil of rumours, rumours that sprang from the agitated reports of women who could not find their Master in the tomb. As the rumours became speculations in passing from street to street, they created an atmosphere like a fog, marvellously depicted for us by Luke (24 ¹⁻¹²). It was the beloved disciple who first 'saw and believed'. The morning mist and slanting beams of the rising sun had dispersed when he entered the rock-hewn room where he had seen them lay Jesus, and the secret lay clear. Things seemed first as they had been on that dread Friday morning. *There lay the grave cloths undisturbed, with the rolled head-turban in its place.* Only Jesus was not there. So the beloved disciple saw, understood, and believed that Jesus in the power of endless life had passed out of the trammels of this physical world into the Unseen. (Christ did not rise from the dead like a man getting out of bed one leg first.) 'Look! Simon look! He is not here! He is risen!' Despair overwhelmed the man who had said: 'I never knew the man' (Mk. 14 ⁷¹): Christ had risen, but not for him. But his friend links their arms and lead the disconsolate to his own home, lit once more with a mother's joy and a sun that would know no setting.

But they had forgotten Magdalene in the garden. Jesus had not. Here is the Gospel of Easter. It is not that Jesus has risen from earth to heaven, but that he has returned from heaven to us, to the earth that had discarded him. And it is sheer joy to watch him come back. On this first day of boundless liberty we find him going, not to those that love him most—they can wait— but to those that need him most. And, first of all, to Magdalene whose mind is reeling back, rudderless in a starless sea, to the vortex of insanity from which (Lk. 8 ²) he had delivered her. Then to Simon, the one man who had no hope of seeing him, not to lash him for his denial, but with his own hand to place pardon in the stricken heart and the key of forgiveness in the trembling hand, that he may unlock the doors of the prison-house and let men go free into the sunlight of the grace of God. Had he not promised this—'I will give you the keys of the Kingdom'?

But perhaps we are most surprised to find that there was time for an afternoon walk to Emmaus, that he might break bread with two of his folk, 'unassigned recruits', who stood for all those in every town and village where such as they would rise from the dead to everlasting joy. And the fuller glory of the

Easter message greets these two when hurrying back to Jerusalem and bursting into the Upper Room with their tidings, they are met by the gathered company of disciples with the Gospel: 'The Lord is risen *indeed*—he has appeared to Simon—no one but Jesus would do that.' Jesus had not only risen; he had come back; but, more than that, he was the same Jesus. And then, Master of life, able to weave for himself at will visible clothing of flesh and blood, he stood in their midst, in the midst of his gathered Church, and the day of Resurrection ends with the triumphant act of consecration whereby their Lord forms them a Church and endows them with the Spirit's light and power. To them Jesus reveals himself as he ever is, till sin be no more. We hear nothing of halo, or robes of royalty, or heralding archangels. He showed them his hands and feet. The Cross is Eternal, and it was Thomas who, a week later, was the first to see that here, just here, is the final revelation unguessed through all the ages 'My Lord—and my God!' (Jn. 20 [29]).

Here began the crowning part of Christ's ministry, so long neglected by us, the ministry of the Upper Room where he would meet his Church on the first day of each week, it may be, until his Ascension. Here he taught them supreme things which they had not been equipped to understand before, and of this teaching we have a record in the Fourth Gospel (15 [18]–16 [15], 14 [1–26]). He bade them know that this was not an ending, but a new beginning; that Pilate and Caiaphas had not said the last word; that he would send his Advocate (15 [26], R.V. margin), that the case would be re-tried, and the verdict would be reversed (16 [8–11]). Who believes in Caiaphas now? Even in the courts of the world, Jesus stands unquestioned, and Pilate is forgotten. This is the work in history of the Holy Spirit, and Jesus said that he would accomplish this.

At their last gathering, Jesus renders up his life and work to his Father in prayer (Jn. 17), which is for us the most precious page of the Bible, and having accomplished his work in the flesh, leaves them in great joy. The following days were very strange. Where was their Master? The answer is given at Pentecost, Peter once again being entrusted with the key of light: 'Let all the house of Israel therefore know assuredly, that *God hath made him both Lord and Christ*—this Jesus whom you crucified' (Acts 2 [36]).

Thou art the King of Glory, O Christ:
Thou art the everlasting Son of the Father.
When Thou tookest upon Thee to deliver man,
Thou didst not abhor the Virgin's womb.
When Thou hadst overcome the sharpness of death,
Thou didst open the Kingdom of Heaven to all believers.
Thou sittest at the right hand of God in the glory of the Father.
Day by day we magnify Thee,
And we worship Thy name ever world without end.

Book List

Jesus of Galilee. F. Warburton Lewis (Epworth Press).
Jesus, Saviour of Men. F. Warburton Lewis.
Jesus the Son of God. Frederic Greeves (Epworth Press).
Jesus and His Church. Dr. R. Newton Flew (Epworth Press).
Jesus and Ourselves. Dr. Leslie D. Weatherhead (Epworth Press).
Jesus as They Saw Him. J. A. Findlay, M.A., D.D. (Epworth Press).
The Mind of Jesus Christ. G. B. Robson (Epworth Press).
Jesus Christ is Alive. J. Scott Lidgett, C.H., M.A., D.D. (Epworth Press).
The Personality of Jesus. W. Deane, M.A. (Epworth Press).
Jesus Christ and the Meaning of Life. W. R. Maltby, D.D. (Epworth Press).
Jesus of Nazareth. Ellis W. Heaton (Epworth Press).
The Light of the World. Greville Cook (Hodder & Stoughton).
A Plain Man's Life of Christ. A. D. Martin (Allen & Unwin).

Appendix

THE STANDING ORDERS, AS THEY RELATE TO LOCAL PREACHERS

CONNEXIONAL
LOCAL PREACHERS' COMMITTEE

The Committee for administering the business of the Local Preachers' Department shall consist of: The President, the Vice-President, and the Secretary of the Conference; the ex-President and ex-Vice-President; the Secretary, the Treasurer and the Deputy-Treasurer of the Department; twenty-one Ministers and twenty-one Local Preachers, elected by Conference; one Minister or one Local Preacher nominated by each District in Great Britain.

DISTRICT
LOCAL PREACHERS' COMMITTEE

The District Local Preachers' Committee shall consist of:

(*a*) The Chairman of the District and the Secretary of the District Synod;

(*b*) Members of the Connexional Local Preachers' Committee who are Members of Society in any Circuit in the District;

(*c*) Ministers and Local Preachers in equal numbers up to a maximum of twelve each, elected by the September Synod; the laymen so elected becoming thereby Members of the District Synod;

(*d*) Local Preachers appointed as Associated Members in accordance with the Standing Orders; who do not thereby become Members of the District Synod.

N.B.—Synods are strongly recommended to take advantage of this Standing Order and to encourage the appointment of such Associated Members.

From among the Members of the Committee so constituted the Synod shall appoint one Minister and one Local Preacher as Secretaries and one Layman as Treasurer of the Committee.

CIRCUIT
LOCAL PREACHERS' MEETING

(a) *Constitution*

The Circuit Local Preachers' Meeting shall consist of:

(*a*) The Ministers and Ministers on Trial and Supernumerary Ministers stationed in the Circuit;

(*b*) The fully accredited Local Preachers who are Members of Society in the Circuit.

Local Preachers on Trial are expected to attend the Meeting, but are not entitled to vote.

The Meeting shall be held once in every quarter.

(b) *Functions*

(1) To consider the state of the Work of God in the Circuit so far as the work of the Local Preachers has relation thereto.

(2) To consider the character of the Local Preachers, their fidelity to doctrine and fitness for the work of the Circuit.

(3) To examine and decide as to the recommendation of Candidates for the office and work of a Local Preacher.

(c) *Regulations*

(1) A candidate for the office of Local Preacher shall be a Member of Society in the Methodist Church and shall in the first place be recommended to the Circuit Local Preachers' Meeting by the Leaders' Meeting of that Society in which he (or she) is a Member, or by a Minister or Local Preacher present in the Local Preachers' Meeting.

(2) He shall then, with the approval of the Meeting, receive from the Superintendent Minister a Note authorizing him to assist a fully accredited Local Preacher in the conduct of Services within the limits of the Circuit. This Note is valid for three months, and, if it is deemed advisable, may be renewed for a further quarter or quarters. A report shall be submitted to the Local Preachers' Meeting by the Local Preacher, or Preachers, who shall have been present at any Services in which the

Candidate has taken part. The Candidate shall also be questioned by the Superintendent Minister, or under his direction, as to his Christian knowledge and experience. Upon satisfactory reports being obtained, the Candidate shall then be received by the Local Preachers' Meeting as a Local Preacher on Trial.

(3) Before any Candidate is finally admitted as a Local Preacher he shall, save in exceptional circumstances, have been not less than twelve months on Trial. Conference recommends that the normal period of probation shall be two years. The Local Preachers' Meeting shall have power still further to extend the period in individual cases if it should see reason for so doing.

(4) While the Candidate remains a Preacher on Trial, he shall, each quarter, conduct a Service in the presence of at least one Local Preacher, a report of which Service shall be submitted to the next Local Preachers' Meeting.

(5) (a) Every Local Preacher on Trial shall, unless for very exceptional reasons special exemption is granted by the Circuit Local Preachers' Meeting, take a Connexional Written Examination before being finally admitted as a Local Preacher. The reasons for which exemption in special cases is given shall be communicated to the Connexional Local Preachers' Committee.

(b) The Connexional Written Examination shall consist of three elementary Papers on the Old Testament, the New Testament and Christian Doctrine respectively, and shall be based on textbooks indicated annually in the Minutes of Conference.

Stress shall be laid on accurate knowledge of the Bible.

(c) The Connexional Written Examination shall be held twice in each year. Candidates, if they so desire, may take the Papers one at a time, and at intervals of six or twelve months. The result in each case shall be reported to the Circuit Local Preachers' Meeting through the Superintendent Minister.

(6) Conference directs that a copy of the Syllabus of Studies be handed to Candidates as soon as they receive a Note, and that they be informed of the Correspondence Courses of Study available for them and be advised to enrol as students. Conference recommends that Local Preachers on Trial should, as a rule, take two years for these probationary studies. (*See* Regulation 14 (*a*).)

(7) (a) Before any Candidate is finally admitted as a Local Preacher he must undergo an Oral Examination conducted by

the Superintendent Minister or under his direction at the Local Preachers' Meeting as to his knowledge of and loyalty to the following doctrines of the Evangelical Faith:

The Fatherhood of God; the Deity of our Lord Jesus Christ; the Person, Mission, and Work of the Holy Spirit; the Universality of Sin; the Atonement; Salvation for all by Grace through Faith; the Believer's Privilege of Assurance and of Perfect Love; the Christian Church; the Future Life.

These doctrines are based upon the Holy Scriptures, and are contained in Wesley's *Notes on the New Testament*, and in the first four volumes of his *Sermons* (*Forty-Four Sermons*), which Sermons must have been read by the Candidate.

(*b*) At the time of the Oral Examination the Candidate shall give an account of his conversion to God, his present Christian experience and his call to preach.

(*c*) During the quarter preceding the Oral Examination, the Candidate shall conduct a Trial Service in the presence of a Minister and a fully accredited Local Preacher, who shall present a written report of that Service to the Local Preachers' Meeting.

(8) The Circuit Local Preachers' Meeting, in determining whether a Local Preacher on Trial shall be recommended to be admitted as a fully accredited Local Preacher, shall give due consideration, not only to the report of the Connexional Written Examination, but also to the Oral Examination and to the report of the Candidate's Trial Service.

(9) Before any Local Preacher on Trial is admitted as fully accredited he shall be approved by the Circuit Quarterly Meeting.

(10) Local Preachers, after being admitted as fully accredited, shall be recognized at a Public Religious Service to be arranged by the Circuit Quarterly Meeting. At the Service a letter signed by the President of the Conference shall be delivered to each Local Preacher so admitted.

(11) It is the duty of a Local Preacher:

    (*a*) To meet in Class, or some equivalent Fellowship.

    (*b*) As frequently as his Circuit appointments permit, to attend Public Worship and to partake of the Sacrament of the Lord's Supper.

    (*c*) To fulfil the appointments given to him on the Circuit Plan; or, if unable to do so, himself to arrange for an accredited substitute, and to report such an arrangement to the Superintendent Minister.

(12) Upon removal from one Circuit to another, every fully accredited Local Preacher is entitled, upon the production of Note of Removal and a copy of the current Circuit Plan from his former Circuit, to be received in the new Circuit not only as a Member of Society but also, without further trial or examination, as a Local Preacher in full standing. The position in which his name shall appear on the Circuit Plan shall be determined by the Local Preachers' Meeting of the Circuit which receives him.

N.B.—This Regulation does not apply to Local Preachers on Trial.

(13) A Lay Pastor, who is a fully accredited Local Preacher, while employed in a Circuit, shall be subject to the jurisdiction of the Local Preachers' Meeting of that Circuit.

(14) The Secretary of the Circuit Local Preachers' Meeting shall:

(*a*) Hand a copy of the Syllabus of Studies, and of the Regulations relating to the Examination for admission as a Local Preacher, to all Candidates as soon as they receive a Note, and advise them to enrol as students in the Correspondence Courses of Study which are available for them.

(*b*) Forward to the Secretary of the Connexional Local Preachers' Committee:

(i) A copy of the Circuit Plan for the January-March Quarter.

(ii) Immediately after each Quarterly Meeting—the name and address of any person who has received a Note, or has been received as a Local Preacher on Trial, or has been admitted as a fully accredited Local Preacher

(d) *Agenda*

The Minutes of the previous Meeting shall be read; and, when approved as a correct record, shall be signed by the Chairman.

The following questions shall then be asked:

1. (*a*) Does each of our Local Preachers continue faithfully in the discharge of his duties as a Local Preacher?

N.B.—If any Local Preacher refuses to take appointments in the Circuit, and if his reasons for such a refusal seem to be inadequate, objection to his standing as a Local Preacher shall be raised when this question is asked, if the objection has previously been notified to the Superintendent Minister.

(*b*) Does he walk worthily of the Gospel?

(*c*) Does he believe and preach our doctrines and nothing contrary to them?

(*These doctrines are defined in Regulation 7 (a).*)

(*d*) Does he observe our discipline?

(*This question has particular reference to Regulation 11.*)

(*e*) Has he competent abilities for our work?

Notes: (1) *An objection to a Local Preacher on the ground that a satisfactory answer cannot be given to any of these Questions shall first be notified to the Superintendent Minister in writing, who shall seek a personal interview with the Local Preacher and inform him of the objection to be made. When this procedure has been observed, the Meeting shall hear and consider the objection.*

(2) *If, in the judgement of the Meeting, the objection is sustained, the Superintendent Minister shall determine and declare the action to be taken; subject to a right of appeal to the District Discipline Committee and to Conference on the part either of the Local Preacher concerned or of the person who brought the charge.*

(3) *The record of the proceedings relating to charges against any Local Preacher shall be kept in a separate Minute Book by the Superintendent Minister of the Circuit, and shall not be entered in the Minutes of the Local Preachers' Meeting.*

2. Has any Local Preacher died?

3. Has any Local Preacher resigned?

4. Has any Local Preacher removed into another Circuit? If so, to what Circuit has he been accredited?

5. Has any Local Preacher come to reside in the Circuit? If so, from what Circuit has he been accredited?

6. Has any Local Preacher on Trial sat for the Connexional Written Examination, or for any part of it, and with what results?

7. Is anyone now on Trial to be admitted on full plan and recommended for approval by the Quarterly Meeting?

8. Who are continued on Trial?

The names shall be entered in the Minutes with the number of quarters during which each Candidate has been on Trial.

Each Local Preacher on Trial shall be questioned as to his studies, and his reading of Wesley's *Forty-Four Sermons* and *Notes on the New Testament*.

The Meeting shall appoint, each quarter, a Local Preacher, or more than one, to be present at a Service conducted by a Local Preacher on Trial, and to submit to the next Meeting a report of that Service.

During the quarter preceding the Oral Examination, the Candidate shall conduct a Trial Service in the presence of a Minister and a fully accredited Local Preacher, who shall present a written report of that Service to the Local Preachers' Meeting.

9. Does any Local Preacher on Trial intend to sit for any part of the next written Examination?

10. What is the report concerning those, if any, who have received a Note from the Superintendent Minister?

11. Who are received on Trial?

12. Is anyone recommended to be given a Note authorizing him to assist a Local Preacher in the conduct of Services?

N.B.—(1) *It is competent for a Leaders' Meeting or for any preacher present at the Meeting to make such a recommendation.*

(2) *The Note shall be for one quarter only; if deemed advisable, it may be renewed.*

13. Have the Local Preachers, and especially those who have been placed on Trial or received a Note, been informed of the Correspondence Courses of Study arranged for them, and have they been advised by the Meeting to enrol as Students?

14. What is the state of the Work of God in this Circuit so far as the work of the Local Preachers has relation thereto?

15. How can we further prepare ourselves and improve our preaching that 'our Gospel' may come unto our hearers, 'not in word only, but also in power and in the Holy Spirit'?

The Conference recommends that in every Circuit an endeavour shall be made by the Meeting to form a Local Preachers' Training Class.

16. Does the Meeting recommend any change in the hours of Service on the Lord's Day?

17. Does the Meeting recommend that any new Preaching Place be put on, or that any Preaching Place be taken off, the Plan?

18. What arrangements can be made for evangelistic work other than the Public Services appointed on the Circuit Plan?

19. Whom do we appoint as Secretary of this Meeting?

N.B.—The September Meeting shall appoint a Secretary whose name and address shall be sent to the Lay Secretary of the District Local Preachers' Committee and to the Secretary of the Connexional Local Preachers' Committee.

20. Whom do we appoint as Representative to the District Local Preachers' Committee?

N.B.—The District Synod may add to the District Local Preachers' Committee one Representative (Minister or Local Preacher) from each Circuit in the District, as an Associated Member of that Committee. Conference recommends, and the Connexional Local Preachers' Committee strongly advises, that Synods shall agree to such additional representation. If the District Synod agrees, the Local Preachers' Meeting each June shall nominate its Representative to the District Committee, and the Circuit Secretary shall immediately inform the District Local Preachers' Secretary of the name and address of the elected Representative.